The Superpowers

The Superpowers: a short history is a highly original and important book surveying the development of the USA and Russia (in its tsarist, Soviet and post-Soviet phases) from the pre-twentieth century world of imperial powers to the present. It places the Cold War, from inception to ending, into the wider cultural, economic and political context.

The Superpowers: a short history traces the intertwining history of the two powers chronologically. In a fascinating and innovative approach, the book adopts the metaphor of a lifespan to explore this evolutionary relationship. Commencing with the inheritance of the two countries up to 1898, the book continues by looking at their conception to 1921, including the effects of the First World War, gestation to 1945 with their period as allies during the Second World War and their youth examining the onset of the Cold War to 1968. The maturity phase explores the Cold War in the context of the Third World to 1991 and finally the book concludes by discussing the legacy the superpowers have left for the twenty-first century.

The Superpowers: a short history is the first history of the two major participants of the Cold War and their relationship throughout the twentieth century and before.

Paul Dukes is Emeritus Professor of History at the University of Aberdeen. His many books include *A History of Russia* (Macmillan, 3rd edition, 1997) and *World Order in History* (Routledge, 1996).

To Daniel and Ruth

The Superpowers

A short history

Paul Dukes

London and New York

First published 2000
by Routledge
11 New Fetter Lane, London EC4P 4EE

Simultaneously published in the USA and Canada
by Routledge
29 West 35th Street, New York, NY 10001

Routledge is an imprint of the Taylor & Francis Group

© 2000 Paul Dukes

Typeset in Perpetua by Taylor & Francis Books Ltd
Printed and bound in Great Britain by University Press, Cambridge

British Library Cataloguing in Publication Data
A catalogue record for this book is available from the British Library

Library of Congress Cataloging in Publication Data
Dukes, Paul, 1934–
The superpowers : a short history / Paul Dukes.
p. cm.
Includes bibliographical references and index.
1. United States–History. 2. Russia–History. 3. Soviet Union–History. 4.
United States–Foreign relations. 5. Russia–Foreign relations. 6. Soviet
Union–Foreign relations. 7. Imperialism–History. 8. Cold War. I. Title.
E178 .D864 2000
973–dc21
                                                      00-055340

ISBN 0–415–23041–1 (hbk)
ISBN 0–415–23042–x (pbk)

Contents

Preface

While there have been many books about the Cold War, there has not yet been one about the relationship of the major participants throughout the twentieth century. Aimed at filling such a gap, this book defines a superpower as able to conduct a global strategy including the possibility of destroying the world; to command vast economic potential and influence; and to present a universal ideology. It adopts the metaphor of a lifespan in an examination of the manner in which the USA on the one hand and the USSR (preceded and succeeded by Russia) on the other have constituted superpowers, as follows. Chapter 1, 'The Inheritance' argues that the subjects cannot be understood without some understanding of their earlier antecedents. The treatment, as throughout the work, is thematic as well as chronological, with attention given to economic and cultural as well as political aspects of the subject. Chapter 2, 'Conception', places a strengthening USA and a weakening Tsarist Russia in the context of imperialism before going on to discuss the impact of the First World War and the Russian Revolution, which led to the formation of the respective ideologies both challenging traditional liberalism, Wilsonism and Leninism. Chapter 3, 'Gestation', describes the manner in which both USA and USSR strove for their world orders along with older and newer rivals before the Second World War brought them closer together as their rivals were defeated or declined.

Chapter 4, 'Youth', examines the onset of the Cold War along with the process of decolonisation. It does not seek to attribute responsibility, but rather to set out the conflicting aims and comparative strengths of the two sides. Chapter 5, 'Maturity', takes the Cold War from the US involvement in Vietnam to the Soviet involvement in Afghanistan as principal examples of superpower engagement in the Third World, where an emerging rival to both of them was the People's Republic of China. It also analyses the Soviet collapse. Chapter 6, 'The Legacy', poses such questions as, is the Cold War over, and how has it been assessed? How have American and Russian analysts placed the superpowers in the context of 'world process' or 'civilisations' and how should they be placed in the context of the end of the millennium? A summary follows as part of an examination of the uses of the past before a few final conjectures are made about the future in conclusion.

This book marks a return to a subject which I first addressed in another work published thirty years ago, and have considered in other books since. In particular, *The Emergence of the Super-Powers* (Macmillan, 1970) now looks like a preliminary sketch, considering the twentieth century in less than fifty pages. *The Last Great Game* (Pinter, 1989) approached the subject making use of the Braudelian concepts event, conjuncture and structure in ascending order of emphasis. Again, therefore, there is comparatively little on the twentieth century. In the present work, apart from the adoption of the guiding metaphor, the treatment is more conventional as well as somewhat fuller. Nevertheless, the structure may be found in Chapter 1, which draws heavily on these earlier works now out of print. What I have called the Great Conjuncture, Wilsonism versus Leninism, reappears in Chapter 2, but in fresh guise. For the rest, the overall approach and most of the material is 'new'. That is to say, although almost none of it has been taken from archives, considerable numbers of publications have been consulted, ranging from the speeches of politicians to the works of novelists and poets. Some key works of yesteryear have have seemed worthy of extended mention.

An enormous debt is owed to them and to more recent publications, including those by fellow historians. To the best of my knowledge and belief, no other work takes the same approach as my own. For example, a book with which I mostly agree, Walter LaFeber's *America, Russia and the Cold War, 1945–1996* (New York, 1997), and another with which to a considerable extent I disagree, John Lewis Gaddis, *Russia, the Soviet Union, and the United States: An Interpretive History* (New York, 1990), both devote no more than a few pages to the period before the outbreak of the Second World War. However, more needs to be said about these outstanding scholars. Walter LaFeber has produced other books giving masterly surveys of US diplomacy as a whole as well as throwing light on a range of particular questions. Moreover, since I first heard an exemplary lecture by him in 1970, I have listened to him and read him with great respect. Meanwhile, John Lewis Gaddis has gained a reputation as one of the leading Cold War specialists with a series of publications culminating in *We Now Know: Rethinking Cold War History* (Oxford, 1997), which has been praised for setting the agenda for future work but also criticised for sounding a note of triumphalism. Among other stimulating colleagues, I would like to include Academician Nikolai Nikolaevich Bolkhovitinov, who has set the highest standards in his studies of early American–Russian contacts as well as demonstrating what could be done even in difficult circumstances. Selecting the material which has seemed most appropriate for my purpose, I have made due acknowledgements in the Notes.

While accepting ultimate responsibility for what is published here, I would like to acknowledge the indispensable assistance that I have received from two good friends, Dr John Kent, Reader in International Relations at the London School of

Economics and Dr Cathryn Brennan, Honorary Research Fellow in History at the University of Aberdeen, both of whom have read the penultimate draft with great thoroughness and insight. My profound thanks to both of them for vital improvements. I would also like to record my gratitude to Professor Clive Lee of the Department of Economics, with whom I conducted a course on The Superpowers, for his useful comments and suggestions, to the students who took that course in successive presentations for their varied contributions, to colleagues in the History Department as well as in the Queen Mother Library for their advice and support, and to members of the Routledge team who have seen the book through the various stages of its production in an efficient and expeditious manner.

Paul Dukes
King's College, Old Aberdeen
31 May 2000

1 Inheritance

Nations and empires, before 1898

There were two superpowers in the twentieth century: the USA and the USSR. At the beginning of the next century, from most points of view, there appears to be only one, the USA. In the future, there may be others: China seems a prime candidate. And in the past, before the superpowers, there were the 'great powers', mainly the European empires but including both the USA and the USSR's predecessor, Tsarist Russia. Already in 1835, in a famous prediction, Alexis de Tocqueville talked of them as 'two great nations' apparently tending towards the same end, if starting from different points, each of which seemed to be 'called by some secret design of Providence one day to hold in its hands the destinies of half the world'. As we shall soon see, we have to go far further back than 1835 in order to understand the origins of the two twentieth century superpowers.

But before that, a brief definition is in order. I suggest the following necessary characteristics. A 'superpower' must be able to conduct a global strategy including the possibility of destroying the world; to command vast economic potential and influence; and to present a universal ideology. Thus, the USA and USSR were involved in an arms race which threatened the ultimate holocaust; were capable of commanding the necessary resources for this purpose while promoting the capitalist free market and the socialist planned economy, respectively; and, more generally, acted as major spokesmen for liberal democracy on the one hand and communist 'Marxism–Leninism' on the other. As we shall see, many modifications may be made to this basic definition, the most important of which can only be explained by examining historically how the superpowers themselves and their predecessors evolved through previous centuries. This will involve going back to medieval times, before 1492, the year of the epic voyage of Columbus when Ivan III was tsar, and then on to early colonial expansion before 1776, the year of the American Revolution, when Catherine the Great was Empress of Russia, looking for the roots of the political culture and other features of both the USA and the USSR.

I have to recognise a considerable difficulty here. There will be those, I have to admit, who will ask why a book which claims to be concerned with the twentieth century should find it necessary to begin with a whole chapter in which this century will scarcely be mentioned. All I can do here is quote the words of Shakespeare, carved on the front of the US National Archives in Washington DC: 'what's past is prologue', and to remind you of some of the references made during the impeachment of William Jefferson Clinton which took place in Washington in 1998–9. These included not only the intentions of the Founding Fathers when they were framing the Constitution of 1787 but also the ideas of Sir Thomas More in the sixteenth century, the meaning of 'high crimes and misdemeanours' as adopted in the High Court of Parliament in the fourteenth and fifteenth centuries, and even the clauses of the Magna Carta of 1215. If the long historical dimension is appropriate for the arraignment of a president, why should it not be appropriate for the comparative examination of the history of his country and that of its great rival? Such an argument receives powerful support from the comprehensive study of *Soviet Diplomacy and Negotiating Behavior*, commissioned by the Committee of Foreign Affairs of the US House of Representatives and published in 1979, which considers the emerging forms of diplomacy under the Greeks, then contributions from Rome and Byzantium, before coming on to aspects of the modern age.[1]

Geography and history (before 1492)

If, as was often alleged during the years of the Cold War, the twentieth-century struggle was indeed one between godless Communism and Christian democracy, there could be little doubt that the Almighty weighted the scales in favour of his principal adherents and against his chief adversaries when he arranged the basic conditions of the USA and the USSR. Historically, Russia's vast size has often been a tremendous handicap, contributing as much as the poor climate and maldistribution of natural resources to the slow pace of its development. On the other hand, waves of invaders up to the Nazi Germans in the Second World War have found themselves swallowed up in the monotonous steppes, while strategic thinkers from the beginning of the twentieth century to the nuclear age have seen the advantages of domination of the Eurasian land mass. Geography, indeed, has been no less evolutionary than history.

In fact, the former Soviet Union, now the Commonwealth of Independent States (CIS) plus the ex-Baltic republics, is about equal in area to the USA plus Canada and Mexico; that is, the North American Free Trade Association (NAFTA). However, the relationship of the two land masses to the sea has been of considerable significance. Although Russia's coastline is very long, much of it is north of the Arctic Circle and not yet of any great use. One of her historic drives has been to obtain a coastline on a navigable sea, first to the White Sea, then to the Baltic Sea, later to the Black Sea and finally to the Pacific Ocean. But only the Black Sea is completely ice-free, while none of Russia's ports enjoys completely open access to blue water. The USA has been much better endowed with exploitable coastline on both Pacific and Atlantic Oceans, remote Alaska being the only seaboard state to be seriously threatened by ice.

While the sea has been more agreeably arranged for the USA than for Russia, a broad comparison can be made between their manner of exploitation of the Atlantic Ocean and the Baltic Sea, the Gulf of Mexico and the Black Sea, the eastern and western littorals of the Pacific Ocean. In the eighteenth century, St Petersburg and other towns on the Baltic, forming the window on the west, maintained Russia's connection with the European civilisation that stretched over the Atlantic to Boston and other ports before and after the American Revolution. The USA's takeover of the Gulf of Mexico, providing more access to the Atlantic in two principal stages during the first half of the nineteenth century, might be likened to Russia's assimilation of the northern and eastern shores of the Black Sea, her outlet to the Mediterranean, a few years before. The Crimea and the northern shore of the Black Sea are juxtaposed here to Louisiana, and the Caucasus to Texas. Continuing this over-fanciful comparison and quickly passing over a superficial similarity between Russia's Central Asia, where some nomadic peoples as well as others more settled were subdued in the late nineteenth century, and America's Far West, where the 'Red Indians' made their last stand at about the same time, we come to the Pacific shores. Vladivostok, although founded in 1860, had some years to go before it could begin to rival San Francisco, and recently has been falling behind rather than catching up. Only the most visionary enthusiast could claim that the Russian Far East could become another California.

Leaving the seas, we move inland along the rivers, which have played an important part in the history of both superpowers. Kievan Russia grew up on the Dnepr, and was infiltrated by Northmen coming up the Western Dvina and other rivers, just as they penetrated North America along the St. Lawrence. With the growth of Muscovy, the rivers rising near Moscow were vital arteries for the new society. These included not only the Dnepr and Western Dvina, but also the Don and the Volga and their tributaries. Outstanding among these became the Volga, whose value would have been even greater had it flowed into the Black Sea rather than the landlocked Caspian. The USA's nearest equivalent to the Volga, the Mississippi, did not achieve its full significance until well into the nineteenth century. Before then, the rivers leading into the hinterland from the conveniently indented seaboard, the James, the Hudson, the Delaware and others, were of most service before the mountains were crossed and the Ohio was among those that came into use. The rivers remote from the first centres assisted exploration and communication, whether the Ob, Yenisei and Lena systems in Siberia, across to the Russian Pacific down the Amur, to a lesser extent into Central Asia along the Syr Daria and Amu Daria, or down to the North American south-west along the Rio Grande and Colorado, up to the north-west along the Columbia, from Northern to Southern California along the Sacramento and San Joaquin. While the heartland rivers were supplemented by canals, those beyond it were not, partly because this would have been less useful in their case, but more because their exploitation was not fully developed before the arrival of transport by rail and, in some cases, by air.

Alighting, we need now to develop further the concept of the heartland in an economic sense (as opposed to the strategic). In North America, this extends from the Atlantic westwards beyond the Mississippi into the prairie, from the Gulf of Mexico northwards near to Canada. The circumstances for agriculture have been mostly favourable. In Russia, a 'Fertile Triangle' tapers from a base line between St Petersburg on the Baltic Sea and Odessa on the Black Sea (since 1991 in independent Ukraine) over towards the Ural Mountains. Russia's heartland is smaller (especially since 1991) and also less productive. While the human factor should not be discounted, two fundamental physical features have been more influential. First, the fact that both St Petersburg and Moscow are to the north of Ketchikan, Alaska, gives a clear indication of the disadvantageous situation of Russia from the point of view of latitude. Second, the vast flattened and distorted rhomboid shape of the former Soviet Union, as opposed to the irregular triangle that is North America, has given it a continentality of climate that increases in extremity towards the east and makes it virtually impossible to farm in deeper Siberia. Moreover, cold is an enemy to the north, as is dryness to the south.

The parts historically played within the agricultural heartlands by the steppe and the prairie, as well as by the respective forests, have been central to the development of both the USA and Russia. Carving and burning out small plots of land in the wooded regions, or farming more extensively in the rolling plains, the frontier people in both societies have struggled against vast natural difficulties in an epic manner. Yet there is one more key difference: the relatively minor importance of mountains during the expansion of Russia. The Urals are in many places no more than high hills, and the Caucasus does not come on to the scene significantly until the nineteenth century, while the mountains of Central Asia and the Far East have always been on the fringe. On the other hand, the Appalachians were important moulding influences in American colonial times and beyond, while the crossing of the Rockies was one of the most momentous episodes in the great trek west.

Turning from the use of the land to that of its contents, we find again that the USA has been better endowed than its counterpart, especially as far as accessibility is concerned. Many of Russia's natural resources are to be found in remoter Siberia. Whereas the USA's northeastern states contained most of the necessary ingredients for early industrialisation, coal and iron were less conveniently located from the Russian point of view. Then, in the ambitious attempt to catch up with its rival during the Five-Year Plans in the 1930s and after, the USSR suffered handicaps beyond bureaucratic incompetence and ruinous purges.[2]

But we must begin nearer the beginning, with the Muscovite period of Russian history following on from the Kievan period after centuries of the earlier development of the Slavic peoples. Some readers will ask again, is this really necessary? Here, I shall try to convert those who still doubt the uses of the past by beginning with a State Department Order made to a specialist at Harvard University. If an important branch of the US government believed that it was in order to spend taxpayers' money on finding out the mainsprings of Soviet behaviour, should the rest of us doubt that this was a worthwhile exercise? Moreover, fortunately, the assignment was carried out by a leading scholar who adapted it for wider consumption as 'Muscovite Political Folkways'. In his article, Edward Keenan argued that Soviet political culture was an update of that developed in medieval Russia and conditioned by the natural conditions of life in the East European forest. Since these threatened survival itself:

> the most significant autonomous actor in peasant life was not the individual (who could not survive alone in this environment), and not even the nuclear family (which, in its extended form, was marginally viable, but still too vulnerable in disease and sudden calamity), but the village, to whose interests all others were in the end subordinated.

The main features of the consequent political culture were:

> a strong tendency to maintain stability and a kind of closed equilibrium; risk avoidance; suppression of individual initiatives; informality of political power; the considerable freedom of action and expression within the group; the striving for unanimous final resolution of potentially divisive issues.

These features, moreover, were to be found not only in the village but also, writ large, in the emergent Muscovite state. And since for it too, the major aim was survival, this state gave its prime attention to policies directed at the avoidance of chaos, at safety first, while the major guarantor of such policies was believed to be a strict principle of centralisation. The centre should hold on to all it could, extending its grasp where possible. But this did not mean a single ruler: as in the village, so in the state, ultimate responsibility was not individual, but collective. While such an aim was more easily considered than achieved – since among powerful aristocratic families extended in clans, there were great regional and dynastic problems sometimes leading to civil war – by about the end of the fifteenth century a kind of resolution had been achieved. This consisted of a coalition of the clans gathered around 'the divinely anointed grand prince of Moscow'. At the same time, however, the evolution of this coalition was accompanied by the emergence of a bureaucracy.

With some justification, critics of Keenan's approach pointed out that he had said little about Byzantine or Mongol influences, about the steppe and colonisation, or about international relations.[3] To take one example a little further, as far as the influence of Byzantine culture and the Orthodox Church was concerned, Keenan argued that:

> It cannot be demonstrated … that during its formative period (i.e. 1450–1500) Muscovite political culture was significantly influenced either by the form or by the practice of Byzantine political culture or ideology. Nor is there convincing evidence that any powerful Muscovite politician or political group was conversant with Byzantine political culture, except perhaps as the latter was reflected in the ritual and organisation of the Orthodox Church, which itself had little practical political importance in early Muscovy and little formative impact upon Russian political behavior.[4]

On the other hand, Dimitri Obolensky writes:

> It is highly significant that Russia entered the European family of nations through her conversion to Christianity, for which she is indebted to Byzantium. The heritage of East Rome was not, as it is sometimes suggested, Russia's 'mark of the beast' that isolated her from medieval Europe: it was, in fact, the main channel through which she became a European nation. Byzantium was not a wall, erected between Russia and the West: she was Russia's gateway to Europe.[5]

Let us leave for now the question of the harsh conditions of the Russian frontier and their influence on Muscovite and Soviet folkways to cross Europe and the Atlantic Ocean to ask a similar question about early influences on the political culture of the other superpower, the USA. Some immediate problems present themselves. First, there is no convenient counterpart to the US State Department Order that led to Keenan's article. To the best of my knowledge and belief, the Ministry of Foreign Affairs of the USSR never commissioned a Soviet scholar to analyse the remote roots of the behaviour of the US government. Second, and much more significantly, far from existing in the late fifteenth century on which Keenan focuses, the USA was not foreshadowed even in the wildest dreams of the 'discoverer' of America in the same period, Columbus in 1492. For many historians, even though they would concede that the Americas were far from 'empty' at that time, to look for explanations of the twentieth-century political culture of the USA in the period before the beginning of the colonial period might still be seen as wild eccentricity. Nevertheless, because it is in the interests of parity, and, indeed because it might have intrinsic validity, the attempt must be made.

Passing over for the moment the period of later clashes and interaction between Native Americans on the one hand and immigrant Europeans and Africans on the other, let us concentrate to begin with on the political culture of the principal promoter of the North American colonies. Towards the end of the fifteenth century, Muscovite Russia was not the only state suffering civil war among powerful families accompanied by great regional and dynastic problems. For England, the Wars of the Roses involving the houses of York and Lancaster fits that description all too well. But for at least one observer, the way forward had already been indicated. Just as Edward Keenan found directions for Russian development already indicated in earlier centuries, so the historical anthropologist Alan Macfarlane has asserted that 'most of the central legal, political, economic, social and demographic premises that were observable in the early nineteenth century were already formed by the fourteenth century at the latest'. The Common Law reached a mature stage of development by the end of the thirteenth century, while the principle that England was not an absolutist state but that the Crown was under the law and responsible to parliament was established even before the Magna Carta of 1215. Medieval England was already a trading nation with a 'shopkeeper' mentality, according to Macfarlane. Moreover, for him, the nuclear family with male primogeniture and a distinctive marriage pattern was almost the same in the nineteenth century as it had been in the fourteenth, and a consequence of this peculiarly English arrangement had led to an unusual level of demographic stability.[6] The nuclear family originating in the insular confines of England, as opposed to the extended family reacting to the severe conditions of the vast Russian forest? Do we find the early roots of the superpower rivalry already sunk deep in such an origin before the European voyages of exploration and discovery at the dawn of modern times?

Early modern colonisation (1492–1776)

Certainly, these voyages bring us to another phase in our search for the origins of the 'two great nations'. Russia was 'discovered' in 1553, and in a manner recalling the more famous 'discovery' of America in 1492. For, just as the expedition led by Columbus was expected to reach the riches of the Orient by way of the western route, over the Atlantic Ocean and beyond, so the expedition of 1553, led initially by Sir Hugh Willoughby and later by Richard Chancellor, was expected to reach the same goal via the north of Norway and the northeastern passage. A further link between the two routes of exploration was embodied by Sebastian Cabot, already known for following in the wake of his father John over to the New World, now governor of the group sponsoring this fresh venture to skirt the shores of the continent already known. Moreover, the letter carried by Chancellor from Edward VI of England and delivered to Ivan IV – the Terrible – in Moscow, also recalled the official purposes of earlier voyages. Addressed to 'all kings, princes, rulers, judges and governors of the earth, and all other having excellent dignity on the same, in all places under the universal heaven', the letter proposed the establishment of commercial relations, arguing that 'the God of heaven and earth greatly providing for mankind, would not that all things should be found in one region, to the end that one should have need of another, that by this means friendship might be established among all men, and every one seek to gratify all'.[7]

At about this time, Muscovite Russia was both a potential object of colonisation and an actual coloniser. A year before Chancellor's arrival in Moscow, Ivan the Terrible had taken the town of Kazan on the Volga from one of the remnants of the Mongol Tatars. Soon afterwards, Cossack freebooters – landward counterparts of Elizabethan seadogs – drove deep into Siberia in the search for gold, furs and other riches. Russian history had always been on the move, and this was just the latest stage in an expansion which had already been going on for several centuries.

As far as the relative significance of English expansion to west and east towards the end of the sixteenth century is concerned, the chronicler Richard Hakluyt gave some pertinent illustrations. For example, Christopher Carleill, Secretary to an English embassy to Moscow in 1568 and one of the most energetic promoters of overseas enterprise in the sixteenth century along with Hakluyt himself, attempted to secure the support of the Muscovy merchants for a transatlantic expedition in 1583 with the observation that:

> As for the merchandising, which is the matter especially looked for, albeit that for the present we are not certainly able to promise any such like quantity, as is now at the best time of the Moscovian trade brought from thence: so likewise is there not demanded any such proportion of daily expenses, as was at the first, and as yet is consumed in that of Moscovia and others.[8]

In other words, Carleill believed that in the not too distant future, the North American colonies could provide the same kind of materials as Russia without the same kind of haggle and hassle. In the fairly near future, too, Carleill and others expected that these same colonies would become a market for goods as well as a supplier of raw materials.

At the death of Elizabeth in 1603, as David Cressy has pointed out in a telling phrase, 'her subjects in North America could be reckoned on the fingers of one or two of her bony hands'.[9] Nevertheless, even before this date, an increasing number of projects for colonies were being put forward, not least by Richard Hakluyt, who enumerated seventy-six separate occupations in five principal categories as the basic manpower requirement for such an undertaking.[10] Such schemes multiplied in the seventeenth century throughout the reigns of the Stuart kings and the republican period under Oliver Cromwell, while Scotland and

Ireland were more fully incorporated in colonial projects in both an active and a passive manner.[11]

France and the Netherlands, along with Britain, caught up and overtook older empire-builders such as Spain and Portugal, in a European-wide movement which might be placed under the general heading of modernisation. Generally speaking, Western Europe was more affected than Eastern Europe, but as we have already seen, Russia was not omitted from the process, although responding to the challenge in a manner more transcontinental than transoceanic. One of the most interesting analyses of this response has been made in a book on *The Well-Ordered Police State: Social and Institutional Change through Law in the Germanies and Russia, 1600–1800*, by Marc Raeff, who tells us how the use of the word 'police' to mean administration in the broadest sense came from classical roots to spread throughout Central and Eastern Europe by the seventeenth century. To a considerable extent, although unwittingly, the emergence of the well-ordered police state was promoted by the Western part of the continent in its internal and external economic activity. Within such a framework, Raeff remarks that 'the colonial experience was of particular interest and relevance, since it gave the administrator from the homeland virtually free rein to shape the lives of the natives for the purposes the colonial government demanded and expected'. We have already noted the formulation of schemes by Richard Hakluyt. For his part, Raeff pays special attention to the Jesuits in South America, remarking how amazing it is with the benefit of hindsight to observe the degree to which they 'prefigured the outlook, aims, and policies of enlightened absolutism in Austria and Russia (especially with respect to peoples deemed to be on a lower level of culture) and those of the well-organised police state'.[12] Needless to say, for Jesuits and enlightened absolutists alike, there was often a wide gap between aspiration and achievement.

An older authority than Marc Raeff, Albion W. Small, points out that cameralism – the body of doctrine behind many police-state policies – came to be an equivalent for Central and Eastern Europe of the mercantilism adopted in much of the West of the continent, especially when the process is described and defined in the following manner:

> The whole internal history of the seventeenth and eighteenth centuries, not only in Germany, but everywhere else, is summed up in the economic policy of the state to that of the town, the district, and the several Estates; the whole foreign history is summed up in the opposition to one another of the separate interests of the newly rising states, each of which sought to obtain and retain its place in the circle of European nations, and in the foreign trade which now included America and India. ... Mercantilism ... in its innermost kernel is nothing but state making – not state making in a narrow sense, but state making and national-economy making at the same time; state making in the

modern sense, which creates out of the political community an economic community, and so gives it a heightened meaning.[13]

To look at Russia in particular, the third phase of the implementation of the great historian V.O. Kliuchevskii's fundamental fact of its history, colonisation in a boundless plain, began in the seventeenth century. First, there was Kievan Rus, then Muscovite Rus. Now there was the expansion leading towards the creation of one of Tocqueville's 'two great nations'. However, the first half of the century was basically a holding operation, a recovery from the traumatic shocks of the Time of Troubles (1598–1613) that threatened to destroy Muscovy soon after the death of Ivan the Terrible. Not only was there internal strife at the end of a dynasty under severe social pressures, but also the threat of takeover by foreign powers, Poland and Sweden. Under Michael, the first Romanov (1613–45), something like order was restored and the invaders pushed back. But it was not until the reign of the second Romanov, Alexis (1645–76), that Russia began to expand again, absorbing much of the Ukraine (or Little Russia, including the ancestral home of Kiev) and consolidating interests in Siberia. At this time, government policies followed a centralising course that was as much traditional as influenced from outside, although innovatory enough to contribute to a schism in the Orthodox church. But more implementation of cameralist ideas, as well as fuller integration with Europe, would have to wait until the end of the seventeenth century and the reign of Peter the Great.[14]

Meanwhile, across the Atlantic, the first successful colonies were being founded and developed along the North American coast: Virginia from 1607, Massachusetts from 1630 and so on. The character of the colonies would vary according to geographical circumstances and the nature of the foundation, opportunities for prosperity and the evolution of local administration. Already, American traditions such as those begun by the Plymouth Pilgrims in 1620 were in process of formation, with ideas of predestination becoming involved in intimations of Manifest Destiny. Walter LaFeber summarises American beginnings as 'Gold, God and Paradise'. 'The birth of Americans as a separate people came out of fourteenth- and fifteenth-century events', he observes, adding: 'The early quests for wealth, personal salvation, westward empire, control of the world's centres of political and economic power, and supremacy in technology led to both the settlement of America and its rise as the globe's superpower.' Already by 1630, John Winthrop in Massachusetts Bay was urging his fellow immigrants: 'We must consider that we shall be as a city upon a hill, the eyes of all people are upon us.' Over and over again, these words have been quoted by American politicians, including Ronald Reagan, to sanction the USA's world mission. As LaFeber points out, far less quoted have been Winthrop's recommendations that 'The care of the public must oversway all private aspects' and that the colonists should be willing 'to abridge ourselves of superfluities for the supply of others' necessities'.[15] Moreover, from the beginning, the Native Americans were not included in the great vision; and soon, seeds of later conflict would be propagated by the import of African slaves to the South. As far as imperial administration was concerned, although the seventeenth century was disturbed enough in the mother country to keep the attention of Stuart and Cromwellian governments nearer home on several occasions, what was known as the Old Colonial system on mercantilist foundations had been developed by the time of William and Mary at the end of the century. Policies were far from rigorous for most of the time – indeed, there was a considerable degree of 'beneficial neglect' – and some kind of harmony was preserved for the most part between the interests of those overseas and those back in the metropolis.[15]

That both the steppe and transoceanic frontiers were subject to pressures from the European core may be illustrated by taking the example of *Unfree Labor: American Slavery and Russian Serfdom*. In his book with that title, Peter Kolchin points out that the two institutions:

> were part of the same historical process, despite the vastly differing societies in which they emerged. Both were products of geographic and economic expansion in areas of sparse settlement. ... In both countries a crisis in the labor supply finally forced landholders and the governments that depended on them to make arrangements that led to the spread and institutionalisation of new systems of unfree labor.[16]

However, recourse to unfree labour does not mean so much backwardness as apartness. Indeed, both Russia and America were dynamic societies from the later seventeenth century through the eighteenth. Peter the Great (1689–1725) and Catherine the Great (1762–96) were associated with two significant and distinctive phases of the consolidation of absolutism along with empire. In the first phase, Russia gained its 'Window on the West' in the shape of the new capital city of St Petersburg and the adjacent provinces on the Baltic Sea; in the second phase, the empire swallowed a large slice of Poland. In both phases, there were probes towards the Black Sea and the Balkans, the Caspian Sea and Central Asia, as well as increased activity right across Siberia and beyond the Bering Strait, over to Alaska and down to California. Further to the east, on the other side of the North American continent, the dissatisfaction of the thirteen colonies at not being able to expand beyond the line of the mountains was to contribute to the frustrations culminating in the American Revolution.

Democratic revolution (1776–1815)

The American Revolution was a consequence of a crisis of empire. From 1754 to 1763, Great Britain fought France for domination in North America and elsewhere. Emerging the victors in 1763, the British had to work out a way of paying for their extended empire, which now included Canada as well as the thirteen colonies and most of the West Indies in the Western hemisphere, India and other places to the East. The government in London decided that the King's subjects across the Atlantic Ocean should be given clearer direction, in particular not only to limit their movement beyond a proclaimed line, but also to help pay for their upkeep and defence. Taxation led to the first complaints about lack of representation. Import duties as an alternative were no more palatable, especially when they were levied to help relieve the financial difficulties of the East India Company: hence the Boston Tea Party of December 1773, leading towards the Continental Congress of September 1774. In April 1775 the 'shot heard round the world' was fired at Concord, and the American Revolution had begun. At first protesting against the unacceptable policies of Parliament, the insurgents turned on their King and opted for independence in the famous declaration of 4 July 1776.

The hostilities allowed the French to attempt to regain through support of the American Revolution what they had lost in 1763. Other imperial powers seized the opportunity to cut the British Empire down to size, with even the Empress Catherine the Great of autocratic Russia participating in an armed neutrality and threatening to send troops over to join in the fight against His Majesty King George III's redcoats. When peace came along with independence in 1783, the United States found it difficult to establish firm government until the Federal Constitution was drawn up in 1787. At its beginning, however, this celebrated arrangement of the legislative, executive and judicial branches of the government was far from being a promoter and guarantor of democracy. Indeed, when the French Revolution broke out in 1789, firm measures were taken to make sure that the pernicious Jacobin spirit did not infiltrate the USA.

The wars raging in Europe then infiltrated the Western Hemisphere. The alliance with France broke down, and there was renewed tension with Great Britain. Yet the USA was able to exploit Napoleon's difficulties in order to acquire the whole of the Mississippi valley and its tributaries in the Louisiana Purchase of 1803. Then, partly as a consequence of the high-handed actions of the British navy on the high seas, and partly as British imperial activity on the North American continent appeared to limit the westward expansion of the USA, a 'second war for independence' was fought in 1812. Officially, peace on Christmas Eve 1814 meant to both sides acceptance of prewar boundaries. Unofficially, the USA's confidence in its own ability to survive and prosper had received a considerable boost. By 1815, the USA was well on the way to becoming a power in the Pacific as well as the Atlantic, with Yankee traders taking over from Imperial Russia the fur trade from Alaska to Oregon and selling their wares over in China as well as back home. By this time too, the application in a 'can do' spirit of new technology ranging from the steamboat to the cotton gin was beginning to open up the continent to dynamic exploitation.

From the point of view of the future superpowers, the Democratic Revolution of 1776–1815 has far more significance for the USA than for Russia. Nevertheless, the long reign of Catherine the Great from 1762 to 1796 marked an important stage in the development of the Soviet Union's Tsarist predecessor. In the first place, her 'enlightened absolutism' was far more than a cover for her hypocrisy, and was nothing less than a skilful attempt to create a constitutional monarchy. Secondly, the lack of success of Russian America should not blind us to the fact that, by the European standards of the period, the Russian economy was one of the most powerful in the late eighteenth century. The legacy that Catherine left was strong enough for her successors and their advisers to negotiate the threat posed by the French Revolution and then to triumph over Napoleon. In 1815, Alexander I was one of the major arbiters of the post-Napoleonic settlement.

Less obviously, perhaps, the period 1776–1815 was one of cultural self-assertion for both the USA and Russia, even if both tended to follow a European lead at the beginning of it. For, if Bernard Bailyn is correct in his observation that 'American culture in this early period becomes more fully comprehensive when seen as the exotic far western periphery, a marchland, of the European culture system',[17] something similar might be said of much Russian culture at that period as well. However, there were also significant differences. First of all, there is the problem of Old Russian Culture, with both its pagan folkways and its Orthodox Christianity. Eighteenth-century Russian writers had to consider this heritage as well as the desirability of the import of foreign models. Eighteenth-century American writers, on the other hand, depended almost entirely on such import, both secular and religious, along with the continual process of immigration. As yet, they had neither assimilated much of Native American culture nor responded fully to the influence of their new setting.

If we concentrate on the radiation of British culture, further points of interest emerge, including the fundamental circumstance that it would often come to Russia in translation through German or other intermediaries. This would obviously mean a considerable time lag in continental cultural transference, although such chronological breaks would often be found on the Atlantic side too. When weeks or even months were necessary for the crossing of the ocean, the periphery could always have the feeling that what was fresh for it was already becoming stale in the core. This would be a short-term reaction. In the longer term, there was a more profound disorientation. For example, as the American Revolution of 1776 approached, at least part of the debate centred around the 'Glorious and Bloodless' Revolution of 1688–9, no longer so vital in England, Scotland and Ireland. For Jefferson and his fellows, the writings of John Locke were more pertinent documents than for their British sympathisers.[18]

As much as time, space was a problem in the adaptation of the metropolitan culture to the frontier. Distance lent enchantment to the view, so that rather than allowing the new environment to influence them, colonists in Russia and America alike more usually attempted to superimpose the metropolitan culture upon the frontier. Let us remember too, that until the end of the eighteenth century, the wilder splendours of nature were not considered to be objects of veneration. Travellers on the Grand Tour normally hurried through the Alps as the price to be paid for the wonders of Italy. Until the arrival of the Romantic veneration of nature in the nineteenth century, then, it was difficult for American and Russian culture fully to come to terms with the grandeur of their own respective frontiers.

Let us take just one basis for cultural comparison, the linguistic. In his *Dissertations on the English Language*, published in 1789, the same year as the onset of the French Revolution, Noah Webster declared: 'I am constrained to declare that the people of America, in particular the English descendants, speak the most pure English now known in the world.'[19] Hence, simultaneously, at least some of the inhibition of and stimulus towards the development of an American literature at a time when Russian literature, we may recall, was also finding difficulty in making its way owing to the persistence of foreign models. For, while Russian would be included in the Indo-European family of languages being identified towards the end of the eighteenth century, its Greek-derived alphabet would continue to cut it off from the Latin-based mainstream, in spite of the effort of Catherine the Great and others.

To sum up so far, towards the end of the eighteenth century the early modern development of Russia and North America as peripheries of Europe, building on the medieval legacy, was coming to an end. The struggle for European empire, in which both transcontinental and transoceanic frontiers played important roles, partly active and partly passive, was reaching a turning point. The American revolutionaries showed that they could adapt the imperial urge before their descendants could give it their own distinctive flavour in the 'manifest destiny' of the nineteenth century. The French revolutionaries, to some extent following in the American wake, completed the introduction of a new political rhetoric along with a new direction for European and world history. The years 1776 to 1815 therefore constituted an important watershed or conjuncture in the rise of the 'two great nations'.

Moreover, two further developments may be placed in this period of about forty years: the first specific realisation of the future significance of the American–Russian relationship; and the intensification of the phenomenon that we have come to know as Russophobia. Direct relations concerned science as well as diplomacy.[20] More generally, just after the beginning of the American Revolution in 1776, the American diplomat Silas Deane observed in 1777 that 'Russia like America is a new state, and rises with astonishing rapidity'.[21] Then in

1780, Russia played a leading part in the armed neutrality which brought about the first diplomatic contacts between the forerunners of the superpowers and made a positive if minor contribution to the successful outcome of the American Revolution a year or so later. Soon after the outbreak of the French Revolution in 1789, one of her European correspondents, Baron Melchior von Grimm, wrote to Catherine the Great in 1790 of a future in which:

> Two empires will then share all the advantages of civilisation, of the power of genius, of letters, arts, arms and industry: Russia on the eastern side, and America, having become free in our own time, on the western side, and we other peoples of the nucleus will be too degraded, too debased, to know otherwise than by a vague and stupid tradition what we have been.[22]

Grimm was inaccurate in other aspects of his prophecy; he believed that the French Revolution would hasten the downfall of Europe, for example. Nevertheless, both he and Silas Deane before him had clearly seen what was happening on the peripheries of the continent.

As far as early Russophobia is concerned, when Alexander I joined an allied coalition against Napoleon in 1805, the fear spread across the Atlantic that, if the French were defeated by the Russians, these latter-day Goths and Vandals would overrun Europe and then threaten the USA. Then, when the Russians and others were defeated by Napoleon at the battle of Austerlitz in 1805, an American commentator exclaimed that the neo-barbarian leaders, the 'Alarics and Attilas of modern times' were 'chained to their mountains'[!]. More generally, an American journalist wrote that the vast expansion of Russia along with the French Revolution would probably determine the future of Europe, looking upon Russia as 'more favourably situated for the prosecution of a boundless scheme of conquest, than any nation that has ever existed'.[23]

'Two great nations' (1815–56)

During the years before and after Alexis de Tocqueville's famous prediction of the future superpowers as 'two great nations' predestined to share world domination, the American people went forth and multiplied. In what seemed no time at all, the USA acquired vast lands to the west of the Mississippi, at the expense of Spain, Russia and Great Britain and, above all, of Mexicans and other Native Americans.

Following the Louisiana Purchase of 1803 from France, the USA consolidated its hold on Florida in 1818, and at the same time acquired from Spain its rights to the Pacific Coast. There as before, the interests of the USA clashed with those of other powers. In 1821, Alexander I of Russia proclaimed his rights from Alaska to San Francisco and thus helped to prompt President Monroe to include in his annual address to Congress of 1823 the three fundamental principles which came to be known as the Monroe Doctrine. The first, aspiring for 'amicable negotiation' concerning the north-west coast with both Russia and Great Britain, was that 'the American continents, by the free and independent condition which they have assumed and maintain, are henceforth not to be considered as subjects for future colonization by any European powers'. The second, with an eye on 'the heroic struggle of the Greeks' for independence from the Turks, was: 'In the wars of the European powers in matters relating to themselves we have never taken any part, nor does it comport with our policy so to do.' And the third, after noting the essential difference between the political system of those powers and that of America, warned that 'we should consider any attempt on their part to extend their system to any portion of this hemisphere as dangerous to our peace and safety'. The reassurance was added, if more to be acknowledged before the nineteenth century came to an end in the breach rather than the observance, that: 'With the existing colonies or dependencies of any European power we have not interfered and shall not interfere.'[24]

In 1846, in spite of a recent election slogan, 'Fifty-four forty or fight', a deal was struck with Great Britain to divide Canada from the Oregon territory at the forty-ninth parallel, and the long-impending war with Mexico finally broke out. By 1848, the USA had incorporated Texas and acquired the territories of New Mexico and California. In 1850, agreement was reached with Great Britain concerning their respective rights to any future isthmian canal in Central America. At this time, US spokesmen were not as assertive in Latin America as they later became. Nevertheless, both the dollar and the Bible were to be found increasingly all round the great ocean as merchants and missionaries followed in the wake of the first intrepid explorers. Of course, there were periods of depression as well as of prosperity, but the overall impression of the years 1815 to 1856 has to be of a rapidly expanding nation sweeping all before it.

In the North American continent, this process was to engulf the original inhabitants. When in 1831 Chief Justice John Marshall could rule that an Indian tribe may not have been a 'foreign state' but it was 'a distinct political society' dependent on US law, President Andrew Jackson challenged his rival to enforce his decision and moved the Cherokees on from a part of Georgia where gold had been discovered.[25] The doctrine that the only good Indian was a dead Indian was yet to be fully enunciated, however, and in any case, brute force was not enough totally to justify the treatment of Native Americans and others standing in the path of what was widely believed to be progress. Building on religious traditions begun with the *Mayflower* and to be developed with the secular admixture of Social Darwinism in the later part of the century, the concept of 'Manifest Destiny' emerged clearly in the roaring 1840s. To put the point simply, God had decided that the USA should carry out a special mission, to civilise as much as possible of the North American continent and beyond. Variations of the idea

abounded in the journalism and literature of the period. To give just one
example, in a lecture read in Boston in 1844 by Ralph Waldo Emerson:

> We cannot look on the freedom of this country, in connection with its youth,
> without a presentiment that here shall laws and institutions exist on some
> scale of proportion to the majesty of nature. To men legislating for the area
> betwixt the two oceans, betwixt the snows and the tropics, somewhat of the
> grandeur of nature will infuse itself into the code. … It seems so easy for
> America to inspire and express the most expansive and humane spirit; new-
> born, free, healthful, strong, the land of the labourer, of the democrat, of the
> philanthropist, of the believer, of the saint, she should speak for the human
> race.[26]

In 1847, a representative of 'the land of the labourer' spoke out on behalf of
US engineers supervising the construction of railroads in the other 'great nation'
which was also in process of development: 'Who knows but in a few years the
now Russian serf may stand a free man … as he beholds the locomotive fleeting
past … and bless God that the mechanics of Washington's land were permitted to
scatter the seeds of social freedom in benighted Russia'.[27] Leaving aside for the
moment the vexed question of the USA's own unfree labour – Black slavery – we
must certainly recognise that from the point of view of railroad construction
Russia lagged far behind: by 1860, there were more than 30,000 miles of railroad
in operation in the USA, and little more than 1,000 in Russia. The gap was great
as far as other indices of industrialisation were concerned. While the total
population of Russia far exceeded that of the USA at mid-century by a ratio of 3:1
(69 million as opposed to 23 million), American natural rates of growth and of
urbanisation were higher. About 65 per cent of the American people were
engaged in agriculture, compared to about 90 per cent of the Russian population.
The reasons for the comparative slowness of Russian growth were partly
geographical, partly institutional: natural resources were unhelpfully distributed,
and the Tsarist government feared social change. Nevertheless, the Tsarist
economy was far from static; there was significant export of grain, for example.
Ralph Waldo Emerson, for one, had no difficulty in including Russia along with
the USA in a celebration of the impact of modern science: 'When its errands are
noble and adequate, a steamboat bridging the Atlantic between Old and New
England, and arriving at its ports with the punctuality of a planet – is a step of
man into harmony with nature. The boat at St. Petersburg, which plies along the
Neva by magnetism, needs little to make it sublime.'[28]

Moreover, the boundaries of Russia were expanding ever more widely after the
final victory over Napoleon in 1815. Finland to the north-west and Bessarabia to
the south-west were more completely incorporated, as were Georgia, Azerbaidzhan and Armenia beyond the Caucasus. Tsarist forces pushed into Central Asia,

while the hold on Siberia was consolidated by comprehensive administrative reforms in 1822.[29] However, while the island of Sakhalin in the Pacific was occupied, the Tsarist government found it difficult to maintain its influence on the North American continent. Major energies were devoted to the maintenance of law and order nearer home, which included East and Central Europe at times of revolution, notably in 1830 and 1848. Tsar Nicholas I himself wrote the manifesto of March 1848, lamenting the outbreak of rebellion and lawlessness in Prussia and Austria and the menace which they presented to 'our holy Russia'. Summoning the people to arouse themselves for 'faith, Tsar and country', he threatened to march the army to the Rhine, but in the end limited his army's activities to intervention in Hungary.[30] (With a different excuse, the move was to be repeated by the Soviet government in 1956.) The alarm of other European powers at the threat posed by Nicholas I in the Black Sea was a major contributor to the Crimean War of 1854–6.

Arguably, the expansionist behaviour of Tsarist Russia was similar to that of the USA. At the time of Nicholas I's intervention in Hungary, let us recall, the USA was bringing to an end its war with Mexico. However, the principal difference lay in the respective ideologies. While 'Manifest Destiny' certainly had its less attractive features, it also proclaimed a democratic impulse. The Tsarist ideology of 'faith, Tsar and country' or of 'orthodoxy, autocracy and nationality' was less generally acceptable. There were very few American intellectual dissidents during the first half of the nineteenth century: many bitter political arguments but all within the same constitutional framework. In Russia, however, there were a considerable number of such malcontents, notably at the death of Alexander I in 1825. At the end of that year, drawing variously on the precedents of the American and French Revolutions, the members of the Decembrist movement staged an abortive revolt. The leaders, we must stress, were members of the nobility. Five were hanged, many more were exiled to Siberia, and Russian society was never the same again.

Tsarist autocracy or republican democracy, comparisons between the future superpowers continued throughout the period 1815–56. As we have already seen, Alexis de Tocqueville's famous prediction of 1835 did not come like a bolt from the blue: Melchior von Grimm and others had made comparable forecasts during the years of the Democratic Revolution. This point may be reinforced by taking a glance at some other predecessors. For example, in 1818, an Englishman named John Bristed brought out in London and New York a book entitled *The Resources of the United States of America*. It was later published in German, in 1819, and in French in 1826 and 1832. John Bristed observed that America 'is rapidly emerging into unparalleled greatness; is flaming upwards, like a pyramid of fire, so that all the Western horizon is in a blaze with the brightness of its ascending glory'. America was playing a waiting game with the Holy Alliance of Russia, Prussia and Austria formed soon after the final defeat of Napoleon in 1815. Then, it would gradually 'bear down all possible opposition from any single foe'. Bristed declared:

> Behold another and a greater Russia here. With a better territory, a better government, and a better people, *America* is ripening fast into a substance, an attitude of power, which will prove far more terrible to the world than it is ever possible for the warriors of the Don or the defenders of Moscow to overcome.

Several other figures, less well-known than Alexis de Tocqueville, had discussed the joint future of America and Russia before his celebrated observation of 1835. In 1827, the US diplomat Alexander Hill Everett wrote of Russia as an immense military empire 'advancing with giant steps to the conquest of the west' which if completed would mean 'a return to barbarism'. Such an eventuality would probably be averted 'because the principle of civilisations and improvement will be powerfully sustained by aid from abroad, that is, from America'. And Michel Chevalier, engineer turned economist and politician, declared in a letter to the *Journal des Débats* in April 1834, two years before the publication of his own book on American civilisation, that there were 'two great figures which are rising today at both ends of the horizon ... two young colossi who watch each other from one shore of the Atlantic to the other and touch each other on the banks of the Pacific Ocean', which would probably soon divide among themselves the 'dominion of the world'. Chevalier also asserted that 'the struggle between the East and the West' was 'the most general fact in the history of the civilisation to which we belong', expressing at the same time the thought that America might be best able to reconcile the two. On the whole, conflict between the two great nations was not foreseen as much as their rise to world power in the place of the nations of Europe. In 1845, ten years after the publication of Tocqueville's *Democracy in America*, the *Journal des Débats* echoed Von Grimm in an editorial leader showing alarm about the American annexation of Texas at the expense of Mexico: 'Between the Russian autocracy in the East and the democracy of the United States thus enlarged in the West, Europe could find itself compressed more than would comport with its independence and its dignity'.[31]

But apprehension concerning the spread of the USA never reached the proportions of that concerning the expansion of Tsarist Russia. This, after all, had roots stretching as far back into history and was exacerbated by Russia's behaviour towards Europe in and around the revolutions of 1830 and 1848. In his *Secret Diplomacy of the Eighteenth Century*, published first as newspaper articles from 1856 to 1857, Karl Marx wrote:

> It is in the terrible and abject school of Mongolian slavery that Muscovy was nursed and grew up. It gathered strength only by becoming a virtuoso in the

craft of serfdom. Even when emancipated, Muscovy continued to perform its traditional part of the slave as master. At length Peter the Great coupled the political craft of the Mongol slave with the proud aspiration of the Mongol master, to whom Genghis Khan had, by will, bequeathed his conquest of the earth.[32]

The Petrine and earlier legacies combined with Catherine the Great's leading part in the partitions of Poland and other expansive policies to produce by the end of the eighteenth century the phenomenon known as Russophobia, which was then to grow stronger in the early nineteenth century.

Another potential conflict detected just before the outbreak of the Crimean War deserves at least summary mention. Edouard de Stoeckl, the Russian chargé d'affaires in Washington DC, believed that an alternative struggle might develop between the major English-speaking peoples. As the historian Frank Golder reported Stoeckl's views as expressed early in 1854, they have an undiplomatic apocalyptic quality more appropriate for some of the enthused sermons of the period:

> It will be a battle of giants, he said, the earth will tremble, commerce will be crushed, the world will suffer; but there will be certain gains to civilisation, nevertheless. Weakened England will stop meddling in other people's affairs and exhausted America will cease to protect revolutionists and to cause trouble to other states. ... The Americans will go after anything that has enough money in it. They have the ships, they have the men, and they have the daring spirit. ... When America was weak she refused to submit to England and now that she is strong she is much less likely to do so.

When the Crimean War actually broke out between Russia on the one hand and Britain, France and their allies on the other around about the time that Stoeckl's note was being received in St Petersburg, the USA refrained from joining in the hostilities; nevertheless, by the time the war was over two years later, in Golder's estimation, 'the United States was the only nation in the world that was neither ashamed nor afraid to acknowledge boldly her friendship for Russia'. But diplomacy and national interest were one thing; attitudes towards a friendly power outside official communication could be another.[33]

To qualify completely as two great nations, the USA and Russia needed not only to command enormous power, but also develop their distinctive cultures as they developed their empires. European models had to be discarded, and indigenous creative spirits fostered. More will be said on this below.[34]

Two great empires (1856–98)

Both future superpowers suffered the experience of war on their own soil early in the second half of the nineteenth century. Russia was invaded again little more than forty years after Napoleon had reached Moscow. On this occasion, hostilities from 1854–6 were confined mostly to the Black Sea and the Crimea. Yet the international consequences were significant, the alignment of the European powers was determined for several years to come, and some of the rivalries exacerbated by the conflict were to influence the nature of the onset of the First World War. Internally, the poor performance of the Russian armed forces was a major reason for the emancipation of the Russian serfs. Similarly, the American Civil War from 1861–5 was to lead to the liberation of the Afro-American slaves. Like most events of its kind, the war was passionate and bloody, and left scars which took a long time to fade. In the short run, the victory of the North accelerated the process of industrialisation, and the achievement by the USA of great power status.

The first shots in the American Civil War were fired just a few weeks after news had crossed the Atlantic of the Russian emancipation of the serfs. Now the abolitionist element in the war aims of the North encouraged some of its journals to reverse completely their previous image of Russian despotism and of the absolute Tsar. For example, *The Atlantic Monthly* declared: 'He is the Greatest of Russian benefactors in all these thousand years – the Warrior who restored peace, the Monarch who had faith in God's will to make order, and a man's will to keep order, the Christian Patriot who made forty millions of serfs forty millions of men – Alexander the Second – ALEXANDER THE EARNEST.' And *Harper's Weekly* could go as far as to compare Alexander II's repression of the Polish Insurrection of 1863 with the attempt of Abraham Lincoln to prevent the South from seceding from the Union, observing that:

> Russia, like the United States, is a nation of the future. ... To two such peoples, firmly bound together by an alliance as well as by traditional sympathy and good feeling, what would be impossible? ... An alliance between Russia and the United States at the present time would relieve both of us from all apprehensions of foreign interference.[35]

Yet beneath the journalistic rhetoric there was a deep-seated mutual suspicion between the Russians and the Americans, which different times would bring once more to the surface. Abraham Lincoln did not change his views of a country where 'they make no pretence of loving liberty', and would probably have been appalled by some of the remarks made about him by official Russia after his assassination, even though he would have been flattered by those of Leo Tolstoy, who wrote that the 'greatness of Napoleon, Caesar or Washington is only moonlight by the sun of Lincoln.'[36] And the Russian chargé d'affaires, Edouard de Stoeckl, could at the same time work for co-operation between his own country and the USA while expressing no confidence in the American political system:

> The experience of recent years has taught us how easy it is to manipulate the universal suffrage in all ways everywhere. In the United States the institution has been cleverly exploited by a bunch of politicians of the lowest class, who through corruption and flattery of the passions of the populace, have come to exercise an absolute control over the elections.[37]

De Stoeckl's condemnation of the absolutism of universal suffrage did not come out of the blue; it was indeed a variation on a theme enunciated by Russian critics earlier in the nineteenth century, and would be enlarged upon by others later.

But there was also a Russian admiration for the USA, stretching back beyond the Decembrists. To give a good later example, however, in 1865, as the American Civil War came to an end, in *Letters to a Traveller* Alexander Herzen took American–Russian comparisons in particular to a new level, also echoing Tocqueville and other predecessors while anticipating later commentators and analysts. He declared: 'Classless, democratic America and peasant Russia, which is moving towards classlessness, remain for me, as before, the countries of the immediate future'. Of Russia in particular he wrote: 'Aside from the village, no one feels any attachment for anything, and everybody either feels or understands that everything else is like a temporary shack that has been given the outward appearance of an old and solid building'. By 'everything else' and 'temporary shack', we are given to understand that Herzen means not only the autocracy of the Tsars and the privileges of the nobility but also the institution of private property. Similarly, the USA was for Herzen a fragment of Europe cut off from its 'native soil, from palaces, from the Middle Ages' and freed from the 'historical shackles of monarchy and aristocracy'. However, he observed that, while leaving certain negative features of European thought and practice such as the class system behind them, immigrants had imported to North America some of the best features, the Common Law, for example. So both Russia and the USA were untrammelled by many burdens of the past, the latter thereby possessing *actual* freedom while the essential spirit of the former was one of the *inner* freedom. Comparing the respective processes of expansion, he declared:

> The United States sweeps everything from its path, like an avalanche. Every inch which the United States seizes is taken away from the natives forever. Russia surrounds adjoining territories like an expanding body of water, pulls them in and covers them with an even, uniformly coloured layer of autocratic ice.

Herzen also made some interesting remarks about the literary evocation of the lives of American and Russian settlers, likening the novels of Fenimore Cooper to Sergei Aksakov's *Family Chronicles*. However, his most striking observation was a prediction, that the problem of the future was not a choice between individual freedom and socialism, but their reconciliation in a higher form of existence. As Herzen put it:

> The North American States and Russia represent two solutions which are opposite but incomplete, and which therefore complement rather than exclude each other. A contradiction which is full of life and development, which is open-ended, without finality, without physiological discord – that is not a challenge to enmity and combat, not a basis for an attitude of unsympathetic indifference, but a basis for efforts to remove this formal contradiction with the help of something broader – if only through mutual understanding.[38]

Unfortunately, Herzen's prediction was not to be fully realised in either the short or the long run. Nevertheless, in the following thirty years or so and then into the twentieth century, some sort of understanding was on occasion approached, if more normally avoided in pursuit of aims far narrower.

Both the future superpowers were expansionist powers during this period. In 1864, the Russian Chancellor Prince Alexander Gorchakov made the accommodating remark: 'The United States in America, France in Algeria, Holland in her Colonies, England in India – all have been irresistibly forced, less by ambition than by imperious necessity, into this onward march, where the greatest difficulty is to know where to stop.'[39] Russia was no exception: in 1860, the Russian imperial standard was raised on the Pacific Coast over a group of huts named Vladivostok, 'Lord of the East'. Nevertheless in 1867, the Tsarist government revealed the limits of its aspirations in the sale of Alaska to the USA, signalling its intention to withdraw from North America and concentrate on the Eurasian land mass. On the other side, although Secretary of State W.H. Seward was at first heavily criticised for his folly in spending $7,200,000 dollars on an 'ice box', he was posthumously forgiven even before the discovery of gold in the Yukon in 1896.[40] And while Russia rounded out its frontiers in Central Asia as much as the mountains and British opposition would allow, the USA not only subdued the rest of the Natives to establish full possession of its large slice of North America while increasing its grip on Central and South America, but also pushed out into the Pacific Ocean, acquiring Hawaii, establishing a firm foothold in Samoa and reaching over to Japan and China. Internal and external expansion were connected, since the official closure of the frontier in 1890 was marked by historian Frederick Jackson Turner and soon followed by the insistence of Captain A.T. Mahan that the USA must look outward: Manifest Destiny was on the move.

Frontiers were far from closed in Russia, which was seized in the late nineteenth century by the spirit of Panslavism as the Ottoman Empire was pushed back and more of its blood relations freed from the Turkish yoke. To be sure, the Kaiser attempted to persuade the Tsar to reduce his concentration on the Balkans and elsewhere in Europe, and to switch his major attention to the Far East. But Nicholas II was to find himself, like his father Alexander III before him, firmly caught up in the Balkan imbroglio that was to lead to the First World War. Europe was one area in which the USA had no possibility of expansion, and successive presidents, whether conscious of it or not, adhered to the less well-known principles of the Monroe Doctrine concerning that continent. But the USA was not isolationist, playing at least a modest part in international conferences in Berlin and The Hague.[41]

Because of the different international interests of the USA and Russia, there was no serious confrontation between them before 1898. Reflecting the harmonious relations of the time, Russian naval officers had sailed into the harbour they dubbed 'Vladivostok' on a steam corvette named *Amerika* in 1859,[42] before giving the same title to the modest land settlement in the summer of 1860. Just a few years later, during his survey of Kamchatka and Chukotka for a projected (but never completed) telegraph route under the Bering Strait, George Kennan came across American cooking utensils, linen, magazines, lithographs and music. When Henry Adams wrote in 1891 that the Americanizing of Siberia was the only challenge the Pacific region offered to the United States, Russians and Americans enjoyed mostly friendly relations in what was still a challenging wilderness even for the indigenous peoples. Nevertheless, relatively, we can see a clear division between the two future superpowers which could produce the first serious disputes between them at the turn of the century. In the year 1898, there were signs of collaboration as the Tsarist government lifted import duties on US agricultural machinery, and President McKinley appointed the first US consul in Vladivostok.[43] Soon, however, antagonism would flare up in Manchuria.[44]

Yet what appeared for the most part to be good relations were undermined less by geopolitical considerations than by a clash of values. George Kennan gave wide publicity to the convict system operating in Siberia. Even more seriously, news began to arrive in the USA from the 1880s of the Russian pogroms, from which large numbers of Jews fled across the Atlantic. And US businessmen, both Jew and Gentile, found themselves up against discrimination when they tried to operate in the Tsarist empire. These latter restrictions were by no means exclusively the consequence of bureaucratic tradition or racial prejudice. The Russian economy simply could not accommodate the Open Door advocated by its most dynamic rival. Between 1860 and 1900, the US population more than doubled to 71 million, a consequence of vigorous natural growth and mass immigration. Wheat production tripled, while coal extraction increased eightfold and the manufacture of steel and rails rose fivefold. By 1898, 55 million barrels of oil were being produced per annum. Of course there were serious setbacks, busts as well as booms, industrial strife as well as harmony, but from 1874, US exports regularly exceeded imports. Europeans in general began to fear 'The American Invaders' and even 'The Americanization of the World'.[45]

The Russians in particular were nowhere in the same league, even though they were far from inert. The emancipation of the serfs of 1861 contributed to a considerable growth in the production of wheat and other cereals, and a sevenfold rise in grain exports in the second half of the nineteenth century. Coal, steel and iron all increased in output, but at a lower level than in the USA, while Russian oil production had barely begun. Only in numbers of people did the tsarist empire outstrip the democratic republic, 125 million by 1897. But nearly 90 per cent of the population were peasants, the low proportion of town dwellers reflecting the lag in industrialisation.[46]

Considering *Russia and America: The Roots of Economic Divergence*,[47] Colin White rejects the term 'modernisation' because it cannot include significant change occurring before periods which can properly be deemed modern, and because it prejudges the importance of its component activities. Nevertheless, he concentrates on what most historians would consider to be modern periods, which also give his work a clear sense of direction. Accepting that there are four phases of economic development – pioneering, commercial, industrial and planning – he adds the key concept of a formative period. During this period, the basic principles of institutional organisation in any given society are established. In White's estimation, the closing date of the formative period was the 1780s for the United States and the 1580s for Russia. In the 1780s, the United States achieved a lasting constitution protecting market institutions, rejected the Proclamation Line holding back settlement beyond the Appalachians, and consolidated their pre-revolutionary core to the east of those mountains. In the 1580s, Tsarist Russia took a large stride towards the establishment of a service state based on serfdom (although the process neared completion in 1649), crossed the Urals into Siberia (although another seventeenth-century process, the movement into the steppe, was also important), and, less clearly than in the transatlantic case, crystallised a core around Moscow (with a significant persistence of openness to attack). White finds neither the neoclassical approach following Adam Smith in which 'economic agents are rational economic men' nor the Marxist analysis based on the class struggle a comprehensive guide to the phases of development, considering that the environment of competition or conflict in which both schools operate ignores the more universal wish for security. Societies are organised not only to promote prosperity but also to lessen or manage risk.

White next examines what he calls 'stylised facts' and asks several pertinent questions. He looks at the size and nature of native populations, reminding us that, while the pre-contact figures for North America vary from 4.4 to as many as 12.5 million, higher at their most conservative than those for Moscow's outliers, assimilation of Red and Black peoples occurred to a much smaller extent than among their counterparts in Russia, which therefore constituted a more complete melting-pot. He makes the necessary point that the opening-up of the respective frontiers was a more complex process than has often been assumed. Recognising that there has been no more impressive saga of modern times than the exploration and settlement by the American and Russian peoples of their respective continental areas, he indicates that the process was much more protracted in the latter case, where spurts occurred both before and after the mostly nineteenth-century action in the former. Government policies as well as variations in basic geography were responsible for differences in the two sets of core–periphery interactions during the pioneering phase. Similar considerations would apply to the later commercial and industrial development. Here again Russia, as it were, missed out on the nineteenth century, reaching the commercial phase only at the very end, a century or so later than the USA, and the decisive industrial phase in the 1930s as opposed to the USA's 1880s.

The reasons for this disparity are among the subject matter for the second and third parts of the book, entitled 'Risk, Resources and Natural Environment' and 'Risk, Regimes and the Human Environment', respectively. These two parts are seen by White as the pith of his book, calling for some of the skills not only of the economist and the historian, but also of the geographer, anthropologist, sociologist, demographer, political scientist, lawyer, statistician and even linguist. (For a full attack on the subject, even further specialities could be called into service, not least those of the literary critic and the philosopher, as we will soon see. Indeed, virtually all fields of human enquiry could be summoned into the discussion, but that could be an unattainable ideal. Limits have to be set somewhere.)

Within the broad limits that White has imposed upon himself, he presents a challenging enlargement of his thesis. Discussing gardens and deserts – that is, the benign and malign influences of the physical environment – he recalls that if these are considered in too simple a manner, the conclusion would follow that Native Americans would have been the first to undertake an industrial revolution. Following several previous authorities, he indicates that the arrangement of natural assets was less favourable in the Russian case. Again, the cards were somewhat stacked as far as the socio-economic impact of natural assets was concerned: 'There can be little doubt that Russian society was more "shocked" than American – more frequently, more severely, more extensively and more inopportunely.' For such reasons, pioneer risk-taking was found to a lesser extent in Siberia than in the Western states. If immediate survival is the major aim, there can be little thought for long-term profit. But, of course, as with all general rules, there must be exceptions, such as the activities of the Stroganovs and other fur-traders, to cite just one. On the other hand, circumstances such as those described by White also account for the differences between the American and

Russian applications of technology, the Yankee 'can do' spirit as opposed to the more fatalist outlook of the Muscovite.

Turning to human factors more generally, White focuses first on the creation of government, the political divergence between autocracy and democracy, and then on the creation of markets, as affected by such factors as opportunities for commercial risk, the distribution of land and resources, and demographic arrangement. As far as the interaction between government and markets is concerned, he again stresses the impact of the environment, for example in the vital sector of transport. At the end as at the beginning, White gives emphasis to the manner in which choice of option has been greatly influenced by the weight of the past. Rather surprisingly, he says little about the converse of his theme, the economic convergence that used to be so popular among some colleagues, particularly those specialising in the industrial and planning phases of development. Is the weight of the past so great that convergence is generally accepted as an impossibility? If so, more than a dozen years after his book was published and more than a decade since the Soviet system began its collapse, what hope is there for the introduction of the advanced market economy in today's Russia?[47]

We will tackle this question later. For the moment, let us note that, in the nineteenth century, Russia lagged behind America in cultural as well as economic development, as numbers of schools and universities increased in both societies, but much more in the USA. In Russia, the preponderance of peasants meant the persistence of tradition, as was clearly revealed in the 'crazy' summer of 1874 when thousands of mostly young crusaders attempted to take the message of modernity to the people. Often dressed as peasants and attempting to put their arguments in a similarly homespun manner, the preachers found few converts and many more sceptics, even opponents. But Russian opposition to Tsarism never ceased, soon moving on from a populist to a revolutionary phase. In the USA, nearly everybody shared the American dream, even many of those who lived an American nightmare in urban and rural deprivation alike. To be sure, violent suppression also contributed to the comparatively low level of protest. But, within the more democratic parameters, there was much more open debate among women as well as men, increasingly stimulated by newspapers and magazines. And there was much more following of fashion, from bicycles to bloomers.[48]

As always from the eighteenth century onwards, clear reflections of American and Russian culture can be found in their literature. We have traced above the first halting steps of both outliers of Europe in the age of the Democratic Revolution. Concerning later development in the national and imperial phases, the critic George Steiner reminds us of the writer D.H. Lawrence's observation that 'Two bodies of modern literature seem to me to have come to a real verge: the Russian and the American', as he himself recommends us to look in the same places for the reconciliation of the modern novel with 'the essential world view of the epic and of tragedy.' In Steiner's view, both frontiers:

> lacked even that sense of geographical stability and cohesion which the European novel took for granted. Both nations combined immensity with the awareness of a romantic and vanishing frontier. What the Far West and the Red Man were to American mythology, the Caucasus and its warring tribes, or the unspoiled communities of Cossacks and Old Believers on the Don and the Volga were to Pushkin, Lermontov and Tolstoy. Archetypal in both literatures is the theme of the hero who leaves behind the corrupt world of urban civilisation and enervating passions to affront the dangers and moral purgations of the frontier. ... The vastness of space brings with it exposures to natural forces at their most grandiose and ferocious ... all these encounters of man with a physical setting which can destroy him in moments of wanton grandeur lie outside the repertoire of western European realism.[49]

Steiner suggests that Tolstoy's *How Much Land does a Man Need?*, in which a greedy settler discovers that the answer is enough to bury him, could have been the nineteenth-century creation of only a Russian or an American. While the scale of Melville's *Moby Dick* has made it seem a very Russian novel to some readers, they might also find in Mark Twain's *Huckleberry Finn* that the Mississippi attains the universal, eternal quality that Russians have always attributed to the Volga. Moreover, Tolstoy's favourite book, at one period in his life at least, was Thoreau's celebration of the natural life, *Walden*.

A final point of departure for discussion could have been Ernest Hemingway's celebrated remark that 'All modern American literature comes from one book by Mark Twain called *Huckleberry Finn*', and Dostoevsky's, that all subsequent Russian literature emerged out of Gogol's *The Overcoat*. The magnitude and influence of both these works are undeniable, but, arguably, additional implications of the above remarks are that Hemingway's urge away from civilisation and back to nature was most clearly foreshadowed by Mark Twain, and Dostoevsky's St Petersburg twilight world, peopled with monomaniac outsiders, by Gogol. Better perhaps, however, to finish on the mundane observation that art reflects as well as inspires, and that, besides frontier and size, American and Russian society were the most formative influences on the literature of the two great nations becoming empires. An analysis of their social systems, of their concepts of world mission, would be of close relevance to a consideration of their novels. The assistance could be mutual, of course, for the epic quality to be found in the history of the superpowers often approaches, sometimes surpasses, that of their art. How could any novel do justice to the saga of the emergence of America and Russia as great powers in the centuries before 1898?

But our conclusion cannot be completed without a return from fiction to 'fact', or at least to philosophy. W.J. Gavin and T.J. Blakeley observed in 1976 that in the nineteenth century the 'American and Russian contexts were radically uncertain or mysterious' and in some way 'realised' that 'this indeterminacy was essential'. Gavin and Blakeley conclude:

> Although some specific questions could be answered, nonetheless the cultural context should always be seen as fundamentally mysterious. It is ironic that only in an uncertain world can one function as a human being. In this case, however, the irony rings true. Perhaps William James said more than even he realized when, at the close of the nineteenth century, he asked for 'the re-instatement of the vague to its proper place in our mental life'.[50]

However much historians might agree with their philosopher colleagues, they are also bound to recognise that 'the vague' is not an easy concept for them to handle. Equally, agreeing with Gavin and Blakeley that the human being is perhaps best defined as a 'questioning animal', I accept the professional necessity to at least suggest some of the answers. Furthermore, while accepting their parallel between William James and Alexander Herzen, I repeat the observation of the Russian that the relationship between their two countries is best viewed as representing 'two solutions which are opposite but incomplete', with a complementary contradiction 'which is full of life and development, which is open-ended, without finality, without physiological discord'. Having attempted to set out the manner in which the future superpowers had developed before 1898, I shall now turn to the manner in which their relationship took a turn for the worse in the following century.

2 Conception

The First World War and revolution, 1898–1921

Imperial showdown (1898–1914)

Having considered the structure of the inheritance, we turn to the great conjuncture of conception. Certainly, we should not carry our basic metaphor too far, and we would not extract much enlightenment from speculating about parentage, even though serious scholars have discussed the femininity of Russia and the masculinity of the USA.[1] In any case, in Chapter 1 we have given a considerable amount of attention to the manner in which Europe made a contribution to the political, economic and cultural development of both the USA and Russia. And so, we would be better off noting simply that it was during the period 1898–1921 that the ideological foundations of superpower, Wilsonism and Leninism, were laid against a background of war and revolution.

Beginning this chapter in the year 1898, we may appropriately take a brief preliminary glance at chronometry itself. A conference in Washington in 1884 proposed that Greenwich time should be adopted as a standard for the world. Many European countries as well as the USA soon accepted this proposal, but France held out until 1911, while Russia continued to adhere to a norm provided by the Pulkovo observatory just south of St Petersburg. This was just over two hours ahead of Greenwich, while, in measurement of days, according to the Orthodox calendar, Russia remained thirteen days behind the West into the early twentieth century; a reflection also of a many-sided backwardness. One of the well-known supporters of the idea of standard time was the German Field Marshal Count Helmuth von Moltke, who just before his death in 1891, pleaded with the German Reichstag to adopt it for military reasons. Germany's five different time zones complicated planning, which the further changes to be met at the French and Russian frontiers made increasingly difficult. Germany duly accepted the great change in 1893, and Europe as a whole sufficiently co-ordinated its chronology and its means of communication for the 'war by timetable' to go ahead by telegraph and telephone as well as train in 1914.[2]

Back in 1898, the light of peace as well as the shadow of war could be detected among the still expanding world empires. On 24 August, Russia distributed a note suggesting an international conference to relieve world tensions. If armaments continued to grow, there would sooner or later ensue 'a cataclysm too horrible for the human mind to contemplate'. But Germany soon declared 'no intention of binding herself in the question of military armaments', while the great powers in general could not avoid noting that Russia had just infringed an earlier agreement with China by seizing Port Arthur, and so they themselves made no immediate arrangements to curb their own ambitions. Even the USA, which also talked of higher principles, could not resist the lure of self-aggrandisement during the war against Spain. In 1899, the first Hague Peace Conference managed to establish a permanent court of arbitration and to adopt two conventions relating to the rules of war, but the century turned without any reduction in the speed of the arms race or in apprehensions about its ultimate destination. The second Hague Peace Conference of 1907 was even less successful in holding back the arms race, even accelerated it. Although it confirmed a prohibition on 'the use of asphyxiating or deleterious gases' while discussing the necessity for the prior declaration of war, seven years later there would be a declaration of war without such warning followed by the use of poisonous gases.[3]

Among other notable events in 1898 were the deaths of Bismarck, the architect of the Second Reich in Germany, and of Gladstone, the former British Prime Minister, considered to be 'the Christian statesman' by future US President Woodrow Wilson, himself then working as a university teacher and writing a book to be published in 1899 with the title *The State*. In this work he put forward Russia as a long-standing exception to the general rule made by the rest of Europe and the USA:

> There can be no reasonable doubt that the power of Russia's Czar, vast and arbitrary as it seems, derives its strength from the Russian people. It is not the Czar's personal power; it is his power as head of the national church, as semi-sacred representative of the race and its historical development and organisation. Its roots run deep into the tenacious, nourishing soil of immemorial habit. The Czar represents a history, not a caprice. ... The measure of the Czar's sovereignty, is the habit of his people..., their humor also, and the humor of his officials.[4]

In 1898 too, a political organisation that would do much to undermine Tsarism and change the course of history, the Russian Social Democratic Labour Party, was founded at a meeting in Minsk. But at this time, its future leader V.I. Lenin was in exile in Siberia, working on the ideas that were to help him ultimately to establish authority over the Bolshevik fraction of the RSDLP and over revolutionary Russia. Needless to say, by this time he was drawing most of his inspiration from Marx and Engels. At the same time, however, in a less perceptible and more complex manner, Lenin and Wilson both were drawing on the heritage of many centuries that we have described in Chapter 1.

In 1898, the six major world empires could be divided into several different categories:

- monarchical (Germany, Great Britain, Japan, Russia) and republican (France, the USA)
- European (France, Germany, Great Britain, Russia) and non-European (Japan, the USA)
- overland (Germany, Russia) and overseas (France, Great Britain, Japan, the USA);
- static (France, Great Britain, Russia) and dynamic (Germany, Japan, USA).

Broad indeed, the last two categories are relative: if Germany's principal interests were continental, it was also heavily involved overseas; many observers of the British Empire, on which the sun never set, would not easily recognise it as static. Nevertheless, relatively, we can see a consistent categorical difference between the future superpowers. Let us glance at each of them in turn after noting in a preliminary manner the consistent categorical difference between them: Russia was monarchical, European, overland and static; the USA was republican, non-European, overseas and dynamic.

The Tsar was less divine than the Emperor of Japan, but nevertheless ruled by a divine right more complete than that of the German Kaiser. Russian policies were carried out by his ministers in his name, and to his greater glory. The heartland of the empire over which he ruled was in Europe, but it also stretched over Asia. The acquisition of Port Arthur and its hinterland on a long-term lease in 1898 clearly demonstrated that the expansionist impulse was not completely sated in the Far East, while there were British fears for Central Asia as the Tsar's agents were deemed to be infiltrating as far as Tibet. The unsatisfied aspiration to acquire Constantinople indicated unfulfilled ambitions in the Near East, while there were harbingers of Russian involvement in the Balkan question. If the Russian empire was static, then, it could be deemed so only in comparison with other empires more dynamic.

For its part, the USA had concentrated on internal expansion for most of the nineteenth century, but was always conscious of surrounding waters. After all, the classical formulation of its foreign policy, the Monroe Doctrine, looks out to the Atlantic Ocean, seeking to maintain it as a barrier for the Western hemisphere. With the frontier officially closed in 1890, more emphasis was soon given to the Caribbean and the Pacific. Still avoiding involvement in Europe, it was nevertheless becoming a great power. But in acquiring an empire, the USA had still to find a global role. 'Manifest Destiny' had been mostly confined to the North American continent and did not easily find its sea legs. What did a republic which had broken away from Great Britain in a principled manner mean by taking on Puerto Rico, Cuba, the Philippines and other possessions of Spain along with Hawaii, some of Samoa and so on? President McKinley gave his own clear answers to aspects of this question. In 1899, he told a group of Methodist ministers that after much sleeplessness and prayer, he had decided that the Philippines could not be handed over either to Spain or to other European empires who were also commercial rivals. Therefore:

> there was nothing left for us to do but take them all, and educate the Filipinos, and uplift and civilize and Christianize them, and by God's grace do the very best we could by them as our fellow-men for whom Christ also died.[5]

The question of imperial acquisition was central to the presidential election of 1900, and an argument that was a mixture of muscular Christianity, Social Darwinism and Manifest Destiny won the day. And only Hawaii was formally incorporated, Puerto Rico becoming an 'unincorporated territory' while the rest were taken temporarily for a transitional period until the peoples involved were prepared for democracy. The new spirit was to be found at its most assertive in Teddy Roosevelt, who succeeded as President after McKinley's assassination in 1901. For example, in 1903, he sent US forces to Panama in order to ensure the opening of the canal. In 1904, in justification of what he had done and what he might do, he added what was to be known as the Roosevelt Corollary to the Monroe Doctrine, announcing to Congress that the USA might be obliged to act as 'an international police power' in the Western Hemisphere.[6] In 1907 he sent the US Navy around the world, with a visit to Japan as a polite warning not to take its recent victory over Russia and domination of Korea as springboards for further expansion. But world war and revolution would have to ensue before an ideology and a policy more completely appropriate for the USA's embryonic superpower could be formulated by Woodrow Wilson.

Before 1914, the major clash with the predecessor of its future adversary would be across the Pacific where the USA struck the Asiatic mainland. For here too was Tsarist Russia, entering fully into the international opposition to the Boxer Rebellion of 1900 as it sent its own expeditionary force to join those of the USA and others in lifting the siege of the diplomatic compounds in Peking. American policy in the Far East was Secretary of State John Hay's Open Door, in line with US traditions and half-way on the road to President Woodrow Wilson's Open Covenants. On the whole, the spheres of interest of the great powers were reconciled with the concept of an economic free-for-all, but there was one major exception. This was in Manchuria, which, after constituting the focus for a diplomatic duel between Russia and the USA, came under the control of Russia and Japan. These two imperial rivals came to blows in the Russo-Japanese War of 1904–5, when an enemy dismissed as 'yellow monkeys' overcame armed forces believing themselves to be the representatives of the white master race. A kind of compromise peace was made at Portsmouth, New Hampshire, with the active participation of President Roosevelt who wanted neither power to predominate, after the Tsar's attention had been drawn back to Europe, not least by the outbreak of revolution.[7]

In what Lenin called a 'dress rehearsal', most of the features of 1917 were revealed in 1905. There was unrest among workers and peasants, soldiers and sailors, Russians and other nationalities, as well as agitation from a whole range of political parties. Warned by his advisers that the alternative before him was military dictatorship, which would be difficult to implement without the certain loyalty of the armed forces, or political reform, which could be easily accomplished through his signature on a piece of paper, the Tsar came to realise that his pen would be mightier than his sword.[8]

As Russia struggled to develop some kind of constitutional regime, it became increasingly sucked into the Balkan vortex. Having dropped his earlier pilot, Bismarck, Kaiser Wilhelm II had for the most part charted his own course, believing that the interests of peace would best be served if he concentrated on Europe and the sea while his cousin Nicholas II concentrated on Asia and the land. Unfortunately, this imperial division of labour had come unstuck with the Russo-Japanese War, and the once friendly cousins were soon at each other's throats.

War and revolution formed by no means a combination exclusive to Russia. As Walter LaFeber notes in his outstanding work on US foreign policy at home and abroad:

> An understanding of twentieth-century US foreign policy requires learning one central theme: just as Americans began to claim Great Britain's title as the globe's greatest power and, at the same time, to demand an orderly world, the globe burst into revolution. The American claim was to be realized, but the demand was never met nor the revolutions ended.

As early as 1898, President McKinley had talked of the danger of 'revolution within a revolution' in Cuba, of a social movement against conservative property holders following the breakaway from Spain. In the Philippines, such a movement actually confronted McKinley and then many of his successors through a large part of the twentieth century. Among them, Woodrow Wilson came to power in 1913 facing an additional threat to US property interests in Mexico. He sent troops to intervene in the Mexican Revolution twice, not to mention elsewhere in Latin America, before sending them overseas to participate in the First World War. At home, in spite of the aspirations of radical politicians, neither Woodrow Wilson nor his immediate predecessors had to face any actual threat of large-scale disturbance. There were enough reforms, and enough fundamental stability, to avert revolution. Again, however, the situation needs to be seen relatively. In both rural and urban America, there had been protests and strikes in both the late nineteenth and early twentieth centuries. Considerable numbers of dissidents had been jailed and not a few killed in the struggle against poverty and injustice. Enough combustible material had been created in the years leading up to the USA's entry into the First World War for the danger of a great conflagration to appear real enough immediately after it.[9]

The First World War and proletarian revolution (1914–21)

The well-known observation of Karl von Clausewitz that 'War is nothing more than the continuation of politics by other means' gained unprecedented justification from the events of 1914–21, the years of the First World War, the Russian Revolution and the consequent Civil War. This was apparent in the original war aims of the belligerents, within the general framework of imperial rivalry. Great Britain sought the restoration of Belgium, the security of France, the guarantee of the smaller nationalities and the destruction of the ambitions of the Central Powers, Germany and Austria-Hungary. Agreeing with these objectives, France also sought the recovery of Alsace-Lorraine, while Russia wanted to secure control of Constantinople and the Straits. Japan was not obliged to enter the war by her alliance with Great Britain, but nevertheless declared war in August 1914 in order to exclude Germany from Far Eastern waters while conquering the German possession of Kiaochow in China and consolidating her occupation of the Shandong peninsula. As for the principal enemy, Germany, in the words of the historian A.F. Pollard: 'The mass of her people had been persuaded that the war was one of defence against a Pan-Slav peril and encirclement by other Powers; but the bourgeois classes looked for *Weltmacht* in the shape of commercial and colonial expansion', while militarists insisted that France must be completely crushed. However: 'Behind such ebullitions was a growing conviction in the Prussian mind that the Prussian system of government could not maintain itself against social democracy without fresh tributes to the efficacy of the sword'. And Austria-Hungary sought to re-establish its failing authority, especially in the Balkans.[10]

We will not follow the military history of the war in any detail. As we all know, stalemate soon ensued on the Western front, while the Russian 'steam-roller' went into reverse on the Eastern. Then in 1917, the future superpowers both played a key role in bringing the great conflict to an end, since:

> The Russian revolution and American intervention together form the turn-ing point of the war even more from the diplomatic than from the military point of view. But the one was needed to complete the other: without the

revolution American intervention would still have left the Entente with a dubious face and a divided mind; without American intervention the Russian revolution would have robbed the Entente of its victory.[11]

The fall of the Tsar early in 1917 was welcomed almost everywhere. But of course on this occasion the great wheel of social change was soon to turn in a different, proletarian manner. When the attempt of the Provisional Government under Kerensky to keep the Eastern front going failed, the ensuing Bolshevik government under Lenin made no attempt to resume hostilities, having come to power with such slogans as 'Peace, bread and land' and 'All power to the Soviets'. And so:

> Russia had gone effectively out of the war faster than the United States came in; but she left a blazing trail behind her, and sparks from the conflagration started a smouldering fire on German soil which was never extinguished. Bolshevik pacifism seemed a ridiculous gesture in face of Prussian arms, but its moral effect was by no means contemptible. 'Looking back', writes the archmilitarist Ludendorff, 'I can see that our decline obviously began with the outbreak of the Revolution in Russia'. After all, the original ground or pretence upon which the war had enlisted democratic support was as its appearance as a war of defence against autocratic Pan-Slavism.[12]

But if Imperial Germany had now begun its decline, Bolshevik Russia appeared to be following its Tsarist and liberal democratic predecessors towards collapse. As far as international relations were concerned, Trotsky, who had begun his work as Commissar for Foreign Affairs with the statement that he would issue a few revolutionary proclamations to the peoples of the world and then shut up shop, painfully learned that Germany was determined to carry on business as usual. So, after an armistice on 15 December 1917, he found it necessary to deal with the representatives of Germany and Austria-Hungary regarding the terms of the end of the war on the Eastern Front at the frontier town of Brest-Litovsk. The Central Powers were anxious to transfer troops from the Eastern to the Western front, Czernin (the chief Austrian representative) observing that 'peace at the earliest moment is necessary for our own salvation, and we cannot obtain peace unless the Germans get to Paris, and they cannot get to Paris unless the eastern front is free'.[13] The Soviet side was unable to stop this troop transfer. However, it could telegraph the negotiations throughout Europe, proposing the evacuation of all conquests, self-determination for all peoples and no indemnities, with the intention of promoting peace and revolution.

While the negotiations at Brest-Litovsk were temporarily broken off, the US President Woodrow Wilson prepared his famous Fourteen Points for an address to Congress of 8 January 1918, conscious that the liberal thunder had been stolen by Bolshevik insistence on open diplomacy and self-determination. So he began with a reference to these negotiations, observing that the time was ripe for a general statement about the conditions for peace. 'The Russian representatives were sincere and in earnest', he declared, while 'a voice calling for those definitions of principle and purpose', which was 'more thrilling than any of the many moving voices with which the troubled air of the world is filled', was that of the Russian people. The American President believed that 'the people of the United States would wish me to respond, with utter simplicity and frankness'. And so, Wilson put forward a programme consisting first of the best possible open covenants of peace, freedom of navigation upon the seas, removal of all economic barriers, reduction of national armaments and adjustment of colonial claims. There followed several points on particular European problems, beginning with the longest, on Russia:

> The evacuation of all Russian territory and such a settlement of all questions affecting Russia as will secure the best and freest co-operation of the other nations of the world in obtaining for her an unhampered and unembarrassed opportunity for the independent determination of her own political development and national policy and assure her of a sincere welcome into the society of nations under institutions of her own choosing; and, more than a welcome, assistance also of every kind that she may need and may herself desire. The treatment accorded Russia by her sister nations in the months to come will be the acid test of their good will, of their comprehension of her needs as distinguished from their own interests, and of their intelligent and unselfish sympathy.

While the following points on Belgium, France, Italy, Austria-Hungary, the Balkans, Turkey and Poland were more or less to be implemented, that on Russia fell far short of realisation. And, as far as President Wilson was concerned, so did the last: 'A general association of nations must be formed under specific covenants for the purpose of affording mutual guarantees of political independence and territorial integrity to great and small states alike.'[14]

On 7 January 1918, the day before Wilson's announcement of his Fourteen Points, having just denounced a German declaration about self-determination and proposed a transfer of the conference to neutral Stockholm, Trotsky had to resume negotiations with the enemy at Brest-Litovsk, even if asserting that the Bolsheviks would make no peace that was not 'just and democratic'. And he continued to find it difficult to negotiate in a traditional manner with the enemy and talked of the ongoing situation as 'neither war nor peace', while at least some comrades wanted to consider nothing but world revolution. Ultimately, Lenin had to persuade a majority of the Council of Commissars including Trotsky that the only possible policy was acceptance of harsh terms offered by the Germans. But having signed the treaty on 3 March, Trotsky gave up foreign affairs on 8 March and turned to the organisation of the Red Army: it was left to Lenin to manage the ratification of the treaty by a congress of Soviets after a three days' debate on 16 March. By the Treaty of Brest-Litovsk, Soviet Russia had to accept the loss of Poland, the Ukraine and the Baltic states as well as of some territory to Turkey. Russia was virtually made a commercial preserve of the Central Powers, while two million or so German colonists in Russia were exempted from allegiance to the Bolshevik government. In the same month of March, the Central Powers also made formal agreements with Finland and Romania.[15] While the conclusion of the World War brought the nullification of treaties made by the Central Powers during it, Poland, the Baltic states and Finland were all lost by Soviet Russia, which found itself largely ejected from Europe.

Already by the spring of 1918, the major contours of what were to become known as Leninism and Wilsonianism or Wilsonism (the latter term's lesser usage being indicated by the variation), were discernible. Of course, they would evolve and mature through the years following, and we will follow this process through to the spring of 1921, when Woodrow Wilson had just left office and Lenin took a new tack. Again, two significant illustrations will be briefly examined, the League of Nations and the Comintern.

For an evaluation of the League and its Covenant, we could do worse than turn to Woodrow Wilson's close collaborator, Colonel Edward M. House, who wrote seven years after the Paris Peace Conference had dispersed: 'It is to be doubted whether there were many sitting at the historic table who realised that with the acceptance of the Covenant a new phase of civilisation had begun and that the League of Nations was its keystone.'[16] Some of the major participants at the conference attempted to introduce reservations. As far as Europe was concerned, Wilson was made to realise that the principle of self-determination might lead to the voluntary acceptance of Bolshevism, and that a 'sanitary cordon' needed to be set up against it from the Baltic to the Mediterranean. In the wider world, he found it difficult to resist the desire of the other victors to share among themselves the spoils of the German colonies, finally agreeing to the compromise that they could do so but under league mandates. The Japanese were passionately in favour of a clause declaring equality of all members of the league without respect to race or colour. This was vetoed at the insistence of Premier Hughes of Australia, although Wilson succeeded in appeasing the Japanese by allowing them to remain in Shandong, China. A French suggestion that the league should have its own military staff and the power to supervise disarmament also failed, as did an American proposal to forbid discrimination in fiscal and economic regulations between one state and another. Moreover, although a specific provision was included to safeguard the Monroe Doctrine in order to forestall some of the criticisms emanating from the US Senate, the necessary two-thirds majority could not be found in that upper chamber of the Congress to endorse President

Wilson's support of Article X, which committed each member of the league to respect and preserve against external aggression the territorial integrity and existing political independence of all other members, and which Wilson saw as the 'heart of the Covenant'. As is well known, the rejection by the Senate of Article X and of the whole treaty helped to bring about the collapse of President Wilson and the triumph of the Republicans in the elections of 1920. And a more general disillusionment could be found among the Allies; the British diplomat Harold Nicolson wrote: 'We ceased to believe that President Wilson was the Prophet whom we had followed. ... We saw in him no more than a presbyterian dominie.'[17] But many of the hopes for a lasting peace continued to rest on the League of Nations. And while the USA sent no more than 'observers' to some of the League's commissions, President Harding and other successors developed a programme for world order by no means completely dissimilar to that of their predecessor. In other words, Woodrow Wilson was now dead, but his spirit lived on.

The Comintern, or Third Communist International, was no hastily impro- vised counterpart to the League of Nations. Lenin had talked about the necessity for its creation as early as 1914, when most members of the Second Socialist International had forsaken the cause of proletarian solidarity in favour of support for their respective national governments as war broke out. And then, in the tenth of his April Theses of 1917, he came out for the foundation of a new revolutionary international. After a pause brought about by such preoccupations as the October Revolution and the onset of the Civil War, Lenin's purpose was no doubt reinforced by the refusal of the Big Three to invite him to join them in Paris, or even, under pressure from White exiles in Paris, to allow Allied representatives to parlay with him at the Turkish island of Prinkipo. He presented a further set of theses to the inaugural congress of the Comintern in March 1919, attacking the imperialism of the Versailles powers and the terror inflicted by the White counter-revolutionaries as well as denouncing bourgeois democracy and parliamentarianism while asserting the dictatorship of the proletariat. In an appeal 'To the Workers of All Countries', the Comintern expressed 'gratitude and admiration' for 'the Russian revolutionary proletariat and its directing party – the Communist Party of the Bolsheviks' before going on to say what needed to be done. The congress considered it the duty of the 'working masses of all countries' to press upon their governments by all means (including, if impossible otherwise, revolution) the necessity to cease intervention and withdraw their armies, to recognise the Soviet Republic and establish diplomatic and commercial relations, and to send to Russia hundreds or even thousands of engineers and other specialists to help the restoration and reorganisation of transport. As well as accepting the need for such immediate steps, Lenin also expressed the belief that the congress could be seen as 'the forerunner of the international republic of Soviets'. And although most of its delegates were from the 'near abroad' and the

West, there were also in attendance 'consultative' delegates from China, Persia and Korea.[18] Undoubtedly, the Comintern was a central part of Lenin's internationalist outlook. According to Trotsky, he always considered the October Revolution 'from the standpoint of the European and world revolution. ... His thoughts never ceased to labour at the task of freeing the workers...' But, needless to say, Lenin also had his critics, even among those often sympathetic to him. For example, Gorky once included him among wooden dogmatists.[19]

Lenin died just before Wilson early in 1924, just one incident in the remarkably parallel lives of the 'presbyterian dominie' and the 'wooden dogmatist'. But their ideas, enshrined as Leninism and Wilsonism, were to live on through most of the twentieth century.

Imperialism: the highest stage of capitalism?

At the beginning of the twentieth century, the world's population amounted to something over 1600 millions, scarcely more than a quarter of some recent estimates for the end of the century, with the last decades seeing the steepest rise. In 1900, more than half of humankind was to be found in Asia, a formidable 'Yellow Peril' for those who saw 'Orientals' as people apart. China alone accounted for about 500 million, the Indian subcontinent for more than 250 million. The 'Dark Continent' of Africa contained about 120 million, Central and South America just over 60 million. Europe amounted to just over 400 million, including the European part of the vast Russian Empire, which as a whole numbered about 125 million people of many nationalities (although the vast majority – up to 110 million – were Slavs). While Russia was scarcely viewed in the West as a full part of the advanced world, by no means all the 80 million or so in North America would be considered part of the earth's upper crust, which tended to be represented mostly by WASPs (White Anglo-Saxon Protestants). Most of the self-styled 'lords of humankind' would be found at the top of the American and European peoples, with only a few additionally from the Southern Hemisphere. And so, the twentieth century dawned with most of the world in the possession of a small minority, mostly West European in origin, white and male, comparatively or very rich, educated or at least literate, and Christian (predominantly Protestant, but also Roman Catholic and even Orthodox).[20]

In that dawn, the vast majority of the world's inhabitants were involved in farming of some kind. Their horizons were limited almost literally, for they were not usually conscious of more than their nearest neighbours. They probably believed that the land should belong to the people, but normally knew only too well that their own patch did not belong to them. They would for the most part have a strong sense of family and of wider community, but were unlikely to have any real idea about how far people at large were actually distributed. And around the year 1900, their sense of time was often governed by the rise and fall of the sun and the waxing and waning of the moon, and by the seasons. But the newer ideas of time were arriving along with the railway, and farmers were increasingly caught up in national and international markets. For example, they could be deeply affected by the going price for grain not only in nearby towns but also abroad. As far as the future superpowers were concerned, there was a substantial divergence. While up to 90 per cent of the Russian population were peasants, little more than 50 per cent of the US population were rural inhabitants, and a smaller percentage earned its living from agriculture. Moreover, while there were at least some rich, educated peasants during the last years of Tsarism (when there were some poor, ignorant farmers in the USA), considerably more of the Russian population would fit the norm of agricultural workers throughout the world.

Moreover, the two urban populations also showed a considerable disparity. In the USA, the total was about 30 millions; New York had reached a population of 3.5 million, Chicago 1.5 million, and they and other cities were growing rapidly. They were swollen by immigration from over the ocean as well as by the depopulation of rural America. More than 5 million Europeans had come to the USA in the 1880s, followed by nearly 4 million in the 1890s; more than half were from Southern and Eastern Europe, Roman Catholics and Jews, compared with the earlier settlers from Northern and Western Europe, who were mainly Protestants (with the major exception of the Irish). From other continents, older immigrants of African origin were being followed by others from Asia, especially China. City slums grew like mushrooms, while political bosses often took over the government of the cities. But although there were some civil disturbances, notably stemming from strikes in the steel industry in 1901 and the coal industry in 1902, through the united armed opposition of the plant and mine owners, some kind of social stability was maintained, especially in contrast with Tsarist Russia, which suffered its 'dress rehearsal' for revolution in 1905. By about that time, the Russian urban population was about 20 millions, with St Petersburg and Moscow by far the largest at well over a million each and growing. Again, we are up against some problems of definition. At least some of the work in the new and old capitals was seasonal, and their population fluctuated.[21]

In agriculture, Russia was a significant player in Europe, especially as far as its grain exports were concerned, but in most respects, especially the technological, it lagged far behind the USA. In industry, Russia produced fewer machines than the USA: for this reason, in 1912 the import of industrial machinery equalled domestic production, while that of agricultural machinery exceeded it. While in 1913 Russia was fifth overall in world industrial production, and in some branches fourth, her overall share of the world's total was less than 5 per cent. Thus, the Tsarist empire was in an advancing but precarious international position when the war broke out in 1914. As Peter Gatrell puts it:

Imperial Russia had to deal simultaneously with the tasks of economic recovery, structural change and rearmament; the attempt to reconcile these tasks, in the midst of an international scramble for influence, exposed the fragile foundations upon which the entire edifice rested.

Rivalry between state and private sectors and too much emphasis on 'a fancy naval programme' were among the reasons why Russian industry could not take full advantage of the opportunities presented by rearmament. And then:

The war, with its sickening consequences for human beings, its appalling consumption of resources, its reliance on mass mobilization and new industrial technology, its extension of government intervention and the breakdown of international cooperation truly marked the beginning of the 'real, not the calendar century', and eventually exposed the recklessness of the gamble undertaken by the imperial regime.

Meanwhile, the USA now accounted for about a third of total world output, including agricultural, and was already in many respects, especially in newer industries such as machine making, the world's leader. If the world's financial capital was still to be found in London, it would not be for long.[22]

The immediate impact on Russia of the outbreak of war was tremendous. A key element in financial policy, the Gold Standard, was abandoned almost immediately, as was another with the loss of revenue following the introduction of prohibition, and rampant inflation soon set in. Foreign loans increased steeply and, even more than before, Russia became the financial client of the other great powers, Britain, France and the USA in descending order of importance. Meanwhile, needless to say, the USA's economy experienced a great war boom.

Comparison between the economic development of the two future superpowers may be summarised under the heading of the imperial showdown of 1914. Competition between the great powers in this field increased enormously towards the end of the nineteenth century, and there was a series of confrontations between individual empires or groups of them. The two future superpowers clashed in Manchuria in particular. But while the USA was flexing its economic muscles, Tsarist Russia was subject to overstrain. In the climax to the showdown of empire, the First World War killed Tsarist Russia, which had already been wounded by the Russo-Japanese War. Soviet Russia was crippled from the beginning by civil war from 1918 to 1921 as the empire fell apart. The human and material losses were horrendous: 13 million people died through famine and disease, while the combined populations of St Petersburg and Moscow fell from 4.30 to 1.86 million. Industrial revolution had gone into reverse, with large-scale production falling by 1920 to no more than 13 per cent of the 1913 level, iron and steel to as little as 4 per cent, while grain production was about two-thirds of the average level in the years leading up to the First World War. A hastily devised policy given the name War Communism could not succeed in disguising the catastrophe. Meanwhile, the USA profited enormously from the First World War before entering it in 1917, when the boom continued. By 1918, moreover, New York was taking over from London as the world's financial capital, appropriately enough since by now the Allies owed the USA more than $3.5 billion.[23]

How did the Soviet and US leaders look upon the phenomenon of empire? With the outbreak of the First World War, Lenin's development entered a new phase. He denounced the German Social Democrats and others in the Second Socialist International who had betrayed their cause to support the capitalists of each belligerent state rather than the workers of the world. He also looked for a comprehensive explanation of the process that had led to war, beginning as always with his mentors Marx and Engels but going on to use more recent writers as well. As he himself freely acknowledged, he turned to the principal work on the subject of imperialism, written in English by J.A. Hobson. Following Hobson and other authorities, Lenin concentrated on the monopolistic economic aspects of imperialism. This phenomenon could be discerned in four principal types. First, there was the concentration of production at a very high stage, which took the form in the advanced countries of cartels, syndicates and trusts. Second, there was the seizure of the most important sources of raw materials, especially coal and iron. Third, monopoly had sprung from the banks, some three to five of which in each of the leading capitalist countries had achieved an important connection between themselves and industry as well as controlling the export of capital. Fourth, there was imperialism in its most customary sense, growing out of traditional colonial policy. Lenin wrote:

> In the numerous old motives of colonial policy, finance capital has added the struggle for the sources of raw material, for the export of capital, for spheres of influence, i.e. for spheres for profitable deals, concessions, monopoly profits and so on, economic territory in general. When the colonies of the European powers, for instance, comprised only one-tenth of the territory of Africa (as was the case in 1876), colonial policy was able to develop by methods other than those of monopoly – by the free grabbing of territories, so to speak. But when nine-tenths of Africa had been seized (by 1900), when the whole world had been divided up, there was inevitably ushered in the era of monopoly possessions of colonies and, consequently, of particularly in-tense struggle for the division and redivision of the world.[24]

Lenin's *Imperialism: The Highest Stage of Capitalism* was written in the first half of 1916. Although he followed the approach of Hobson and took many of his examples and much of his supporting evidence from the history of Britain and the USA, he still concentrated on German data from the Austrian Rudolf Hilferding's

Finanzkapital and other sources. This would be partly the consequence of his residence in nearby Bern and Zürich, Switzerland, and partly the consequence of his previous area of concentration. Though moving towards a global outlook, Lenin's attention was still focused on Central and Eastern Europe.

As we have seen, Wilson approached globalism from a different point of departure, the British–American tradition, which gave far less prominence to the role of the state and much more emphasis to the pluralist nature of the nation's existence, as well as being less explicitly theoretical. At first, Wilson followed Gladstone in a belief in imperial dominion and therefore 'approved of the nation's imperialistic ventures, confident that the example of order and discipline would benefit the Filipinos and Puerto Ricans'. In office, nevertheless, as well as intervening in Mexico and elsewhere, he strove in some ways 'to set right the wrongs of imperialism he found on the nation's record' and came to see the attendant selfishness and rivalry as root causes of the First World War. In his struggle to gain Senate support in 1920, he wrote: 'Every imperialistic influence in Europe was hostile to the embodiment of Article X in the Covenant of the League of Nations. ... I hold Article X to be the essence of Americanism.'[25] In this new attitude towards 'imperialistic influence', Wilsonism as it was to emerge from 1917 was not completely different from the Leninism that was to mature at about the same time. Both ideologies rejected European concepts not only of 'empire' but also of the 'balance of power'. J.A. Hobson's ideas had a considerable influence on both men. Yet Lenin gave strong emphasis to the economic aspect of imperialism, while Wilson stressed that of human rights. In this latter connection, there was a wide gap between 'bourgeois' and 'proletarian' concepts of democracy born of the scarcely overlapping intellectual settings in which the concepts had arisen.

In later chapters, we will see how this divergence evolved throughout the rest of the twentieth century. For the moment, let us pause simply to note that by 1921, old ideas of empire were already obsolescent and that Wilsonism and Leninism presented themselves as alternatives. Moreover, both of these ideologies were applicable at home as well as abroad. At times of national emergency, the US President was in his own way as keen on control of the 'commanding heights' in the economy as was the Chairman of the Soviet of People's Commissars.

The spread of liberalism

In 1913, James Bryce, author of *The American Commonwealth* and many other books, set out a global liberal vision. He observed that the whole world was governed by active minorities who originated ideas and compelled the attention of the multitude. He spoke of almost every part of the earth's surface, except the territories of China and Japan, being owned or controlled by a few European races, adding:

Similarly, a few European tongues have overspread all the continents, except Asia, and even there it seems probable that these few European tongues will before long be learnt and used by the educated classes in such wise as to bring these classes into touch with European ideas.

Even in the USA, where democracy had made its greatest strides forward, Bryce asserted, there was a chosen few within the chosen few, an élite within the élite, and further time would have to elapse before the people came fully into their own.[26]

While the bias and limitation of Bryce's outlook is apparent enough, there remains little doubt that the twentieth century dawned without most of the world's people being aware of the fact. Nevertheless, there was a keen consciousness among a small minority that such innocence could not last. Already, musicians were into a movement *molto vivace* bending their ears towards the authentic songs of the 'folk', while, even further off beaten tracks, anthropologists were enjoying field days as they gathered material to demonstrate how men had risen above 'the brute level'.[27]

Yet it was in such a milieu, albeit long ago, that one of the most authentic voices of the American establishment, the *New York Times*, found its 'man of the year' on 1 January 1901. Celebrating in a vigorous manner the rugged individualist spirit of transatlantic civilisation, the leading article declared:

> Away in some immensely distant age there was a hairy fellow living in a cave, who one day picked up the fallen branch of a tree and used it as a club to kill a wild goat for his dinner. If we knew him we should erect a statue to him as a father and founder of the arts that have come to such development in the Nineteenth Century, for his was one of the earliest triumphs of man over nature, a first and hopeful act that put him fairly on the way to the lordship of creation.

The *New York Times* went on to discuss seventeen different aspects of its basic theme, the achievements of the nineteenth century, beginning with THE ADVANCE OF LIBERAL INSTITUTIONS, POWER TRANSFERRED TO THE PEOPLE and the movement FROM ABSOLUTISM TO CONSTITUTIONS. Next came THE PUBLIC SYSTEM OF EUROPE, the permanent concert of nations, along with THE MIGHTIEST FIGURE OF THE CENTURY, 'the most massive, conspicuous and terrible "Napoleon Bonaparte"' and THE HOLY ALLIANCE, the 'preposterous' idea of Alexander of Russia for collaboration with his fellow sovereigns stimulating 'the germinal ideas and the unconquerable impulse of constitutional liberty'. Then, from the USA, there was THE MONROE DOCTRINE, a warning against European aggressions in the Western Hemisphere recently reasserted by President Cleveland as 'applicable to every stage of our national existence', and the development of THE GREAT REPUBLIC, a system and institutions formed by the Declaration of Independence, the War of the Revolution and the Constitution which 'we have never wished to change'. For all, there was THE END OF A COSTLY DELUSION, divergence from the gold standard, whose general adoption had been closely connected to the economic rise of the USA in particular. The *New York Times* asserted next that 'the world of science has been more profoundly affected and learning helped on further in the true path … than by any other philosophical discovery since man appeared on earth' by the THEORY OF ORGANIC EVOLUTION, which revealed MAN'S ANCESTRY from the creation of 'the simple single cell of protoplasm' onwards. CHEMISTRY LIGHT-HEAT indicated some of the other great strides forward in science, while THE GREAT INVENTIONS, including the telegraph, telephone and photograph, helped along with the railway and the steamship to make the world a smaller, more accessible place. ADVANCE IN MEDICAL SCIENCE could be detected in cellular pathology, anaesthesia, the germ theory of disease and antisepsis. The significant development of the century in THE FINE ARTS was the romantic movement, the attempt to express the emotions, while THE GREAT WRITERS included Hawthorne from the USA and Pushkin from Russia among many others from the countries in between. Philology had used the comparative method to determine the family relationship of languages, and in particular to trace 'the history of the great Indo-European group to which our own belongs'. Finally, EXPLORATION AND DISCOVERY had infiltrated Africa in particular, leaving no part of the world untouched except for the polar extremities.

From our vantage point of the end of the century, we would probably want to put forward other individuals besides Napoleon and 'the hairy fellow living in a cave' for special mention. Among these would have to be Charles Darwin, who was mostly responsible for the 'theory of organic evolution'. Moreover, 'chemistry light-heat' could hardly hint at the process leading from Becquerel's discovery of radioactivity, Marie Curie's conclusion that radioactive atoms were unstable and Sir J.J. Thomson's detection of the electron as a component of the structure of the atom, all in the last few years of the nineteenth century, through to Lord Rutherford's conclusion in 1911 that matter was mostly empty space and that, in particular, the atom consisted of a nucleus surrounded by various kinds of particles. This was soon hailed as the greatest advance in our understanding of matter since the time of the ancient Greeks. And it led onwards to the splitting of the atom with all its ominous implications in 1945. Unfortunately, even before then, especially in 1914–18, some science had become the handmaiden of war. The *New York Times* argued that the nineteenth century had seen so much change that the twentieth should begin with a period of deceleration and consolidation. In fact, the pace was to quicken almost beyond belief and comprehension.[28]

Another addition to the list of the *New York Times* could have been the impact of the newspaper, now to be found in many parts of the world, although mostly in

Europe and the USA. Four countries produced more than a thousand newspapers at the beginning of the new century, in ascending order as follows: France, 2,400; the UK, 2,902; Germany, 3,278; and the USA, 15,904. Far and away, then, the most active centres of journalism were to be found in New York and other American cities. Paradoxically, perhaps, the popular press was to be found largely in the hands of a small number of individuals, most notoriously William Randolph Hearst. Beginning with the *San Francisco Examiner*, Hearst built up a large newspaper empire exercising great influence. Competing with Joseph Pulitzer's *New York World*, Hearst's *New York Journal* sought the ever more 'sensational headline'. Among the most famous were those of mid-February 1898: 'Maine Blown to Atoms in Havana Harbor: Over One Hundred of her Crew Killed', 'Destruction of the Warship Maine was the Work of an Enemy', and so on. As the sinking of the ship was accompanied by sabre-rattling comment, the widespread cry went up, 'Remember the Maine', and war with Spain over Cuba and other parts of her empire soon broke out. Of course, the popular press could not be blamed exclusively for the Spanish–American conflict, nor for the US imperial expansion which followed it. Nor, on the other hand, could such developments be given the credit for all of the rise in US newspaper sales to more than 15 million a day by 1900. Undoubtedly, however, a new relationship was being developed in the USA between the people and a new establishment. This relationship, which was to become more complex later in the century with the development of new media, was already far from a simple case of the few manipulating the many. In its attempt to control public opinion, the press often reflected and intensified it.[29]

Even in Russia, the Tsar did not have everything his own way. Louise McReynolds has written of newspaper publishers catering for middle-class readers who were 'consuming, curious, nationalistic, boasting the time and money for both useful information and escapist entertainment, and enjoying more opportunities to determine the course of their own lives'. Assessing the significance of this phenomenon, she observes:

> The mass-circulation press had served a vital function under the Russian autocracy. It established an institution between private individuals and the state in which a public opinion could take shape and find expression. In the West, commercial journalism developed only after writing of constitutions and formation of representative parliaments, and its political utility has been viewed from its relationship to the expanding electorate. Russians, however, had to depend more heavily upon commercial print communications to develop an opposition to the autocratic form of government.

We must not exaggerate the influence of the Russian press. In 1914, the peak year, less than a thousand newspapers were produced with a total daily circulation of not much more than a million (as opposed to the USA's 15 million already by

1900). And there was a system of censorship, which had accounted for the closure of more than a thousand newspapers and the imposition of nearly a thousand fines in the peak years 1905–10. Nevertheless, we can talk with confidence of a varied public opinion in existence in Russia before the Revolution of 1917 and the imposition of a much more rigorous censorship.[30] Lenin himself was later to write that after the Revolution of 1905:

> Millions of cheap editions on political themes were read by the people, by the masses, by the crowd, by the 'lower orders' more greedily than ever before in Russia. … Merchants stopped dealing in oats and began a more profitable trade – the popular cheap pamphlet. Popular books became a *market* product.[31]

Lenin of course had an axe to grind, and would want to emphasise political publications which in fact were not such good business. But, his political preoccupations apart, Lenin would share at least some of the views of many other educated Russians about the literary tastes of the 'lower orders'. As Jeffrey Brooks has argued:

> Popular commercial literature was useful to the newly literate common readers in understanding the modern world. It contained information that was not readily available elsewhere to the lower classes. Its authors spun dreams of material success and individual advancement embellished with much fable and fancy. The repudiation of this literature and the market values it contained by educated and semi-educated people stemmed from a wider hostility toward the market system, with its attendant inequality and strife.[32]

Comparison with American popular literature is instructive:

> Unlike the heroes of the monomyth and classic figures of Western popular culture such as Tarzan … the Russian heroes do not return from their adventures as masters of two worlds or with boons to bestow. They return humbly as ordinary men. Their voyage to an outer world of freedom and adventure does not affirm the value of individual heroism, but instead demonstrates the superiority of society over the individual, even, and particularly, over the extraordinary individual.

Equally, 'The outlying regions of Russia were portrayed as a less friendly environment than the American writers' frontier. American writers often showed the landscape of the frontier to be strikingly beautiful and sometimes endowed it with great serenity. Untamed nature in the Russian fiction, on the contrary, frequently seems threatening.' On the other hand, 'The dominant trend in the popular culture of the prerevolutionary era was toward the development of values similar to those found elsewhere in the industrialized world.'[33]

In the USA, the desire for a natural existence was satisfied and stimulated by such works as Zane Grey's *The Spirit of the Border*, first published in 1906 and followed by many other stirring tales (up to 20,000,000 sales for all his books) as well as *Tarzan* by Edgar Rice Burroughs, which first appeared in 1914 (25,000,000 sales in 56 languages). Popular song followed the lead of popular literature in a search for lost simplicity with such well-known titles as 'In the Good Old Summer Time' and 'Little Gray Home in the West'.[34] But a sizeable minority, mostly African-American and alienated from the cultural mainstream, reflected deeper emotions in the blues and other early jazz forms along with 'Hot Gospel'. And there were other forms of entertainment for the masses before 1914, live vaudeville and the canned 'movies' or the 'flicks'. On 4 April 1913, *The Times* of London expressed concern about the cinematograph's possible 'perversion into an agency for pandering to all the lowest instincts of untaught humanity'. Spectator sport could also provoke violence as well as provide public diversion.

At home, traditional revelries were being supplemented by the phonograph with its cylinders and the gramophone with its discs. Broadcasting by radio began later, J.C.W. Reith suggesting in 1926 that:

> As it was in the United States, prosperous and relatively unrestrained by the War, that broadcasting arose, the principal causes must be sought in the growing dislike of farmers and country-people for the old, self-centred isolation, and the almost universal interests of modern youth in practical science. The monotony of working hours, since machinery has replaced handicraft, has probably accentuated the need for variety and interest to fill leisure hours.

American traditions of a minimum of governmental control over individual enterprise combined with advertisement on the grand scale as customary and acceptable meant that many stations were set up as a boom in broadcasting arrived in 1921–2. In Russia, radio was to be released for the general public in 1924, Reith pointing out how the Russian government:

> realising the great possibilities of broadcasting as a means of direct communication with all classes of an enormous and scattered population, promoted the establishment of wireless clubs and of technical advice offices and provided for the equipment of halls and open spaces in and around which a great number of listeners could be gathered.[35]

By this time too, the cinema was coming into its own in both the USA and the USSR. But we must not run ahead of ourselves, and should return to the early twentieth-century norm of public communication, the printed word.

As far as 'high' literature was concerned, Russian realism continued from the nineteenth into the twentieth century. The transition was embodied by Anton Chekhov, who was keen to stress that he was neither liberal nor conservative, that for him any trade mark or label was a prejudice. The keynote of his stories and plays is more alienation from the new world than commitment to it. Meanwhile, an audacious new note was being struck by Maxim Gorky. His early work (1895–1901) 'took the Russian and foreign reader by storm and was one of the greatest booms of the European market' in the evaluation of D.S. Mirsky, who goes on to say that Gorky's publications then became tendentious and revolutionary until the publication of his autobiographical trilogy beginning with *My Childhood* in 1913: 'objective, dispassionate, unsweetened paintings of Russian life'.

While realism remained to the fore, a new movement was emerging to transform the appearance of Russian literature. Consisting of several different currents, the mainstream of the movement was labelled 'modernism'. Certainly it gave emphasis to themes neglected in the nineteenth century, and could be characterised as 'largely an assertion of the spirit of Dostoevsky as against that of Tolstoy'. Then there was Futurism, a new movement finding eloquent expression in the person of Vladimir Mayakovsky, 'a poet with powerful lungs and a voice like the roar of waters … a poet of the street and of the open air'.[36] After 1917, Mayakovsky's work would take a new tack. Even before 1917, what Mirsky called the 'tendentious' and the 'revolutionary' was coming increasingly to the fore.

To turn to 'high' literature in the USA, we have to recognise that it is something of a misnomer, since its greatest name was the internationally popular Mark Twain. Another contrast with its Russian counterpart would be the less disturbed nature of the society inspiring it, although the contrast was relative. In 1900, after worldwide travel, Mark Twain himself wrote: 'I bring you the stately matron named Christendom, returning bedraggled, besmirched, and dishonored from pirate raids in Kiao-Chou, Manchuria, South Africa, and the Philippines, with her soul full of meanness, her pocket full of boodle, and her mouth full of pious hypocrisies.' Penetrating criticisms of the internal situation were made in 1906 by Upton Sinclair and Jack London. In *The Jungle*, Sinclair exposed the appalling conditions for man and beast alike in the meat-packing plants of Chicago. In *The Iron Heel*, London warned of the dangers of a fascist America, but also set out an ideal of a socialist commonwealth. Lamenting that 'modern man lives more wretchedly than the cave-man', he also argued that 'wonderful machines that produce efficiently and cheaply' should be controlled rather than destroyed. London also celebrated the advantages and drawbacks of a rawer nature in *The Call of the Wild*. Even the élitist Henry James could tour the USA in 1904 and find it a huge unkempt garden 'rank with each variety of the poison-plant of the money passion'. Before 1914, critical fiction and 'muckraking' journalism had died down, while literary 'modernism' and 'futurism' did not immediately strike as deep into the USA as into Russia.[37]

But the First World War was to narrow the Atlantic gap, and to send influences across the ocean in the other direction. While its effect was shattering on Europe in so many ways, for the USA it meant emergence on to the world stage to an unprecedented degree, both for its literature and its popular culture. Sinclair Lewis found wide fame through his criticism of the narrowness of small-town life in *Main Street* in 1920, and it would not be long before Scott Fitzgerald and Ernest Hemingway began to make their great reputations with broader themes. Feet began to tap to syncopated rhythms as eyes opened in wonder at motion pictures. Earlier fears about the 'Americanization of the world' would grow, even if counterbalanced by the threat of world communism unleashed by the Russian Revolution.

Challenges to liberalism

War and revolution made a tremendous impact in cultural life as in political and economic life. In the USA, the minimum of governmental control over individual enterprise, which had been an important tradition, was at least temporarily overthrown, while advertisement on a grand scale was used for governmental propaganda. As Woodrow Wilson's words just before his war message early in 1917 were reported:

> when a war got going it was just war and there weren't two kinds of it. It required illiberalism at home to reinforce the men at the front. We couldn't fight Germany and maintain the ideals of Government that all thinking men shared. ... 'Once lead this people into war', he said, 'and they'll forget there was ever such a thing as tolerance. To fight you must be brutal and ruthless, and the spirit of ruthless brutality will enter into every fiber of our national life, infecting Congress, the courts, the policeman on the beat, the man in the street.'[38]

Just over a week after the USA entered the war, on 14 April 1917, the President set up a Committee on Public Information, composed of the Secretaries of State, War and Navy with a civilian journalist, George Creel, as chairman. Designed as the official source of news relating to Allied war activities, it issued a daily *Bulletin* to help the press tell the right story. Just over a year later, towards the end of April 1918, it helped to create a National Board for Historical Service at a conference of historians in Washington, DC. Maps, pamphlets and moving pictures were prepared to show why the USA was at war, while 'a patriotic speaking service' of 'four-minute men' was set up who 'by arrangement with the purveyors of public amusements made brief talks before their audiences'.

There had been no such restrictions on freedom in the USA since the Alien and Sedition Acts of 1798. Even during the years of neutrality up to 1917, there was apprehension about four million unnaturalised citizens of the Central Powers resident in the USA, often deemed to be 'enemy aliens'. The country was subject to a barrage of enemy propaganda, while the activities of enemy agents seemed to indicate the need for vigorous action.[39] Almost as soon as the USA entered the war, radio and telegraph were taken over by the government. Old internment and treason laws were used before the introduction of new legislation in 1917 and 1918. Loosely drawn statutes were introduced providing up to twenty years' imprisonment for anybody publishing 'any language intended to bring the form of Government of the United States or the Constitution into contempt, scorn, contumely and disrepute'. War hysteria led to convictions for criticisms of the Red Cross and for doubts concerning the utility of knitting socks for soldiers. In a case officially listed as '*U.S.* v. *Spirit of '76*', a film showing Redcoats putting their bayonets in, the judge sentenced its maker to ten years in prison for questioning 'the good faith of our ally, Great Britain'. Translations of political views and comment touching the United States or any other nation engaged in the war were to be filed with the post office at a mailing point for all foreign language publications. About 6,000 out of 4,000,000 'alien enemies' were interned or put under restraint. 1,532 persons were arrested under the Espionage Act of June 1917, and about 600 of them actually convicted.[40]

The Russian Revolution had added a powerful new dimension to the hysteria which was to develop into the postwar Red Scare of 1919. In September 1919, President Wilson suggested that 'the world is now one single whispering gallery'. 'All the impulses of mankind are thrown out upon the air and reach to the ends of the earth', he added, warning that, in spite of its oceans of insulation, even the USA was vulnerable to the 'propaganda of disorder and discontent and dissolution throughout the world'.[41] From November 1919 and January 1920, spurred on no doubt by the explosion of a bomb outside his own home, Attorney General A. Mitchell Palmer deported more than 500 suspect aliens and issued about 3,000 arrest warrants. The most famous case was that of Eugene V. Debs, who had previously stood on several occasions as socialist candidate for the presidency and who had opposed the war from the beginning. But he was not convicted and sentenced to ten years in a Federal prison until after a speech denouncing the war as the work of capital in September 1918. Needless to say, there were citizens of the USA who were more enthusiastic than Debs about the Russian Revolution, ranging from those who came together to found the Communist Party of North America in May 1921 to such eccentric individuals as William Brown, who gained considerable notoriety by resigning as Bishop of Arkansas to become the self-styled 'Episcopus in partibus Bolshevikium et Infidelium'. And, while the trade union movement was often anti-Bolshevik, the IWW (Industrial Workers of the World) took a more supportive stance as it sought to establish 'one big union'. So-called 'Soviets' were set up in Butte, Montana and Portland, Oregon, and various kinds of industrial action were taken. The 'Red Menace' appeared particularly threatening in the General Strike in Seattle in 1919, and Mayor Ole Hanson became a national hero after taking firm action and uttering such observations as:

> Bolshevists believe in destruction of nationalism, loyalty and patriotism and the adoption of a sentimental, sickly, unworkable, skim-milk international-ism. Loving no country, they excuse themselves by saying they love all coun-tries alike. Polygamous men have ever used the same excuse ... Bolshevism would disarm and Chinafy our great people ... Bolshevism teaches and its votaries practise immorality, indecency, cruelty, rape, murder, theft, arson.[42]

Alarm was so great that danger was detected in the use of certain textbooks in schools, even of certain languages in public or over the telephone. In no less than twenty-five states the display of the red flag was a specified offence.[43]

Over in Russia, where the waving of the red flag was soon to become a civic duty, according to Mirsky: 'The World War remains almost unreflected in Russian literature, and Russia has little to compare with the War literature of the Western nations.' Moreover, 'The revolution of March 1917 remained as alien to the Russian imagination as the War.' However, 'Not so the Bolshevik revolution of eight months later and the ensuing civil war' which brought about 'the division of all intellectual Russia into two hostile camps' later becoming 'a geographical division' between those who remained at home and those who emigrated. For the most part, those under thirty stayed while older generations were divided between the two camps. Although 'the years of the civil war witnessed the almost complete disappearance of prose fiction ... since 1921 a galaxy of young novelists have come up who choose their subjects almost exclusively from the revolution, the civil war and contemporary Soviet life'. Meanwhile, 'For the Russian theatre the period was one of rapid development and of remarkable achievement. But the drama did not keep pace with it.' Gorky and Mayakovsky were as successful as anyone in this respect.[44]

Generally speaking, the Soviet vision was even more comprehensive than that of the other 'hostile camp'. For cultural revolution was an all-embracing aspect of Communist ideology, including political and economic activity. For example, to maintain the link between factory and farm, school and state, education would be polytechnical and ideological. And as Peter Kenez and David Shepherd observe:

> When Lenin wrote about culture he had in mind not just high culture or its low, or popular antipode, but also technical civilization, material

achievements. This understanding was not idiosyncratic, but was shared by most of the Russian intelligentsia. In this sense electrification, an efficient postal system, trains running on time, good roads, personal hygiene, and so on were obviously aspects of culture. Culture also meant an internalization of the industrial discipline that Lenin very much admired in the West, and especially in the United States. By contrast, Lenin associated with backward Russia the opposite of discipline, spontaneity (*stikhiinost*), and greatly distrusted it. For the Bolsheviks bringing education to the masses and acquainting them with the achievements of Western civilization were inseparable.[45]

Late in 1922, however, Lenin was to say: 'People dilate at great length and very flippantly on the notion of "proletarian culture". We would be satisfied with real bourgeois culture for a start, and would be glad if we could dispense with the cruder types of bourgeois culture, such as bureaucratic or serf culture.' He pointed out that:

at the very time when here in Moscow a few tens of thousands of people are enjoying a brilliant theatrical performance, throughout the country millions are still striving to spell their names, and have to be told that the earth is not flat but round and that the world is governed by the laws of nature instead of by witches and sorcerers jointly with the Heavenly Father.

While aspiring to the elimination of superstition and religion, Lenin came to realise that the making of the 'new Soviet man', rational, dedicated and internationalist, would take some time.[46]

But some of his supporters could not wait. 'Only the proletariat will create new things, and we, the Futurists, are the only ones to follow in the footsteps of the proletariat', declared the poet Mayakovsky. 'Streets are our brushes, squares are our palettes', he proclaimed, and some of his artistic comrades put his words into action, for example, painting red and purple in celebration all the grass, trees and flowers in front of the Bolshoi Theatre. Most Futurists were Communists, but were regarded as too individual and undisciplined by the Soviet authorities, which attempted to develop with no great success a more reliable 'proletarian culture'. Another group associated with the revolution were the 'peasant poets', of whom the best-known representative was Sergei Esenin, 'only transiently attracted by the conceptions of mystical socialism', but at best with 'an exquisitely piercing lyrical accent', combining 'wistful and uneasy melancholy' with 'a dare-devil "hooliganism"'.[47]

One of the most powerful embodiments of the new spirit was the 'dynamo-numental' building designed for the headquarters of the Third International by the Constructivist architect Vladimir Tatlin. The materials were to be steel and glass, created by fire and symbolising the power of a sea of flame. A huge steel spiral was to coil round the entire tall building as a symbol of vertical Communist dynamics as opposed to the horizontal embodying bourgeois greed. Three glass stories were to be suspended from the spiral in the shape of a cube, a pyramid and a cylinder, each revolving non-stop, every day, month and year respectively. From the cube on top, broadcasts were to be made to the workers of the world, while messages to those in Moscow would be reflected from cloudy skies. However, as a metaphor of the failure of cultural revolution in general, the 'Tatlin tower', although planned to be twice the height of the Empire State Building in New York, came no nearer to realisation than a small-scale model.[48] Here in miniature, the predicament of the Russian Revolution was clearly set out, its aspiration far greater than its achievement. While the 'Tatlin tower' reached no more than a few metres in Moscow, the Empire State Building scraped the sky of New York.

In the conclusion to this chapter, as in its introduction, we must not take our metaphor too far. For example, if the First World War had fully demonstrated the impact of industrial warfare, it fell far short of the awesome power of nuclear weaponry. Yet if a moment has to be chosen for the conception of superpower, it should probably be found roundabout the end of 1917 and the beginning of 1918. By then, the prewar liberal vision of Lord Bryce had been shattered, and the global outlooks of the leaders of Soviet Russia and the USA first clashed. On the one hand, there was Wilson's belief in a world made safe for democracy; on the other hand, Lenin's belief in world proletarian revolution. The American President wanted the League of Nations to arrange the affairs of mankind, the Soviet Chairman aimed at the formation of the Third International. Wilson was devoted to the Open Door and freedom of economic activity everywhere. For Lenin, capitalism had reached the highest stage of its activity and was on the brink of collapse. It would be succeeded by socialism, a system in which the dictatorship of the proletariat would lead to the end of capitalist exploitation of humankind by capitalists. But for this purpose to be achieved, a new Soviet man (and woman) would have to be created with an outlook completely different to that of people under the old regime. A new world outlook would have to accompany the proclaimed new world order. In the short run, however, there was more evidence of the spread of Americanism. To quote H.L. Mencken on this subject in 1926:

> Of late the increase in travel and other inter-communication between Eng-land and America has tended to halt the differentiation of the two dialects. It was more marked, perhaps, before the World War than since. But if it ever vanishes altogether the fact will mark a victory for American. The American cinema floods England (and the rest of the English-speaking world) with American neologisms, but there is very little movement in the other direc-tion. Thus the tail begins to wag the dog.[49]

On 'American Fiction' in particular, Virginia Woolf made the comparison between the English tradition whose centre was 'an old house with many rooms each crammed with objects and crowded with people who know each other intimately ... ruled all the time, if unconsciously, by the spirit of the past' and America, 'a new land, its tin cans, its prairies, its cornfields flung disorderly about ... while the people are equally diversified into fragments of many nationalities'. For Woolf, Americans were 'instinctively making the language adapt itself to their needs': she considered that not much foresight was needed to predict that 'when words are being made, a literature will be made out of them'.[50] In the room of her own, apparently, Woolf was unaware that such a literature had already been made. It would not be long before American culture, neologisms and all, was breaking through not only to the more sequestered corners of the English-speaking world but around the whole globe. The same might be said of American capitalism, while, as we shall soon see, the USA was still putting forward its plans for international order after the departure of President Wilson from the White House.

In other words, as far as future superpower was concerned, conception had taken place, and now gestation would have to take its course. But in the short run, there could be little doubt that one of the embryos was going to be more vigorous than the other.

3 Gestation

New world orders and the Second
World War, 1921–45

New world orders (1921–33)

For both future superpowers, the years following 1921 have often been thought of as a period of isolation. In fact, isolation was by no means complete on either side: indeed, each had a concept of world order including itself but tending to exclude the other. At a time when old rules of international relations had been broken and new rules scarcely devised, let alone established, there was certainly much concern among the other powers about the global roles to be played in international relations by both USA and USSR, as more new world orders were proclaimed to confront older empires. Italy from 1922, Japan from 1931 and Germany from 1933 all put forward plans for expansion threatening to upset, in a more violent manner than either the USA or USSR, the pre-war status quo which Britain and France in particular strove to maintain.

In his first message to Congress, delivered in person on 12 April 1921, President Warren G. Harding misread one of the keywords as he called for a return to 'normalcy' (perhaps giving unwitting emphasis to the inaccessibility of 'normality'). At home, this meant reduction of expenditure and taxation, and of government interference in general. Abroad, this would mean rejection of the League of Nations. However, the President declared, 'we make no surrender of our hope and aim for an association to promote peace, in which we would most heartily join'. To this end, he was soon to sign treaties with Germany and other former enemies. And, in preparation for what a historian soon after that time called 'the high-water mark' of his administration, Harding sent out invitations in July 1921 to an international conference to convene in November in Washington DC on the limitation of armaments.[1]

About a month before Harding's message, at the tenth party congress in March 1921, Lenin announced the introduction of the New Economic Policy (NEP). Only 'in countries of developed capitalism' was it possible to make an 'immediate transition to socialism'; but in Russia there was still 'a minority of workers in industry and a vast majority of small cultivators'. In such a country, a socialist revolution could be successful only on two conditions: the timely support of a comparable event in one or more leading countries; and a compromise between the ruling minority proletariat and the majority peasantry. NEP was as close to Soviet 'normalcy' as possible in the circumstances. Rejecting the League of Nations (as well as being rejected by it), Lenin and his comrades continued to place their hopes for revolution on the Comintern.[2]

The People's Commissar for Foreign Affairs, Georgii V. Chicherin, expressed disillusionment with Wilsonian idealism in an interview of February 1921, adding: 'We are of the opinion that the new administration of Harding will also adopt a more realist attitude towards Russia. Harding stands nearer, I think, to the pulse of American business and can interpret Americans' actual needs better.' As far as the Washington Conference on the Limitation of Armaments was concerned, however, Chicherin was less optimistic, giving his government's view in July 1921 that 'the absence of the Russian Government from an international deliberation on this subject will result only in having the decisions, which have been taken for Russia and to which the Russian Government in its absence is a stranger, ignored by it'.[3]

Arthur Rosenberg gave a Comintern view of the Washington Conference in a newspaper article in February 1922: 'Disregarded by the world, like an old and faded ballet dancer, the Washington Conference has peacefully passed away.' While 'any doubting Thomases who ... steadfastly refuse to believe in the tremendous feat alleged to have been accomplished at the Conference must be declared ripe for the lunatic asylum', the results were in fact nearer to failure. Neither China's weakness nor Japan's strength had been adequately addressed. Great Britain had yielded to the USA, while France was 'fishing in troubled waters', intriguing with Japan. As for President Harding, having 'staged his disarmament comedy in order to hoodwink millions of American farmers, petty bourgeois and workers', he could not admit failure so 'expressed his satisfaction with the various scraps of paper and told his audience that Washington has triumphed', claiming that mankind had entered on a new phase. Both the USA and Great Britain were reluctant to take the alternative path of confrontation with Japan 'while the world is in the throes of an economic crisis and its peoples rather wearied'.[4]

In retrospect, the Washington Conference clearly demonstrated that the gestation of US superpower was well under way, while its Soviet counterpart was barely showing at all. Treaties were signed guaranteeing the Open Door and instituting a 5–5–3 ratio for the major navies in the Pacific – the American, the British and the Japanese – among other arrangements, with no mention of Soviet Russia. However, even before its 'scraps of paper' were drawn up, the older empires had shown that they were not prepared to pass away just yet. Generally alarmed about the threat of communism, more than a little suspicious of American motives, they were specifically prompted by the fact that Germany could not pay for the First World War to the extent laid down after Versailles.

Following an earlier conference of the Supreme Council of the Allies from 18–22 December 1921 in London on the subject of German inability to pay reparations, another in Cannes from 6–13 January 1922 decided to discuss this question, along with European security and reconstruction, at Genoa later in the year, and to invite Soviet Russia and the United States to join in. Possibly under the influence of Boris A. Bakhmetev, the still active ambassador of the Russian Provisional Government in Washington DC, US Secretary of State Charles E. Hughes turned the invitation down, expressing concern that the conference would not be primarily economic but political, and adding, with respect to Russia:

> that this Government, anxious to do all in its power to promote the welfare of the Russian people, views with the most eager and friendly interest every step taken towards the restoration of economic conditions which will permit Russia to regain her productive power, but these conditions, in the view of this Government, cannot be secured until adequate action is taken on the part of those chiefly responsible for Russia's present economic disorder.[5]

By this time too, the US administration appears to have come to the conclusion that, while communism continued to pose a threat, Soviet Russia did not.

For its part, the Soviet government made a long response at Genoa on 11 May to a Memorandum of the other powers in attendance. This response expressed the view that the isolation of Russia was leading to 'political consequences which are no less disastrous than its economic consequences'. On propaganda, it stressed that the most subversive variety had been carried on by means of the organisation and despatch of armed bands by certain neighbouring countries which had been signatories to the very Memorandum which now sought to impose discontinuance from subversive propaganda as a unilateral obligation on Russia. On financial obligations, the response recalled the principle that 'Governments and administrations created by revolutions are not bound to respect the obligations of the Governments which have been overthrown'. It recalled that revolutionary France had repudiated its National Debt, and that the Tsarist government had rejected the claims of foreign nationals for compensation for losses suffered during the revolution of 1905. As far as the First World War was concerned, debts arising had been automatically cancelled by the withdrawal of Russia which 'having had no share in its advantages, could not be expected to share its cost'. With that exception, Soviet Russia would repay state debts provided that the losses incurred by intervention and blockade were recognised. Regarding such counter-claims, the response recalled the decision of the Court of Arbitration of Geneva on 14 September 1872, by which Great Britain was obliged to pay the USA $15.5 million for losses caused by the privateer *Alabama* during the American Civil War. On private property, the Soviet delegation commended the Memorandum for its recognition of Russia's sovereign right to regulate within her own territory as she saw fit her system of ownership, economy and government, but lamented the fact that it went on 'in flagrant contradiction' to make the Russian state 'the sport of chance'. There could not be an impartial arbiter in the conflict between two forms of ownership assuming 'for the first time in history a real and practical importance'. Meanwhile, the Soviet government would attempt to deal in an even-handed manner with the problem of concessions, but foreign powers must cease talking to Russia in the language of victors to the vanquished, and approach her 'on a footing of equality'. The response stated: 'Russia is ready to consent to substantial concessions to foreign Powers in order to ensure the success of the negotiations, but only on condition that equivalent concessions will be made by the other contracting Party in favour of the Russian people.'[6]

Arnold Toynbee's overall verdict was as follows:

> Although the Genoa conference led to no positive results, it was interesting as the first general European conference after the war of 1914–1918, and because economic and financial problems were approached from the point of view of reconstruction, and not of reparation. It was also interesting as the first attempt at a settlement between the European governments and Soviet Russia. At Genoa the difficulties which proved crucial on later occasions were already encountered.[7]

Soviet Russia's response to the wall of incomprehension encountered at Genoa was to sidestep it, by signing an agreement at nearby Rapallo on 16 April 1922 with the major European power that had been excluded completely – Germany. The two pariah powers renounced reciprocally all claims to war indemnities of any kind, while Germany abandoned hopes for compensation for losses incurred by her subjects as a consequence of Russian socialisation of private property 'provided that the Soviet Government does not satisfy similar claims of other States'. Diplomatic and consular relations were resumed, and economic relations were to be regulated 'with mutual feelings of goodwill'. As for the USA, Secretary of State Hughes showed that his government's position had not changed by 15 May 1922 as he rejected an invitation for participation for a proposed meeting of experts at the Hague to consider questions arising at Genoa.[8]

At the end of October 1922, the Italian Fascist march on Rome led to the seizure of power by Mussolini. Domestic disarray gave Il Duce (the leader) his opportunity, but he was able also to refer to slights to the national honour at the Washington Conference and elsewhere as well as the threat posed by Bolshevism.

Although the focus of international attention in 1922 had been on Europe, the wider world had not been forgotten. In an interview given to a visiting American towards the end of the year, Lenin said that he did not expect much of a sequel to the Washington Conference, but was certain that there would be a clash of some capitalist powers, perhaps between Japan and the USA. He asked American farmers to send wheat, in exchange for which Russia could put furs on their wives. On 20 December 1922, the official creation of the Union of Soviet Socialist Republics reflected the consolidation of the concerns of Lenin and his comrades for Asia as well as Europe. About six months later, in June 1923, Karl Radek gave a report on the world political situation to the Comintern Executive Committee alleging that Japan, the USA and Great Britain were already all infringing the agreements made in the Washington Treaty, as well as suggesting that Soviet Russia was in danger since the size of armies and of military budgets was greater than before the war and that the revolutionary movement was in danger both in Europe and Asia. Early in 1924, the Soviet Government protested about US naval vessels entering Soviet waters, first at Kamchatka in the Far East and then at Batumi in the Black Sea. Later in 1924, as China joined Great Britain and a number of other states in recognition of the Soviet Union, there were complaints in the Soviet press that the USA was attempting to dominate China to the exclusion of the USSR.[9]

Meanwhile, the problem of German reparations had not gone away, and the Dawes Plan was adopted to do something about it in August 1924. The payments were to be reduced, and a US $200 million loan handed over to prime the pump of German production. While American investors subscribed over $1 billion, ten times the amount needed, in just a few days, one of their fellow-citizens, a communist from Chicago named Harrison George, attacked General Dawes, a bank president in the same city, as an 'International Open-Shopper' whose report leading to the plan was ' a charter of enslavement to the Morgan banks of, firstly, the German working class and, ultimately, the Workers of all Europe'.[10]

Late in 1925, after several preliminaries and a considerable amount of nego-tiation, European powers signed the Locarno Pact guaranteeing the German–French–Belgian frontiers while France made a similar commitment to Poland and Czechoslovakia. Gustav Stresemann, the German Minister for Foreign Affairs, wrote soon afterwards:

> The man in the street, seeing the harbours empty, the barracks deserted, the armament industries destroyed and the richest areas of his country overrun by foreign troops, found it hard to understand that it was not his own secu-rity but that of his armed neighbours, old and new, that stood in need of a guarantee.

But the point was taken by the Belgian representative at Locarno, who de-clared it impossible 'to keep a rich and powerful people disarmed by duress and in a one-sided way for an indefinite period, while its former enemies in Europe remain armed to the teeth'. Neither the USA nor the USSR was involved in the

Pact, but neither could 'The Spirit of Locarno' be preserved without them.[11] The Soviet economist Eugene Varga commented:

> Locarno is one of the many attempts being made to patch up the ever-increasing antagonism of interests among the European powers. The attempt was rendered necessary by the anxiety to remove all political obstacles hampering the investment of American capital. On the other hand Locarno represents an endeavour to organise a united front of all the capitalist countries of Europe against the Soviet Union, which is now going ahead at truly American speed. If we are to understand Locarno, we must regard it from the points of view of the three decisive world powers: the United States, the Soviet Union, and the British Empire.

In Varga's view: 'For the United States Locarno is a direct continuation of the London Dawes agreement.' But as well as providing security for American capital, he considered that Locarno also represented an attempt to organise a European capitalist united front against the Soviet Union under the leadership of Great Britain, conscious that its imperial dreams were fading.[12]

France was even more concerned, and Premier Aristide Briand wanted the USA to enter with it into at least the spirit of Locarno. But President Calvin Coolidge and his Secretary of State Frank Kellogg were averse to any bilateral declaration, and proposed instead a broader pact denouncing war as a means of settling international disputes. Both the USSR and Germany, along with many other nations, signed the Kellogg–Briand Pact of August 1928, which appeared to advance the cause of peace but in fact became one of the pieces of paper with which the inter-war period was littered. More solid hope appeared on offer to Weimar Germany when the Young Plan of June 1929 succeeded the Dawes Plan of 1924 as a means of relief for the burden of reparations.

A few months later, however, such plans collapsed as the Wall Street Crash of October 1929 accelerated the arrival of the Great Depression. Even the almighty dollar suddenly appeared impotent. While waiting for the global economic situation to improve, President Hoover strove to maintain the world's strategic balance, as Japan in particular expressed dissatisfaction with the naval ratios imposed by the Washington Conference of 1921–2. Unhappy about US immigration restrictions and no longer compensated by US loans, Japan's ever more militaristic appetite grew for expansion on the Asiatic mainland. By the end of 1931, its army had invaded China and seized Manchuria, where the puppet state of Manchukuo was set up in 1932. President Hoover resisted pressure to act against Japan, arguing that it was already threatened by 'a Bolshevist Russia to the north and a possible Bolshevist China' to one side, while aware that mutual suspicion impeded collaboration with Britain and other imperial powers. He was also concerned with the Red threat in Latin America, especially in Mexico and Nicaragua.[13]

Meanwhile, the Reds themselves believed that they were posing less threat than they were offered. That is to say, after the possibility of war with the UK was perceived in 1927, the Soviet government did not feel that its security was enhanced by its signature of the Kellogg–Briand Pact of 1928. Under the leadership of Stalin, and with a new Foreign Commissar, Maxim Litvinov, from 1930, the USSR turned inwards for the construction of socialism in one country with the First Five-Year Plan as the USA attempted to struggle out of depression through capitalism in one country.

Then in January 1933, Weimar Germany was overthrown with the advent to power of Hitler. He made it very clear that his principal struggle was against the Jews, most significantly to be found in the world Marxist conspiracy but also playing leading roles in international finance and journalism. The greatest threat for Hitler, then, was posed by the USSR, but dangers lurked in the USA, Great Britain and elsewhere – indeed, almost everywhere. And so, the new world orders would soon be on the road to a greater showdown in both Asia and Europe than that which had taken place between the imperial great powers in 1914.[14]

New showdown (1933–9)

President Monroe's message to Congress of 2 December 1823 had stated that US policy in regard to Europe was 'to consider the government *de facto* as the legitimate government for us; to cultivate friendly relations with it ...' A hundred years on, this principle was infringed as Monroe's successors were inhibited from recognising a *de facto* European power for fifteen years or more, as after 1917 the Russian Revolution appeared to be a much greater threat to the American Republic than had the French Revolution in the years following 1789, or Tsarist Russia in the early 1820s.

In 1921, as we have seen, views of future world order had been set out by President Harding and Chairman Lenin. Harding's hopes for a return to 'normalcy' were based on the success of the Washington Conference on disarmament of 1921–2 and on the expansion of American business through the Open Door coupled with the increasing influence of the dollar. Lenin, on the other hand, believed it necessary to introduce the New Economic Policy. That is to say, in order that the ultimate aim of world revolution might be preserved by the Comintern, an immediate compromise must be made with the peasant majority in Soviet Russia and commercial, even diplomatic relations set up with capitalist powers. There were problems from the first in the realisation of these two visions. For example, the policies of Harding and his immediate successors could not be easily reconciled with those of the other world powers and the USA held aloof from the League of Nations, while the Comintern was seen as a constant if somewhat indeterminate threat to stability everywhere outside the USSR. Moreover, stability was never really achieved in Europe, where Italy under Mussolini from October 1922 boasted of the Mediterranean as *mare nostrum* and Weimar Germany could never establish a presence to West and East that would satisfy itself without alarming its neighbours. In Asia, the situation was even more problematic as Japan reinforced its presence in a disintegrating China. There were rumblings of anti-colonial discontent in much of Asia and beyond in what was to become known as the Third World. By the end of the 1920s, the arrival of the Great Depression and the launch of the Five-Year Plan had spelled ruin for 'normalcy' and for NEP alike. Replacement concepts of order came to be associated with the names of Franklin D. Roosevelt and Joseph V. Stalin.

We will not subject these two individuals to such close scrutiny as Wilson and Lenin, since both claimed to be the heirs of their predecessors. However, while we are aware of Stalinism as a distinct entity, there has been little reference to Rooseveltism. This difference may be explained by FDR's emphasis on the pragmatic approach and by Stalin's on the ideological, in turn a reflection of diverging traditions. But there are shorter-term considerations, too. While both the First World War and the Great Depression were formative experiences for Rooseveltism, they were far less influential than the Russian Revolution and the failure of NEP for Stalinism. While the New Deal aimed at the recovery of a vigorous economy that had evolved over centuries without any abrupt social or cultural changes, the Five-Year Plans sought to create a new economy, society and culture out of the ruins of predecessors which were being undermined even before the depredations of internal and international conflict. Hence, to a considerable extent, the Soviet emphasis on secret agencies and build-up of armed forces, even the gulag and the purges, irrespective of the darker side of Stalin's personality and any intrinsic totalitarian tendency in his outlook. However, while the less malign situation in the USA did not in itself make Roosevelt a more agreeable person, nearly all of us would agree that Stalin was a better exemplar of Lord Acton's dictum that 'Great men are nearly always bad men'. In any case, to make objective pronouncements on the men themselves as distinct from the circumstances in which they operated is extremely difficult. We are on firmer ground in observing that both FDR and Stalin took their inheritance both long-term and short-term and adapted it at a time of crisis for the purpose of resisting rival new world orders while arriving at rapprochement with each other.

At Franklin D. Roosevelt's entry into the White House in March 1933, there was still much opposition to the idea of coming to terms with the communist rival. The State Department had strong doubts about the observance of civilised norms by Stalin and his entourage, as well as a bureaucratic inclination towards unnecessary obfuscation; FDR himself complained that some of his advisers appeared more concerned about the spelling of the word 'commissar' than about the major points at issue. Among these points were the repayment of debts and Soviet policy on religion. Moreover, organisations ranging from the American Legion to the American Federation of Labor wanted to keep their distance. On the other hand, at least some business circles were in favour of tying the official knot with the headquarters of anti-capitalism, realising that hard-headed commerce could pierce the clouds of Bolshevik rhetoric. The President believed in the practical necessity of establishing official contacts between Washington and Moscow.[15] Finally, in November 1933 the USA accorded the USSR diplomatic recognition. Thus ended the isolation of the future superpowers from each other: but only just. Through the years 1933–8, actual contacts were sparse.[16]

For both powers, as far as general isolation was concerned, it had been neither constant nor comprehensive before 1933, and did not come immediately to an abrupt end afterwards. Although Roosevelt made only brief reference to a foreign policy of 'the good neighbour' in his inaugural address, the USA remained the leading capitalist power and creditor throughout the world. Exclusion from the dominant system was neither desirable nor possible. So, while the new President at first took the USA off the gold standard and withdrew from a London Economic Conference that aimed at the establishment of a new international standard, his Secretary of State from 1933–44 was a determined Wilsonian in favour of the worldwide Open Door. 'A freer flow of trade', declared Cordell Hull, raised living standards and thus eliminated 'the economic dissatisfaction that breeds war'.[17]

Almost as night follows day, political interest followed the economic interest. Yet, as much and as long as possible, this policy meant avoidance of any international involvement likely to lead to war in any continent beyond the Western Hemisphere. In other words, the Monroe Doctrine was still very much alive as far as North and South America were concerned, especially where there appeared to be the threat of communist influence. For the USSR, on the other hand, vainly seeking to introduce a new socialist order, the search for security in ever more threatening circumstances became paramount. The old historic danger of conflict on two fronts, which had often confronted the Tsars, now confronted the Soviet government as disturbing developments took place in both Asia and Europe.

Having taken over Manchuria, some Japanese leaders wanted to take expansion further, and, among these, especially in the army, were those who believed that this would make war with the Soviet Union inevitable. The Soviet government hoped that its recognition by the USA would lead to some agreement about the containment of Japan. But the State Department reassured its Japanese counterpart that no such eventuality would ensue. For its part, after Hitler came to power in Germany in January 1933, the Soviet Union quickly set about signing non-aggression pacts with its immediate neighbours in 1933 and 1934, while assuring its partner in the Rapallo agreement that this policy should in no way be interpreted as 'an attempt to encircle any country, since every State belonging to a given region may join in these pacts'. At the same time, the Soviet Union accepted an invitation to join the League of Nations in September 1934, attempted to improve relations with Great Britain, and signed a mutual assistance treaty with France by May 1935.

Not every other power was as concerned with the possibility of war on two fronts as the USSR. The USA, for one, did not really have to worry too much about war on any front. Nevertheless, there were those in the Roosevelt entourage who were looking for a 'New Deal' in foreign as well as in domestic policy, who believed that the time had come for their country to weigh up both the responsibilities and the opportunities presented by the wider world. Most of them, like Cordell Hull, were Wilsonian in outlook, very conscious that the USA had replaced Great Britain as the world's leading power, looking across the Atlantic rather than the Pacific from their stronghold in the Western hemisphere. On the other hand, however, there were isolationists who succeeded in putting Neutrality Acts through Congress in 1935, 1936 and 1937, keeping the USA aloof from the gathering storm in Europe and Asia alike. But an attempt to balance the US budget through reduction of government expenditure in 1937–8 threw the New Deal off course, and was part of the reason for the government's embarking on a programme of expenditure denounced even by a New Deal supporter as 'battleship and war frenzy'. Already, however, FDR had more than enough reason to adopt a policy of 'armed neutrality'.[18]

In October 1936, Japan signed an anti-Comintern Pact with Germany. In July 1937, Japanese forces embarked on a conquest of what was left of China. On 5 October, Roosevelt called for a 'quarantine' against the encroaching 'epidemic of world lawlessness'. On 3 November, a conference was convened in Brussels by the League of Nations to discuss the Japanese problem. On this occasion, unlike in 1921, the Soviet government was invited to send representatives, although Foreign Commissar Litvinov suspected that the USA was aiming at a reconvention of the Washington Treaty powers. In the event, not surprisingly, the Japanese refused to attend. Again, not surprisingly, when Litvinov called for joint action with the USA, France and Great Britain against Japan, Germany and Italy, he met with a cold rebuff.[19]

There were two strategies for expansion in Asia open to the Japanese armed forces, the northern and the southern. At the end of July and beginning of August 1938, they unsuccessfully probed the Soviet defences in the region of Lake Khasan. In November 1938, Japan proclaimed a Greater East Asia Co-Prosperity Sphere directed explicitly against 'Bolshevism', even if also aimed more widely. Then, in May 1939, the Japanese armed forces made a larger-scale attack across the River Khalkin Gol in the Soviet satellite Mongolian People's Republic, but were beaten back by the Red Army in July. Their fingers burned in the north, at the battle which became known as Nomonhan, the Japanese armed forces turned their attention to the south. Defeated by one of the future superpowers, the USSR, they now embarked upon a policy which was to provoke the entry into the Second World War of the other, the USA.[20]

Meanwhile, a new showdown was leading towards the opening of the conflict over in Europe. In 1936, the Spanish Civil War began. The Soviet Union gave some help to the Republican government, but the United States held back, while Italy and Germany gave full support to the fascist insurgents. 'With dictators nothing succeeds like success', observed Hitler, who took over Austria in March 1938. Great Britain and France, which had so far attempted, like the USA, to stay on the sidelines, now realised that they could stand idly by no longer. And so, Premiers Neville Chamberlain and Edouard Daladier went to negotiate with Hitler and Mussolini in September. The result was the infamous Munich Agreement, which conceded the former German part of Czechoslovakia to Hitler, while Mussolini was unopposed in the Mediterranean. The USSR expressed its willingness to stand up for Czechoslovakia, but was rebuffed. The USA decided not to participate, although President Roosevelt gave Chamberlain his moral support and unsuccessfully proposed an international conference on disarmament and equal access to world markets.

In March 1939, Hitler took Prague and the rest of Czechoslovakia. Great Britain and France now gave their guarantees to Poland, and belatedly entered into inconclusive negotiations with the USSR, where Litvinov was replaced as Foreign Commissar in May by V.M. Molotov, who was less accommodating to the West.[21] On 23 August 1939, about a week before Hitler's invasion of Poland on 1 September, a non-aggression pact was signed between Nazi Germany and the Soviet Union. As Poland collapsed before the onslaught from the west, the Red Army moved in from the east to occupy most of the former Tsarist empire from the Baltic to the Balkans.

The Second World War (1939–45)

On 3 September 1939, both Great Britain and France declared war on Germany. While the USSR fought against Finland in the Winter War of 1939–40, a lull of 'phoney war' followed the fall of Poland in the West until *Blitzkrieg* quickly subdued France in June 1940. Then, Hitler turned his attention to the east, broke his non-aggression pact with Stalin without warning, and launched Operation Barbarossa on 22 June 1941. Future US President Harry S. Truman observed that, while he did not wish to see Hitler victorious under any circumstances, he also considered that the USA should promote stalemate by supporting whichever side appeared to be losing. There was no doubt about that in the short run, as *Blitzkrieg* seemed to be heading for another early victory. However, without any great sympathy for the Soviet Union, there were those in the USA who were profoundly alarmed as Hitler pronounced his crusade against 'Jewish bolshevism' to be a War for Race Extermination.[22] As far as the other future superpower was concerned, he wrote:

> We have no chance of eliminating America. But it does lie in our power to exclude Russia. The elimination of Russia means, at the same time, a tremendous relief for Japan in East Asia, and thereby the possibility of a much stronger threat to American activities through Japanese intervention.[23]

Because of the Nazi–Soviet Pact of August 1939 and the ensuing Winter War between the Soviet Union and Finland (widely popular in the USA as the only foreign country to repay its debts), relations between the future superpowers had dwindled from minor to minimal. The day after the Nazi invasion of 22 June 1941, however, Acting Secretary of State Sumner Welles reiterated condemnation of all dictatorship, but nevertheless singled out Hitler's armies as 'today the chief dangers of the Americas'. On 30 June Welles discussed the question of US aid to the USSR with the Soviet Ambassador Konstantin A. Oumansky. Diplomatic moves were immediately made to iron out some of the differences between the two past and future rivals. On 31 July, President Roosevelt's representative Harry Hopkins met Stalin and Litvinov at the Moscow Kremlin. Stalin asked for a list of vital supplies, which Hopkins promised that the USA and Great Britain would provide as soon as possible. Stalin pointed out the difficulty of ports of entry: Vladivostok was dangerous because it could be cut off at any time by Japan; Archangel was unapproachable for much of the year because of the ice problem; and road and rail communications through Persia were inadequate. Then, on 15 August 1941, Roosevelt and Churchill promised to 'continue to send supplies and material as rapidly as possible' while requesting a 'high representative' meeting in Moscow in order to facilitate speedy decisions regarding 'the apportionment of our joint resources'. Thus, although indirectly, began the fateful relationship of the Big Three.[24]

Three could sometimes be something of a crowd, and two could normally collaborate more easily. On 8 August 1941, FDR travelled to Newfoundland for his first meeting with Churchill. The outcome was the Atlantic Charter, proclaiming freedom of the seas and economic opportunity, from fear and want, as well as a postwar 'general security' system. Churchill was mostly in agreement, although insisting on due respect for 'existing obligations', fearing, not without cause, that the USA wanted the Open Door to include access to the British Empire. Clauses in the Lend-Lease agreement joined aspects of the earlier 'destroyers for bases' deal to begin to prise open what had earlier been a closed system of imperial preference. But Stalin was less accommodating: for him, almost needless to say, freedom in any shape or form was far from welcome. Moreover, he was still reeling from Hitler's treacherous invasion of the USSR, and found it difficult to enter into any further relationship, however much he needed Western aid.

But the Big Three relationship was brought closer after the USA was brought into the war by another surprise attack. Of course, FDR's government had been disturbed by the Japanese proclamation of the Great East Asia Co-Prosperity Sphere in November 1938. Disquiet grew when, following the outbreak of hostilities in Europe, Japanese forces moved from their Chinese stronghold into French Indochina in September 1940. On 13 April 1941, yet another piece of paper later to be torn up was signed in the shape of another non-aggression pact, this time between Japan and the Soviet Union. In July, the Japanese forces took over what was left of French Indochina. The USA sent more aid to the Chinese resistance forces, and further provoked Japan by cutting off vital supplies, especially oil. While negotiations continued, both sides prepared for war. Nevertheless, the attack on Pearl Harbor on 7 December 1941 came as an almost complete surprise. Also unexpected was Hitler's declaration of war on the USA four days later, even though unofficial American involvement in Atlantic hostilities had been growing. At this time, Hitler still believed that nothing succeeded like success and that lightning strikes could still bring down the future superpowers if Japan pressed home its attack and American aid to the Soviet Union was stopped. However, this was not to be.

As Warren F. Kimball has pointed out:

> By the end of 1941, the basic pattern had emerged. Neither Britain nor the United States were willing to jeopardize their own security and interests in order to aid the Soviets, but for the remainder of the war, Roosevelt saw American interests advanced by pushing for more, while Churchill, with a different set of interests to protect, consistently held back.[25]

Nevertheless, even if their relationship was far from ideal, on New Year's Day 1942 the Big Three, along with others not so big, issued a Declaration of the United Nations, expressing a common resolution to fight the Axis powers of Germany, Italy and Japan all the way through to victory with no separate peace. As from the beginning, they decided to concentrate on the enemies in Europe and the Atlantic, then turn to those in Asia and the Pacific. However, as 1942 wore on, harmony between the Big Three could not be maintained. Stalin vainly sought a guarantee of the Soviet frontier as it stood in 1941, including a considerable section of Poland and the Baltic states. To appease him, Roosevelt promised the opening of a second front before the year was over. This commitment was impracticable, but in any case Churchill was unhelpfully opposed, proposing an invasion of North Africa as an alternative. Roosevelt came round to support this action, accepting that a direct strike at France would be premature. But the US Chief of Staff and head of the Combined Chiefs of Staff, General George C.

Marshall, was not alone in his frustration and desire to give more priority to Asia and the Pacific.[26]

Then in January 1943, at a secret meeting with Churchill at Casablanca, Roosevelt accepted that the opening of a second front in France was still too formidable a proposition, and that another alternative strike should be made, this time at Sicily and Italy. But he also announced that the Allies would insist on the 'unconditional surrender' of the Axis. Meanwhile Stalin and his spokesmen had been protesting vigorously that they had borne the brunt of the enemy attack, indeed up to 80 per cent of it, and that to cross the Channel should not constitute any greater difficulty for the world's leading naval powers than Soviet resistance to the greatest land invasion in human history. Now, however, they were able to reinforce rhetoric with the greatest bargaining counter of all, military success. Turning back the German forces from their sieges of Leningrad and Stalingrad in the winter and going on to defeat them in the epic tank battle of Kursk in the summer, the Red forces had turned the tide in the broad Russian steppe just as their Allies were setting foot on the island of Sicily.

At least some experts had previously argued that the Soviet Union was on the way to defeat: now a growing number of them were coming to realise that it was poised for victory. On 22 August 1943, an intelligence report prepared for the US Joint Chiefs of Staff added to the first fundamental aim of destroying 'German domination of Europe' a second of preventing 'the domination of Europe in the future by any single power (such as the Soviet Union), or by any group of powers in which we do not have a strong influence'. Failure to achieve both these aims would mean that 'we may consider that we have lost the war'. The very next day, the US and British top brass agreed to send troops over immediately to join in the race for Berlin if it looked as if the Red forces were going to win it. At this point the Allied forces were being held back by their German opponents, and the surrender of Italy on 8 September 1943 had little more than token significance.[27]

By this time, to paraphrase Churchill, the Western Allies realised that present 'jaw jaw' would impede the eventuality of future 'war war', and so they agreed to meet their Soviet counterpart at Tehran in late November 1943. Apart from the impending problem of the race to Berlin, there were several other points at issue. Who was to 'police' Germany and occupied Europe as a whole? Was the Western refusal to allow Stalin a say in the affairs of liberated Italy a pointer towards the establishment of spheres of interest? En route to Tehran, Roosevelt met Churchill and the Chinese Nationalist leader Chiang Kai-shek, leading to a joint declaration demanding the unconditional surrender of Japan, which would also have to give up its ill-gotten gains in China and beyond. Again, Churchill grew alarmed at the postwar prospects for Hong Kong and other integral parts of the British Empire. At Tehran itself, there was more talk than decision, but yet another commitment was made for a second front, while the shape of Europe and Asia after the defeat of the Axis became a little clearer. If a specific problem such as the frontiers of liberated Poland and the complexion of its government allowed no easy solution, hopes were held out for the future discussion of all outstanding problems in an amicable manner. Now that the Comintern was disbanded, could the United Nations Organisation become an effective replacement for the failing League of Nations?

While the Soviet forces pushed with difficulty beyond their pre-war frontiers towards what would become their postwar deployment, the Western Allied army still found the going heavy in Italy. Meanwhile, the Western Allied air forces fought for the mastery of the skies and the destruction of the enemy's potential on the ground. By the summer of 1944, enough had been achieved for the greatest seaborne invasion in history to be launched on D-Day (6 June). Initially, Operation Overlord was far from a complete success, however, and much bitter fighting was to ensue on all fronts. Paris was liberated on 25 August 1944, but more than eight months would elapse before Berlin finally fell.

Meanwhile, subtle shifts were occurring in the relationship of the Big Three. To put the point bluntly, in the estimation of the USA, old empires, in particular the British and the French, were on their way down, while the Soviet Union was on its way up. Sensing the threat to his power, Churchill flew to Moscow in October 1944 and made a percentage deal with Stalin on the postwar Balkans, adopted as follows: Great Britain would have 90 per cent influence in Greece, while Yugoslavia would be controlled 50–50; the Soviet Union would have 90 per cent influence in Romania, 75 per cent in Bulgaria and Hungary. The British Prime Minister advised against using the phrase 'dividing into spheres' in case Americans might be shocked, although he and they well knew that the Monroe Doctrine had made one of the biggest such divisions of all. Churchill and Stalin also agreed that Germany must be split up and deindustrialised.

A victor for the fourth time in a presidential election in November 1944, Roosevelt was a sick man, fearing that his hopes for the Atlantic Charter and the United Nations might not be realised. Moreover, the war was not going well for the USA, in either major theatre. After the invasion of the Philippines in October 1944, US forces met determined resistance from the Japanese, and thousands of civilians were killed in the crossfire. In December, the Battle of the Bulge saw an almost successful German counterattack driving the Western Allies back from the German frontier, while the Red Army moved ever nearer Berlin. This was the background to the Yalta Conference, to be discussed below.

On 13 February 1945, just after the conclusion of the Yalta Conference, ostensibly to help their Soviet partner but also to remind him how powerful they were, the Western Allies destroyed Dresden in an unnecessary air bombardment which resulted in the deaths of many civilians, including refugees. From 19 February 1945, with great difficulty, US forces retook the Pacific island of Iwo Jima. After the next island hop, a heavy toll of GIs was being levied in Okinawa, and continued through to June. By then, FDR had died on 12 April and VE Day had come on 7 May. As the new President Harry S. Truman waited for the Soviet Union to honour the pledge made at Yalta to enter the Pacific War, and US forces incinerated large parts of Tokyo and other Japanese cities in heavy 'conventional' air attacks, he was also about to be informed of the successful testing of the promised atomic bomb. He passed the news on to Stalin at the Potsdam Conference in July. The dropping of A-bombs on Hiroshima and Nagasaki on 6 and 9 August brought VJ Day more quickly than had been previously hoped and feared. There was just time for the Soviet Union to fulfil its promise of declaring war against Japan three months after VE Day.[28]

The Second World War had been truly global, to an extent much greater than its predecessor. The First World War had seen little action in Asia and the Pacific. Now that the hopes of the Washington Conference were completely dashed, they were to become major theatres of conflict, and the USA was much more involved than first time around, its status as the leading world power amply confirmed. As for the Soviet Union, in spite of staggering losses which appeared to be leading it towards the fate of its Tsarist predecessor, it was to rise in triumph to reclaim the Tsarist empire (except for Finland) in Europe and the Far East, and more.

The Soviet Union and Nazi Germany were involved in a mortal struggle from 1941–5. Had Hitler's forces defeated those of Stalin, the USSR would have been no more. In such a case, the Berlin–Tokyo axis would have joined, and the threat to the USA would then have been extremely serious. To look at the war as it was rather than as it might have been, there can be no doubt where the major sacrifices were made for the ultimate victory. 'The War for Race Extermination' hit hardest in Eastern Europe and the Soviet Union, where up to 5 million Poles and 27 million or more Soviet citizens lost their lives. Many of these were on the field of battle, but the majority were innocent victims. The 'Final Solution' of the gas chambers began with the extermination of Red Army prisoners and went on to account for up to 6 million Jews. Countless millions were eliminated through incineration of whole villages and other forms of wholesale slaughter. This is not to deny the significance of other deaths, whether in Europe or Asia. In particular, the number of Chinese who perished through the years of the Japanese occupation and civil war from 1931–49 is incalculable.[29]

Capitalism and socialism in one country

Economically, the period falls into three sections: 1921–9, before the Great Depression and the introduction of the First Five-Year Plan; 1929–41, up to the full outbreak of the Second World War; and 1941–5, through to the end of the Second World War.

In our discussion of new world orders and world showdown so far, we have necessarily made a considerable amount of reference to their economic aspects, mostly to the capitalist and very little the socialist. This imbalance has not been the consequence of deliberate bias, however, but has followed from the consideration that capitalism was a world system while socialism was taking its first faltering steps in one country. However, we have already noted the disastrous attempt to institute 'War Communism' in Soviet Russia at a time of civil and international strife, and will devote a preponderant amount of space in this chapter to its sequels. First, however, a few words are necessary about the USA.

After the boom brought about by the First World War there was a short, sharp recession in 1921, but with the return of economic 'normalcy' the 1920s became years of prosperity with the expansion of consumer industry in particular. As a consequence of mass production and low prices; 'This was the decade in which the refrigerator, the radio, the gas or electric stove, and most notably the automobile became a part of most households in America.'[30] Yet, along with the urban poor, who were by no means small in number, most farmers did not share in the general prosperity. Expenditure on food tended to remain constant, and there were not many more mouths to feed, especially since immigration was curtailed and European countries put up tariff barriers to safeguard their own agriculture. Even US agriculture had not kept full pace with industrialisation, although the tractor was well on its way to overtaking animal-drawn machinery. Family farms still predominated, even if some were bigger and more modernised than others.

Speculation in the stock market both revealed and intensified weaknesses in the economy. By 1929 this had grown to the scale of a pyramid sale, with every investor believing that quick profits could be made without anybody having to pay the price. Overconfidence suddenly became panic in September and October. Following the Wall Street crash, the Great Depression set in.

Meanwhile, the Soviet economy had been experiencing its own return to 'normalcy'. In a speech to the Tenth Party Congress in the spring of 1921, as we have seen, Lenin said that the socialist revolution could be successful only on two conditions: support from further socialist revolution in other countries; and a compromise between the proletariat and the peasant majority. Obviously, in the absence of the first, emphasis would have to be given to the second in a policy which was first called the New Economic Policy (NEP), and was soon claimed by some of its supporters to be leading towards the construction of 'socialism in one country'. NEP's main feature was the reintroduction of the market along with the replacement of compulsory deliveries of grain by a fixed quantity paid as a tax (later commuted to a tax in money). But the 'commanding heights' – that is, large-scale industry and trade, including foreign trade, modern transportation and finance – were to be retained by the state. NEP came to an end from 1928–9 with an attack on the richer 'kulaks' and extreme pressure on the rest of the peasantry to collectivise, as part of the introduction of the First Five-Year Plan.[31]

Before those fateful years, in 1926, Harvard Economics Professor Thomas Nixon Carver wondered why the USA equipped and directed its workers more efficiently than other countries. His response to the question was:

> First among the factors in prosperity of the American people and its wide diffusion must be mentioned the democratic spirit or the absence of the spirit of caste. American democracy ... presents an open road to talent wherever it exists, whether in the newly arrived immigrant, the child of a ditch digger, or the homes of the educated and the wealthy. This means ... the fullest development of human resources.[32]

Two years later, Columbia History Professor Bartlet Brebner concluded after a short visit to Russia that villages, not cities, were the true centres of Russia. And so:

> The Russian peasant is the ultimate dictator of Russia. In his family patriarchal authority has been strong. In his village commune the heads of families have settled local affairs. In his state the Little Father or the Strong Man of the Communist Party has stood for government. That has been, and is, an oligarchical despotism, often paternal and benevolent, but easily capable of violent lapses to tyranny and blood.

Therefore, 'The present revolution can be understood only if one remembers that it is a revolution in which all Russians and all Russia are the active, if controlling, elements.'[33]

Columbia Economics Professor Rexford Guy Tugwell, the future New Dealer, took a close look at agriculture, insisting like his historian colleague that 'it is quite impossible to understand Russian culture unless the village is accepted as the core of comprehension'. However, in a much understated forecast, he went on to say: 'It will be surprising if the old folkways and the old miseries are not altogether greatly changed in the decade now being entered upon.' For, 'Low-yielding fields and miserable stock have reduced the whole peasantry to a standard of life so mean as to be almost beyond the American comprehension' and bringing 'animals and people into a relationship much too close for the American taste.' Moreover, since 1913 yields per acre had declined, and the situation of the peasant could well be worse than it was before the First World War. Nevertheless, grain followed by timber and oil were Russia's chief exports. Most peasants could not be blamed for having seen but dimly the necessity for 'a drastic change, and for bringing it about – with ruthlessness if need be'. For, concluded Tugwell:

There was a period of unreason and disaster, so awful in retrospect that all who bore any of its responsibility want now above all to have it forgot. But that is past. The spirit now is reconstructive; and its results seem as certain as those of most human enterprises of so vast a sort.[34]

Stuart Chase, Director of the Labor Bureau Inc., observed that 'In Russia a factory is a landmark; it is pointed out as one points out a castle or a skyscraper in other lands. There are probably more factories in Pennsylvania than in all Russia combined.' Over 80 per cent of Russians were peasants, while no more than 3 million out of 150 million people worked in factories, 2 out of 100 as opposed to 8 out of 100 in the USA. Since 1923, the State Planning Commission, or Gosplan, had taken over 'the functions of an earlier super-power board'. (At this time, 'super-power' was a term used to describe the workings of an electricity grid.) A 'five-year program' running from 1 October 1926 to 1 October 1931 called for a 78 per cent increase in industrial production along with a 30 per cent increase in agricultural production. With such emphasis, it was hoped to close the famous 'scissors': 'to give the peasant an adequate flow of textiles and hardware in return for his wheat and his beef; to bring industrial prices into reasonable alignment with agricultural prices'. While most targets were being reached, it was noticeable that iron and steel were lagging, and it looked like another two or three years would elapse before the 1913 levels could be attained. Generally speaking, 'probably nobody really knows whether Russia is falling down faster than she is being built up'. Incentives would be necessary for all targets to be reached. But Russian workers did not have 'the Yankee knack. The tradition of the East is all against it.' Therefore, efficiency and scientific management were combined in what Russians called 'rationalization': 'After Lenin, Henry Ford, as the supreme rationalizer, appears to be the patron saint of industrial Russia.' (Henry Ford himself, in *Moving Forward*, wrote that 'we think Russia needs modern industry in order that the wealth of the country may be opened up. Otherwise it will remain one of the sore spots of the world.') In conclusion, Gosplan would have to be given another five years before 'we can definitely determine whether this courageous and unprecedented experiment is destined to be a landmark for the economic guidance of other peoples the world around, or just another memorandum for the waste basket of history'.[35]

Another five years of NEP was not given, owing to the forced pace of collectivisation and the introduction of the First Five-Year Plan from 1928 to 1929. In the expert view of Mark Harrison:

The NEP economy could have yielded further economic expansion and restructuring of production relations, with rather less industrial growth, more agricultural revolution and more attention to living standards. The latter tasks could not be reconciled, however, with the task of rapid, large-scale industrialization.

And so the abandonment of NEP 'was a political choice, but it had an economic logic'.[36] Some months later, the Great Depression put something of a damper on Stalin's definition of Leninism as the combination of Russian revolutionary sweep with American efficiency. It would also encourage him to think of the dangers posed to socialism in one country by unstable world capitalism. In a famous speech of 1931, he warned of the dangers of backwardness: 'To slacken the tempo would mean falling behind. ...We are fifty or a hundred years behind the advanced countries. We must make good this distance in ten years. Either we shall do it, or we shall go under.' The ensuing period, through to the outbreak of the Second World War, gave all too much evidence of the pressures of catching up, with extreme social dislocation accompanied by the gulag. Millions lost their lives in forced labour, while a few thousand sacrificed themselves to the cause voluntarily.[37] Nevertheless, with a lower level of foreign trade and expertise in the 1930s than in the 1920s, the USSR developed heavy industry, including an up-to-date armaments industry, with special emphasis on rearmament from 1939 onwards.

In the USA, too, there was increasing emphasis on preparing for war from the late 1930s onwards. Indeed, there is a considerable case for the argument that the Great Depression was not fully overcome before then, that Franklin D. Roosevelt's New Deal constituted no more than a partial recovery, less than fully integrated with the rest of world capitalism. For all the alphabet soup of its many stratagems and agencies, from the NRA (National Recovery Administration) onwards, this was no revolution, certainly not a socialist revolution as alleged by some of FDR's opponents, who should in fact have been grateful to the President for saving capitalism rather than undermining it. To be sure, there were parallels to Soviet planning in some of the New Deal's projects, notably in the control of water resources by the Tennessee Valley Authority and the Grand Coulee Dam in the Northwest, but altogether the reforms did not bring full employment nor produce any significant redistribution of income. Meaningful reduction of inequality, and that for middle rather than low incomes, came with progressive tax rates imposed during the war.

Before looking at the economic significance of the war, a brief glance at the demographic impact of the New Deal and the Five-Year Plans. Surprisingly, the regional distribution did not alter as much as might have been expected. But there was a decided move to the cities in both cases, the rural–urban ratio in the USA moving from 30:70 in 1920 to 23:77 in 1940, while the percentage of Soviet city dwellers moved from 18 per cent in 1926 to 28 per cent in 1939. Generally, the Soviet population increased from 147 millions in 1926 to 170 millions in 1939. For all its expansion in the interwar period, the Soviet peoples suffered a deficit of more than 30 millions, most of this accounted for by the First World War, the Revolution and Civil War, and the famine and epidemics consequent upon them, but no small amount resulting from the drive towards collectivisation and the forced pace of industrialisation.[38] Meanwhile, in the USA the total population increased from 106 millions in 1920 to 132 millions in 1940.

After then, as Douglass C. North puts it:

> Between 1941 and 1942, when we suddenly became involved in global war, we again became a full-employment economy, remarkably illustrating how we could expand output and productive capacity and reorient ourselves to prosecute a war in a fashion and to a degree that amazed our allies and dismayed our enemies.[39]

This expansion and reorientation involved planning and direction which went further than in the First World War and would have been unacceptable as part of the New Deal. As a consequence, world capitalism was to an unprecedented degree American capitalism.

There were even signs that the USSR's socialist economy was becoming dependent upon US aid. In 1943 and 1944, Lend-Lease military, industrial and food supplies amounted to as much as 10 per cent of the Soviet gross national product. Jeeps, trucks and field telephones were largely provided by the USA throughout. However, with the command economy imposing its grip even more than during the 1930s to relocate, intensify and improvise an enormous effort, the tools for the Soviet victory were mostly homemade, including all the artillery, seven-eighths of the tanks and amoured vehicles, and five-sixths of the aircraft. The sacrifices made by the Soviet peoples in terms of lives and extreme discomfort defy the imagination. Moreover, if the Second World War advanced the cause of American capitalism by leaps and bounds, it dealt the cause of Soviet socialism an enormous setback.[40]

From universal revolution to new realism

In broad parallel with economic developments in the period 1921–45, cultural developments may also be described in three chronological subdivisions: 'universal revolution' in the 1920s, followed by two successive phases of a new realism, during the 1930s and then throughout the war years.

In the Editorial Preface on 1 September 1926 to three new volumes (making up with their thirty-two predecessors the Thirteenth Edition of *The Encyclopaedia Britannica* of 1926) J.L. Garvin declared that there had been 'no more momentous and transforming years in the experience of mankind' than those from 1910 onwards:

Old Empires and dynasties have vanished; new nations and systems have appeared. With this, science and invention have gone forward with accelerating speed to wonderful results. All industrial life is searched by questioning and full of new developments. In this short epoch the former fundamental conceptions of time, space, matter and energy have been dissolved or modified. Speculation on the possibilities of further scientific discovery and of its practical addition to human power never was more daring. Medicine and surgery have made at least an equal advance in their resources for the defence, repair and prolongation of human life. Civilised taste, fashion and habit present very visibly a thousand interesting contrasts with their former modes. The new generation differs quite radically in many ways from the pre-War notions of its elders. Philosophy, literature and art re-examine with more unsparing scrutiny the mysteries of human being and purpose and the problems of human relations. Wide and signal as have been the changes in the world's external circumstances, still more general and profound have been the changes in the world's thought and feeling. In 15 years, as a result of physical conflict unparalleled for scale, violence and intensity; partly of the subsequent mental reactions; partly of the full and manifold working of influences which had begun to appear before the War, there has occurred a universal revolution in human affairs and the human mind.

As far as the future superpowers were concerned, their relative situation in the middle 1920s was evocatively illustrated by Garvin. While seeking the mutual aid and understanding of the English-speaking peoples, an aim furthered by the joint dedication to King George V and President Calvin Coolidge, and suggesting that 'the relations between Great Britain and America are of decisive significance for the general future of the world and are well capable of determining either way for all mankind the choice between peace and chaos', Garvin also argued that 'for the sake of the best relations between America and Britain under present conditions, it must never be forgotten that though England is the mother country of the language and law of the United States, all Europe is the mother-region of the racial blood and feeling of the United States – now the strongest society relatively to others that has arisen since the Roman Empire'. Quite a reminder from a citizen of the British Empire (as well as something of a slight to members of the United Kingdom other than England and to non-European citizens of the USA). Noting that from the ruins of other former empires many new states had arisen, and that to enforce editorial judgements on consequent contested issues would be premature and presumptuous, Garvin went on to observe for example that 'no finally impartial view of the Russian revolution can yet be formed when Russians themselves still differ violently or are silently perplexed, drifting with events, shunning convinced opinion'. No doubt to reduce the apartness of Russia, 'Commissary [sic] Trotsky himself had been persuaded to write the biography of

Lenin, whose career, whatever else may be thought, had been one of the astonishing features of modern history'.[41]

Among other distinguished contributors was Albert Einstein, pointing out that 'space and time are welded together into a uniform four-dimensional continuum'. While we must be careful not to make over-fanciful connections, we may be justified in asserting that the chaos of the Russian Revolutionary and post-First World War situation encouraged the acceptance of 'relativity' in its vulgar sense. The same influences might have encouraged the entry on 'atomic energy' to suggest that mankind might 'one day discover supreme material power, or cataclysmic annihilation'.[42]

While relativity was given a warm welcome in the USA, the Soviet establishment had reservations. A more traditional concept of time, it seems, was necessary for the Russian Revolution.[43] Nevertheless, among the interesting offshoots of the 'popular-scientific' understanding of Einstein and his theory was *Einstein and Religion: The Application of The Principle of Relativity to the Investigation of Religious Phenomena*, a work by the ethnographer V.G. Bogoraz (pseudonym TAN) published in 1923. Ranging widely through religion and shamanism, sleep and dreams (with a reference to Freud) and enlivened by drawings of a spirit in pursuit of the human soul and other subjects, Bogoraz boldly asserts that:

> Only the theory of relativity allows the possibility of using a method of measurement for religious phenomena, since it establishes as a basic principle that each system X, each field of enquiry has its own time, and that only from this point of view is it possible to research into units of measurement in the field of religion.[44]

Turning to other major figures involved in the 'universal revolution', we find the *Encyclopaedia Britannica* contribution on 'Psychoanalysis: Freudian School' written by none other than Sigmund Freud himself, insisting that this new science was far from 'a convenient panacea' for all psychological disorders.[45] Nevertheless, what had been a minor tendency before war and revolution became a powerful direction after them, throughout both future superpowers. In this context, we may note how Freud's version of psychoanalysis became accepted in the USA, at least in elite circles, while it rose and then fell in the Soviet Union as conception was followed by gestation. In other words, Freudianism turned out to be incompatible with 'Marxism-Leninism', that is, Stalinism. Yet, as we may also see, the process of advanced industrialisation had comparable effects on psychological thinking in the USSR and the USA alike. Development was by no means entirely conditioned by collectivism on the one hand and individualism on the other.

The outcome in the Soviet Union was decided by more than intellectual debate alone. There was also a *force majeure* external to the debate working against Freud and psychoanalysis, and in favour of Ivan Pavlov and behaviourism. The triumph of the salivating dog over the neurotic human being was achieved without any active participation from his master, since far from being a Bolshevik, Pavlov appears to have been a single-minded researcher indifferent to the cause. But, while his reputation flourished largely owing to his intrinsic worth as a scientist, he also received favour from on high.

Perhaps the whole process was illumined in his own inimitable fashion by the future 'Leader' himself, J. V. Stalin, who in 1919 remarked that 'The whole world has definitely and irrevocably split into two camps: the camp of imperialism and the camp of socialism.' On the one hand, there were America and Britain, France and Japan, with their capital; on the other was Soviet Russia, the young Soviet republics and the growing proletarian revolution in the countries of Europe, without capital. But by 1924, he argued that the socialist camp must learn from its rival, since 'The combination of Russian revolutionary sweep with American efficiency is the essence of Leninism in Party and state work.'[46]

Let us be clear about this: the dynamic part of the 'camp of imperialism' was already seen in 1924 as the USA. And let us look closer: what was 'American efficiency'? The answer here is clear enough: the doctrine and system developed by an American engineer Frederick Winslow Taylor, and described by him most completely in *The Principles of Scientific Management* published in 1911. In 'The Immediate Tasks of the Soviet Government', first published in 1918, Lenin himself had declared: 'The Russian is a bad worker compared with people in advanced countries. ... We must organize in Russia the study and the teaching of the Taylor system and systematically try it out and adapt it to our own ends.'[47]

Taylorism was not so far removed from behaviourism, for which, without due modesty, the American psychologist John B. Watson gave himself credit in the Thirteenth Edition of the *Encyclopaedia Britannica* of 1926 (although also making some acknowledgement of Pavlov as helping to provide the keystone of its arch). Later academic assessment shared his own view: 'Watson was the first and most important spokesman of a radical theory and practice that dominated American psychology for nearly half a century'; and Watson 'lent a vitality and power to the objective psychology movement that it might otherwise have lacked'.[48]

In our search for greater understanding of the inter-war mind, certainly, Freud by himself is not enough, especially if Peter Gay is right in maintaining that Freud

> had no use whatever for the celebration of irrational forces, or for the primi-
> tivism that would evade the dialectic of civilization by abandoning civilization
> altogether. He had not laboured in the sickroom of the human mind to join
> the party of disease; he had not descended to the sewer of human nature to
> wallow in what he had found there.

Sadly, no doubt, but also truly, the First World War and the October Revolution and its aftermath threw up much 'irrational ... primitivism', and the 'sewer of human nature' was in full flow not just among 'primitive' peoples. Here, we might have to call in as a research aid the work of Freud's sometime collaborator, Carl Jung, with his concepts of the 'collective unconscious' and others.[49]

As far as history is concerned, emphasis is to be given to the passage of time rather than structural analysis. To put the point as simply as possible, following the First World War and the Russian Revolution, while politicians in the USA held out the promise of a return to 'normalcy' involving continued cultural as well as economic progress, Lenin and his adherents wished to create new Soviet human beings (*homo sovieticus*) and to bring revolution to the whole world. Circumstances turned out to be so unfavourable, however, that their survival even in Russia was for several years in doubt, and then had to be maintained in the context of world capitalism. NEP was a necessary compromise on salient points of the Bolshevik programme, therefore, from means of production through to concepts of freedom. But the debate on how to reconcile dialectical materialism with the leading concepts of the postwar world continued as a necessary part of Soviet adaptation to the global context, consisting of three major components: Europe, the USA and the rest. Thus it was throughout the 1930s as the Five-Year Plans and the New Deal developed mass-production along Taylorian lines more popularly known as 'Fordism', a process continued with patriotic overtones into the Second World War and beyond.[50]

In fiction, the process went much further. Evgenii Zamiatin's anti-Utopian novel *We*, completed in 1921 and part of the inspiration for George Orwell's *1984*, is set far in the future at a time when Taylor is considered '*the* genius of antiquity' and an 'even more glorious feat' than the subjugation of 'the whole of planet Earth to the power of OneState' is about to be accomplished, namely 'by means of the glass, the electric, the fire-breathing INTEGRAL to integrate the indefinite equation of the universe'.[51]

At the end of the 1920s, the American poet John Gould Fletcher completed his book *Europe's Two Frontiers: A Study of the Historical Forces at Work in Russia and America as They will Increasingly Affect European Civilization*. 'For the past ten years, the situation of Europe has been both grotesque and tragic', he wrote, continuing: 'Since 1921 ... she has become like a patient suffering from shell-shock who acts irresponsibly and has no coherent purpose in life. ... Of the two new world-philosophies offered her, she has chosen neither.'[52] For at least two centuries, American and Russian streams of influence had been working on Europe and Asia. They were now reaching their culmination. What were their fundamental psychological characteristics? The special delight of Americans was 'not in thought, but in purely physical activity' – 'The whole course of American history may be summed up as the history of the spread of the pioneer and of his type of mind into every department of human effort.' Even when the American was in repose, 'he must somehow feel that his body, if not his mind, is exerting itself'.

And so, 'The true, the classic American symbol is the rocking-chair', symbolising alike 'domestic comfort, and nomadic restlessness'.

On the other hand, in Fletcher's view, 'the Russians ... tend to have very little interest in physical activity'. 'A fund of Mongolian inertia' probably accounted for this lack of activity, which could be overcome only if some great end was in view. Thus, 'The Revolution owed its success entirely to a few clean-cut practical actions thrown athwart a raging torrent of unpractical ideas and theories; Lenin and Trotsky rather saved Russia from herself, than created a new Russia.' A wise and witty French observer had remarked that 'the Russian conversation is, in times of food shortage, in itself equal to meat and drink'. And the specific symbol of Russia was probably the samovar: 'Ready at all times of the day and night to provide hot water, it stimulates but does not nourish, like the endless Russian conversations', providing only 'hot water'.

And so, 'the conflict that is being fought out today between America and Russia is a psychological one'. Although other great continents would not follow either path, however, there was a tendency for Europe while 'awaiting a new political Messiah ... in its decadent cosmopolitanism' to pass by gradual infiltration under the sway of the USA, and for Asia to be 'ready to turn the weapons of the West against the West itself, while remaining at heart far more akin to the spirit of non-individualistic fatalism which has successfully guided Russia'. Basically, 'Europe has no longer the economic force nor the creative will to resist America. Asia has no longer the spiritual fervour nor the united faith to hold back Russia.' In the conditions of population explosion and 'the mushroom-like growth of industrial capitalism', such a division could lead to war. In these circumstances, the duty of all intelligent persons in both frontier societies was to 'oppose the tides of Bolshevism and of Americanism that are now sweeping the world'. They 'must save America and Russia from themselves', and 'strive to inform both America and Russia with a purpose alien to their whole historical development'. For: 'It is Russia, not America, that needs an Emerson to lead it towards individual self-reliance. It is America, not Russia, that needs a Dostoevsky to show it the value of common submission to the mysterious powers that govern the development of all spirituality.'[53]

John Gould Fletcher makes little or no mention of writers in the 1920s. He completed his book just before the Great Crash in the USA and the impact of the Five-Year Plans in the USSR, before the onset of new realisms, in the 1930s and then through the Second World War. For, just as in political and economic life, there are also breaks in cultural development around 1929 and 1941. To give a simple example, we associate the US 1920s with the Charleston and Scott Fitzgerald's *The Great Gatsby*, the 1930s with 'Buddy can you spare a dime?' and John Steinbeck's *The Grapes of Wrath*. In the USSR, the 1920s are comparatively relaxed, with Ilf and Petrov's *The Twelve Chairs* licensed to satirise varied aspects of life under NEP. Then: 'The combination of repression and bureaucratisation set the tone for the next era of Soviet history, which ran from the early 1930s up to the death of Stalin in 1953.'[54] The new period saw heavy emphasis on 'socialist realism' defined in 1933 by Anatolii Lunacharsky as 'to describe not reality as it is, but reality as it will be'. Even though they do not conform to all the prescribed principles, Mikhail Sholokhov's well-known *Quiet Flows the Don* and *Virgin Soil Upturned* could be cited as exemplars, but there are any number of other novels celebrating the construction of Soviet socialism.

Throughout the 1920s and 1930s, the press, radio and the cinema all flourished in the USA, and Hollywood in particular made a great impact in the wider world, as is well known. For Lenin, the cinema was 'the most important of all arts', but not for aesthetic reasons. On the contrary, film was to be exploited as a means of political education, another product of advanced Western technology which, like the Taylor system, could be adapted for the purpose of building socialism in backward Russia. But Eisenstein's 'Potemkin' had to give way in popularity to 'Robin Hood' as presented by Douglas Fairbanks.[55]

Radio did not become a mass medium in the USSR before the 1930s. Lenin had called it 'a newspaper without paper or wires', but plans for its widespread dissemination came to very little in the short run. By 1937, there were 3.5 million receivers, nearly all of them speakers connected to a single station.[56] The newspaper itself did not prosper as was first hoped. Useful for rolling cigarettes or for sanitary purposes (especially welcome to some when containing photographs of the leaders), its contents were often above the heads of its intended readers who could not assimilate the ideas of Karl Marx even in simplified form.

The old culture persisted, including the church, if not without some update. Jerome Davis, Professor of Practical Philanthropy at Yale, observed in 1928 after a visit to Russia: 'There can be little question that the church in Russia today is one of the freest platforms for the expression of opinion which exists in the country. Most of the priests are not educated sufficiently to take full advantage of this opportunity.'[57] In 1937, a census taken of the people as a whole was widely believed to reveal that more than half of them were still religious in their outlook, even after years of much propaganda, some persecution and not a little announcement of positive progress towards atheism. But secular heroes were updated, the old Russian knight reincarnated in Chapaev, a leader in the Civil War, or in explorers and aviators – counterparts to Charles A. Lindbergh.

Back in the USA, the old culture had also been accompanied by a new realism in the 1930s, at the movies, on the radio and in the press. Officially, the Federal Arts project was set up in 1933 to proceed 'on the principle that it is not the solitary genius but a sound general movement which maintains art as a vital, functioning part of any cultural scheme'. A far cry from traditional individualism, the project employed many artists in activities ranging from decoration of public buildings through arrangement of art exhibitions to compilation of the paintings, songs and other products of the American 'folk'. As well as famous artists like

Thomas Hart Benton depicting the social life of the West and South, there were 'a host of eager young men who refused to abandon their native regions for either the Left Bank or Greenwich Village and who recorded in paint what the regional novelists of an earlier generation had recorded in fiction'.[58] Recorded on wax, blues and jazz singers such as Leadbelly and Jelly Roll Morton now found themselves in the Library of Congress.

Over in the Soviet Union, unfortunately, like everything else, architecture, art and folk culture had been subjected to the powerful influence of the Leader, J.V. Stalin. Even he, however, found it necessary to compromise with tradition to an unprecedented extent in an attempt to rouse the people after the Nazi invasion, urging them in a speech of 6 November 1941 to find inspiration in 'the manly images of our great ancestors' from Alexander Nevsky to Mikhail Kutuzov. On the very first day of the war, 22 June, the Acting Patriarch condemned the 'Fascist Bandits' and blessed the people 'with heavenly grace for their heroic battle'. Such patriotic words, and the reception given them, persuaded Stalin to allow for the election of a new Patriarch in August 1943 and to set up in September an official Council for the Affairs of the Russian Orthodox Church under an atheist chairman, who was soon dubbed 'Narkombog' (People's Commissar for God).[59]

In the USA too, patriotism was encouraged in speech and print, radio and cinema. At work, demands were taken to new levels. *A Guide to Victory on the Homefront* declared: 'No one of us consumers can escape his wartime duty. We must be at our battle stations twenty-four hours a day – lest we leave the furnace burning too high while we sleep.' As in the First World War, there was propaganda and censorship as well as the crusading spirit. In this latter regard, along with ideals such as freedom from war, want and fear went the narrower belief in the all-round superiority of American civilisation. In 1943, for example, Vice-President Henry Wallace traced the course of social justice through the Old and New Testaments of the Bible to its 'complete and powerful political expression ... our nation ... formed as a Federal Union a century and a half ago'.[60]

Wendell Wilkie, FDR's Republican opponent in the presidential election of 1940, was commissioned by the President to fly around the globe in 1942. In Moscow, he found Stalin 'a hard man, perhaps even a cruel man, but a very able one', and Russia 'a dynamic country, a vital new society, a force that cannot be bypassed in any future world'. There was nothing he had ever wanted more to believe than that it would be 'possible for Russia and America, perhaps the most powerful countries in the world, to work together for the economic welfare and the peace of the world.' Such aspirations were widely shared among the wartime allies as the years of gestation neared their end and the moment approached for the birth of superpower. We must now turn to investigate why those hopes were so completely dashed after the allied victory.[61]

4   Youth

Cold War and decolonisation,
1945–68

From Big Three to Super Two (1945)

The word 'super-power' was defined in 1926 as the 'systematic grouping and interconnection of existing power systems'.[1] At that time, the term was applied to describe the working of an electricity grid, but it was possibly, and by no means inappropriately, at the back of the mind of W.T.R. Fox, who made the first recorded use of it in a book entitled *The Super-Powers* published in 1944. The subtitle of the book was 'The United States, Britain and the Soviet Union – Their Responsibility for Peace'. In 1980, Fox wondered why he could have made what later appeared to have been the elementary mistake of including Britain along with what he had termed the other two, peripheral powers.[2] The peripheral designation was one of the reasons for Fox's error in 1944, when there was still considerable acceptance of Britain and Europe as the centre of the world. Moreover, in a sense the christening came before the birth, since one of the essential attributes of superpower, the ability to wreak global destruction through nuclear warfare, had yet to emerge. Also, in 1944 the British Empire had not seemed to be on the brink of collapse, nor was it then quite as clear as it later became that the major ideological clash would be between updated Wilsonism and Leninism.

But if at first Fox included Britain in his new category, several observers of the international scene including Adolf Hitler, Charles de Gaulle and Bertrand Russell soon pointed out that there would be no more than two great powers after the end of the Second World War, the USA and USSR. However, none of them could predict the manner in which these two would come to exert such preponderant influence in the postwar years, and the manner in which the term superpower (without the hyphen) would gain general acceptance in the West. Soviet use of the term was somewhat reluctant, probably because it had no place in Marxist-Leninist vocabulary. Objectively, too, there was the misleading implication that the USSR was the equal of the USA in every sense. Most obviously, the socialist economy had a vast amount of catching up to do before it could complete its task of overtaking.

The leaders of the allies, the UK, the USA and the USSR, would probably have agreed with W.T.R. Fox in 1944, even early in 1945, when they came together for the Yalta or Crimea Conference. An examination of their views as expressed at the meeting allows us to form an impression of their world outlooks at that time. At the beginning, Churchill suggested that the Big Three should speak in alphabetical order. Stalin agreed, pointing out that, according to the Russian alphabet, Churchill would speak last. Here was a reminder that, both literally and figuratively, the Soviet and Western Allies did not speak the same language. Taking them in the order which the British statesman had in mind and which was actually adopted, let us turn to his observations first.

Not surprisingly, Churchill stood stoutly by the British Empire. He was most agitated by the possible threat posed to it by the opening of the question of trusteeship over colonial and dependent peoples. While the Union Jack flew over the territories of the British Crown, he would not allow any piece of British soil to be put up for auction. After all, in one of his wartime speeches, he had talked of the possibility of the Empire and Commonwealth lasting for a thousand years. But he also pointed out on several occasions that he was responsible to his Cabinet and Parliament, and ultimately to the people; he could be voted out of office quite soon. He was also concerned about postwar great power alignment, acknowledging that the British Empire might not be able to stand alone. He therefore considered its participation in a wider English-speaking union along with the USA, and at least voiced the possibility of the UK playing a leading part in a more integrated Europe.

As far as that continent in particular was concerned, he wanted a restoration of France, so that the balance of power could be restored, and, for the same purpose, the reduction of Germany, with special penalties for Prussia, which he saw as the root of most of the evil. While unenthusiastic about the Poles themselves, he insisted that Britain was most concerned with the fate of Poland as a matter of honour, as it had entered the war to defend that country from German aggression. Since it had not been able to achieve much in 1939, it should strive to make up the deficiency in 1945. Thinking back to the First World War, he was anxious that Bolshevism should not penetrate the Balkans. He also believed that imperial responsibilities as well as the desire to remain a world power obliged Britain to take an interest in the Asian as well as the European theatre of war.

Roosevelt was probably not much more preoccupied with Europe than with the Pacific, where the USA's war had started and was still being significantly fought. As a former naval man, he would be very conscious of the fact that the Battle of Leyte Gulf off the Philippines in October 1944 had been the biggest in history, and that more would have to come before the final victory over Japan. But an overriding thought was the realisation that the USA now discharged global responsibilities to an extent much greater than before and significantly greater than its Allies. Hence a vision of a New Deal for the whole world, guaranteed by the United Nations Organisation, in which the USA would participate in a vigorous manner compensating somewhat for its failure to join the League of Nations after the First World War. Conscious of his predecessor Woodrow Wilson's unsuccessful policy of an Open Door for American business in a world made safe for democracy, Roosevelt was anxious to move further in this same direction. This aim could mean some tension with the empires of Europe, as well as trouble in the first location of the Open Door, the Far East. The special relationship with Latin America, where the doors were not open to interlopers from outside the Western hemisphere, would have to be preserved. As far as Europe was concerned, the President certainly wanted Germany to be made to pay. He encouraged Stalin to propose a toast to the execution of 50,000 officers in the German army. He expressed the view that the USA did not want German living standards to be higher than those of the Soviet peoples. Germany should certainly be dismembered, although it might be utopian to talk of complete decentralisation. On Poland, Roosevelt referred to the necessity of giving assurance to the millions of its former citizens who now lived in the USA, but recognised the Soviet need for security as well as the various Polish desires for restoration.

Stalin paid several compliments to the Poles, with brave fighters, outstanding scientists and great artists among them. The Soviet Union was still conscious of the bad treatment meted out to the Poles by Tsarism, he observed (although making no mention of the 10,000 or so Polish officers murdered by his own regime), and was anxious to redress legitimate grievances. Yet twice within thirty years, the Germans had attacked through Poland and a barrier had to be set up against any further repetition. The Soviet peoples would not forgive Stalin and Molotov if they turned out to be less reliable spokesmen than Curzon or Clemenceau (both of whom had suggested frontiers for Soviet Russia after the First World War to the west of where they were in 1939). Allowing for Stalin's rhetorical exaggeration, and noting that he made no mention of the Soviet invasion of Poland after the Nazi–Soviet Pact of 1939, we still have to recognise that he was giving voice to an intense enough apprehension. He appears to have been moving to a tacit acceptance of spheres of influence in postwar Europe, thinking back to his 'percentages' deal with Churchill in 1944 and making no more than token suggestions for Soviet representation in decisions concerning liberated Italy and France. On Germany, he was more insistent than Churchill and Roosevelt that 'the Germans were savages and seemed to hate with a sadistic hatred the creative work of human beings'. All too conscious of the vast task of postwar reconstruction, he was much more determined than his two colleagues on reparations. Incapable of harbouring any immediate hopes of world revolution, Stalin was nevertheless at least as much heir to Leninism as was Roosevelt to Wilsonism and therefore probably hopeful that at some future time there might be a global role for communism. But in the shorter run, he was considering at most an extension of his own idea of 'socialism in one country' as a guarantor of Soviet resistance to the infiltration of harmful outside influences. Going back explicitly beyond the Russian Revolution of 1917 in his argument, he sought in Asia the recovery of land and sea lost in the Russo-Japanese War of 1904–5. Hence, his commitment to join in the war against Japan as soon as possible after the Allied victory in Europe.[3]

Somewhat surprisingly for a self-styled Marxist-Leninist, although not so surprisingly for the central figure of a 'cult of personality', Stalin said to his British and American counterparts that 'as long as the three of them lived none of them would involve their countries in aggressive actions, but after all, ten years from now none of them might be present. A new generation would come into being not knowing the horrors of war.' As we now all know, two of the Big Three were to depart from the centre of the world stage in a matter of months, Roosevelt through death and Churchill by way of a general election. Personal continuities were therefore all too quickly broken, as Stalin had to realise as he met Truman and Attlee at Potsdam.

While the Oder–Neisse line was accepted as the western boundary of Poland (if only on a 'temporary' basis), there was agreement also on zones of occupation in Germany and arrangements for reparations.[4] These were realistic decisions on the basis of possession being nine points of international law. Nevertheless, the ideological element remained strong in the policies of the successive Big Threes. As far as American statesmen were concerned, N. Gordon Levin observed in the revolutionary year of 1968:

> what seems clear is that Wilsonianism, even while losing the battle over the League of Nations, eventually triumphed in the long-term struggle over the ultimate definition of the nature of twentieth-century American foreign policy. Wilson established the main drift toward an American liberal globalism, hostile both to traditional imperialism and to revolutionary-socialism. Many who had been associated with Wilson, or who had accepted the essentials of his world view, such as Herbert Hoover, Cordell Hull, Franklin Roosevelt, and John Foster Dulles, would continue in later periods to identify America's expansive national interest with the maintenance of a rational and peaceful international liberal order. Ultimately, in the post-World War II period, Wilsonian values would have their complete triumph in the bipartisan Cold War consensus.[5]

Needless to say, Leninism remained the guiding ideology of Soviet foreign and domestic policy throughout the Cold War period, even if subject to Stalinist distortions. Adapting the observation of N. Gordon Levin, one could put the point like this:

what seems clear is that Leninism, even while losing the battle over the League of Nations, eventually triumphed in the long-term struggle over the ultimate definition of the nature of twentieth-century Soviet foreign policy. Lenin established the main drift toward Soviet revolutionary-socialism, hostile both to traditional imperialism and to liberal globalism. Many who had been associated with Lenin, or who had accepted the essentials of his world view, such as Stalin, Molotov, Khrushchev and Gromyko, would continue in later periods to identify the USSR's expansive national interest with the maintenance of a rational and peaceful international socialist order. Ultimately , in the post-world War II period, Leninist values would have their complete triumph in the CPSU Cold War consensus.

Meanwhile, although Churchill remained a towering figure after the death of Stalin, his preference for 'traditional imperialism' could not withstand the pressures of the movement that came to be known as Decolonisation. In 1941, while discussing the Atlantic Charter, Roosevelt said to Churchill: 'I can't believe that we can fight a war against fascist slavery, and at the same time not work to free people all over the world from a backward colonial policy.'[6] In 1942, FDR tried to push Churchill towards acceptance of Indian independence in order to forestall fomentation of revolt by Japan. Churchill threatened to resign, protesting: 'I have not become the King's First Minister to preside over the liquidation of the British Empire.' Moreover, the Prime Minister's concern for the balance of power had already shocked his colleagues in October 1943, when he had spoken to the Cabinet for three hours stressing that Britain 'mustn't weaken Germany too much – we may need her against Russia'.[7]

On this point, arguably, Churchill was simultaneously out-of-date and before his time, both harking back to the Great Game of empire involving Victorian Britain and Tsarist Russia, and seeking to anticipate a new Great Game where he believed that the major players would be the UK, the USA and the USSR. But he exaggerated the part to be played both by himself and by his country. During the period immediately before the end of and then after the Second World War, the UK increasingly revealed its comparative weakness during the administration of Churchill's successor, Clement Attlee. The USA strengthened its own position while supporting the movement towards decolonisation as long as it did not threaten stability in Latin America or strengthen its major adversary, the USSR, also a consistent supporter of decolonisation except in its own backyard. While for Stalin, in the words of Alec Nove, the process of decolonisation was 'in some sense a fraud' and the Indian nationalist leader Nehru was 'probably a Western agent',[8] from Khrushchev onwards, the Soviet Union took a great interest in what was to be considered the Third World largely created by decolonisation at the same time as maintaining its grasp on Eastern and Central Europe.

The Cold War and decolonisation constituted a dual process, and must be considered together in any examination of the superpowers in the first flush of their youth. 'When did the Cold War begin?' has been a question more frequently asked than 'Where did the Cold War begin?' Yet place has almost as much importance as time, if we look at the rivalry of the USA and the USSR in the context of decolonisation. While primary emphasis at first was given to Europe, especially Germany with a focus on Berlin, the Middle East was of importance, too, as for example in the case of Iran. The significance of Asia grew considerably after the Chinese Revolution of 1949, which exacerbated the US–Soviet conflict during the ensuing Korean War and complicated the situation in South-East Asia for many years. To repeat the point simply, the Cold War is more accurately evaluated as a global process when considered together with decolonisation.

As far as the timing is concerned, 1945 would be far from everybody's choice as the starting date for the Cold War. Some would say 1947, the date of the Truman Doctrine and Marshall Plan together with the consolidation of Soviet encroachment in Eastern Europe; others would point to 1948, when that encroachment was reinforced after Stalin's break with Tito and the Berlin Blockade. There is a case for 1949, when the Soviet Union acquired the bomb, and for early 1950 when the culmination of a change of direction in US policy was indicated by the adoption of the paper known as NSC-68, the US master plan drawn up before the outbreak of the Korean War and implemented fully thereafter. However, as we go on in this chapter to examine these milestones on the road of the great conflict, we must not forget the inference of preceding chapters, that the nature of the clash, wherever and whenever it came, would be heavily influenced by what had gone before.

From Berlin and Hiroshima (1945–)

The race for Berlin had a symbolic as well as strategic significance, exemplified by the attachment of the Soviet banner to the top of the burned-out Reichstag following the warm embraces of the Soviet and Western Allied troops at the River Elbe. Almost immediately, however, a certain coldness crept into inter-Allied relations, with the American and British Generals Eisenhower and Montgomery turning down an invitation to a victory banquet issued by their Soviet counterpart Zhukov after the signing of the Four-Power Declaration on the defeat of Germany on 5 June 1945.[9]

Undoubtedly, Berlin was soon to acquire a special meaning as a centre of the Cold War and of the intelligence and security mania connected with it. Churchill talked of 'the special importance that the capital of the Third Reich is bound to possess' following the end of the war, and disagreed with Eisenhower's decision to hold his armies back from a final assault on it, while Stalin appears to have adhered to the view attributed to Lenin that 'he who has Berlin has Germany, and he who has Germany has Europe'. Here, as in no other place, the KGB confronted the CIA at the frontier outpost of the West surrounded by territory occupied by the East. Providing material for a vast number of spy novels, Berlin also presents the historian of the years following the Second World War with a case study of outstanding significance, through to the construction and destruction of the famous Wall.[10]

However, the emotional and intellectual impact made by this European city falls short of the feelings and thoughts evoked by a counterpart at the edge of Asia, Hiroshima, to the awesome significance of which we now turn. Stalin at Yalta committed the Soviet Union to entry into the war against Japan three months after victory in Europe, which was formally announced on 9 May 1945. Fifty years after, Gar Alperovitz argued that by July 1945, 'a combination of assurances for the Emperor and the shock of a Russian declaration of war appeared quite likely to bring about the surrender long before an invasion could begin'. And, in the view of Robert A. Pape, 'Japan's military position was so poor that its leaders would likely have surrendered before invasion, and at roughly the same time in August 1945, even if the United States had not employed strategic bombing or the atomic bomb'. For Alperovitz, therefore, three questions arise about the use of the atomic bomb at Hiroshima on 6 August and Nagasaki on 9 August. Did the US leaders believe that there was no other choice? Did the bomb have to be used without notification and against cities? Was the bombing of two cities necessary?

Alperovitz gives answers as follows. First, Admiral William D. Leahy gave his opinion in 1950 that 'the use of this barbarous weapon at Hiroshima and Nagasaki was of no material assistance in our war against Japan. The Japanese were already defeated and ready to surrender.' His own feeling was that 'in being the first to use it, we had adopted an ethical standard common to the barbarians of the Dark Ages.' And Dwight D. Eisenhower wrote in 1963 of his belief 'that Japan was already defeated and that dropping the bomb was completely unnecessary ... that Japan was, at that very moment, seeking some way to surrender with a minimum loss of "face"'. Thus, Alperovitz's own negative answer is reinforced by quotations from two of the leading servicemen of the time. Second, Alperovitz expresses his view that 'it would have been possible to issue a much more explicit warning and to attack a non-urban target first, as George Marshall proposed'. Again in his own words, 'had there been a less intense rush to end the war before the Russians came in, the issue of a second city might have been posed more thoughtfully'.

Having considered a number of other alternative explanations, Alperovitz comes to the following conclusions. First, Secretary of State James F. Byrnes 'clearly saw the weapon as important to his diplomacy *vis-à-vis* the Soviet Union'. Second, Byrnes and Truman postponed Potsdam and then took a hard line there in anticipation of use of the A-bomb. Third, in this specific context and similarly, Byrnes 'arranged for the elimination of language offering assurances for the

Emperor' in negotiations with the Japanese. Fourth, Byrnes then saw the use of the A-bomb as a way to end the war before the Red Army could enter Manchuria. Fifth, Japan was looking for peace, but there was 'fear that the war might end in a manner that would make Moscow the peacemaker'.[11]

Although his book goes into the subject in enormous detail, there remains, of course, an alternative interpretation focusing upon the circumstances and atmosphere at the time the decision to drop the bomb was taken rather than retrospective commentary or analysis. Certainly, too, because of deep-set mutual suspicions already in evidence in Berlin and elsewhere, there is at least a case for beginning the Cold War even before the defeat of Japan, which would also have a considerable impact on the process of decolonisation as its armed forces withdrew from South-East Asia.

Kept out of Japan and Western Europe at the end of the Second World War, the Soviet Union was in any case in no fit condition to embark upon widespread expansion. Early in 1946, a memorandum on Soviet capabilities was prepared in the US Navy Department:

> The Red Fleet is incapable of any important offensive or amphibious operations ... a strategic air force is practically non-existent either in materiel or concept ... economically, the Soviet Union is exhausted. The people are undernourished, industry and transport are in an advanced state of deterioration, enormous areas have been devastated, thirty percent of the population has been dislocated. ... Maintenance of large occupation forces in Europe is dictated to a certain extent by the necessity of 'farming out' millions of men for whom living accommodations and food cannot be spared in the USSR during the current winter. This also aids the popular opinion that the USSR is a tremendous military power, thereby influencing political decisions to a degree out of proportion to the USSR's actual present offensive potential. ... The USSR is not expected to take any action during the next five years which might develop into hostilities with Anglo-Americans.[12]

Subsequent research has reinforced this grim assessment, which should be carefully read and pondered by all those adhering to the view that the Soviet Union was bent on expansionist policies immediately after the end of the Second World War. As far as human losses were concerned, in contrast to the USSR's 27,000,000 or more, the USA's death count was at most 425,000, tragic indeed yet at least sixty times less.[13] Materially, as Thomas G. Paterson puts it:

> The United States military establishment ranked supreme in the early Cold War period. Its air force was the largest and the most capable; its navy was first with twelve hundred warships and fifty thousand supporting and landing craft; its troops occupied territory and bases across the globe, including

Japan, Germany, Austria, and new outposts in the Pacific. Public pressure for demobilization forced the Truman administration to reduce military forces faster than it wished to (from 12 million in 1945 to 1.5 million in 1947), but defense needs and security were not impaired because other nations were heavily devastated and the Soviet Union also demobilized (from 12 million to 3 to 4 million). Then, too, the military expenditures for fiscal years 1947 and 1948 represented one-third of the total United States budget as compared to its miniscule defense budget and might in the 1930s. The United States after 1945 was a military giant, and few denied it. While the USSR held power confined largely to one region, eastern Europe, the United States had become a global power.

'The awesome atomic bomb had a potential rather than real place in the military arsenal', Paterson adds, but essentially 'it created fear and anxiety and loomed in the background as a symbol of United States technological genius and destructive ability to which other nations would aspire.'[14] Military might and threat were accompanied by political power. While Latin America remained a US preserve, Japan also was firmly placed within the US sphere of influence, with the USSR kept out completely. The USA also had a strong presence in Korea while struggling to keep a hold over China. Over in Europe, the USA exerted control over Italy and a part of Germany while France and Great Britain were becoming dependencies. UNO = USA would be an over-simplified equation, but with the votes of nearly twenty Latin American clients in their pocket, the US representatives at the new world forum could appear as the voices of moderation and reason while the frequent vetoes of the Soviet delegation gave the impression of doctrinaire extremism.

US Secretary of War Henry Stimson put his finger on the nub of the problem confronting his fellow Americans in 1945 when he criticised many of them for their anxiety 'to hang on to exaggerated views of the Monroe Doctrine and at the same time butt into every question that comes up in Central Europe'. With very little support, he suggested that through bilateral US–USSR negotiations both sides could reach agreement about each of them having its own sphere of security. He believed that 'Our respective orbits do not clash geographically and I think on the whole we can probably keep out of clashes in the future.'[15]

So not everybody would agree that the Cold War was already under way in 1945. Certainly, there were later pointers, not least the famous pronouncement on 'The Sources of Soviet Conduct' by 'X', alias George F. Kennan, Counsellor in the Moscow Embassy from 1944 to 1946, based on a long telegram that he had sent from to Washington early in 1946. 'X' suggested that the basis for 'the Kremlin's neurotic view of the world affairs' was 'the traditional and instinctive Russian sense of insecurity', explosively mixed since 1917 with 'Oriental secretiveness and conspiracy' as well as communist ideology. Guided by Marxism,

'X' wrote, 'the men in the Kremlin have continued to be predominantly absorbed with the struggle to secure and make absolute the power which they seized in November 1917'. The same ideology 'taught them that the outside world was hostile and that it was their duty eventually to overthrow the political forces beyond their borders'. Moreover, 'the powerful hands of Russian history and tradition reached up to sustain them in this feeling'. At the same time, 'there is ample evidence that the stress laid in Moscow on the menace confronting Soviet society from the world outside its borders is founded not in the realities of foreign antagonism but in the necessity of explaining away the maintenance of dictatorial authority at home'. In the face of such intransigence, 'the main element of any United States policy must be that of a long-term, patient but firm and vigilant containment of Russian expansive tendencies'.

The very next contribution to that of 'X' in the July 1947 number of the journal *Foreign Affairs* is by one of Stalin's advisers, Eugene Varga. Devoted to 'Anglo-American Rivalry and Partnership: A Marxist View', it is far from suggesting equality between the two capitalist powers. With the biggest war budget and strongest armed forces in the world and bases all over it, together with the secret of the atom bomb, 'the United States is the land in which militarism is most in vogue. Big business is bent on using the country's military power for the economic subjugation of the world.'[16]

Varga's essay echoed the message sent to Moscow in late 1946 by the Soviet Ambassador to the United States. According to Ambassador Nikolai Novikov, a bi-partisan reactionary foreign policy in the Congress departed from 'Roosevelt's course for cooperation among peace-loving countries' to give consistent support to President Truman, 'a politically unstable person but with certain conservative tendencies'. The offensive nature of US strategic concepts was illustrated by plans for 228 bases, points of support and radio stations in the Atlantic Ocean, and 258 such outposts in the Pacific Ocean. China was being formed into 'a bridgehead for the American armed forces', which were infiltrating both Far and Near East. In Germany, no measures were being taken to eliminate two groups which had given great support to Hitler, the monopolistic associations of industrialists and the large landholders. An unreformed imperialist Germany could well become part of US plans for a future war. And direct calls for such a 'third war' were being given at public meetings and in the press, accompanied by an anti-Soviet campaign mounted 'to create an atmosphere of war psychosis among the masses'. Support for 'England' could not disguise the tensions with this declining great power nor the basic aim of world domination.

The view from the USA's alleged rival, the UK, may be examined via another communication from Moscow early in 1946, this time to London, from Frank Roberts, the British chargé d'affaires. Along similar lines to Kennan, Roberts wrote that 'one fundamental factor affecting Soviet policy dating back to the small beginnings of the Muscovite State' was 'the constant striving for security of a State with no natural frontiers and surrounded by enemies'. Moreover, Russia had always been a more backward state than her neighbours, and even in 1946, 'the Soviet Union, despite its prestige in the world, is more backward than not only Britain or the United States, but than most other European countries'. Nevertheless, Russia had expanded enormously over the centuries and imperial rivalries, exacerbated by the clash between liberalism and autocracy, had dogged relations with Britain. But not until 1945 were Russia and Britain face to face. Now, with other empires at an end and other states crippled, 'the only other world power is the United States, and there is clearly no reason why Britain and Russia should be brought to combine against her as a menace to their interests or to the peace of the world', especially since there was a greater ideological gulf between Britain and Russia than even in the nineteenth century. No doubt, the Soviet Union's long-term aim was to become 'the most powerful State in the world', and this would involve attempts 'to keep the Americans and ourselves apart' and 'to weaken capitalist or social-democratic countries in every way'. In particular, the Soviet Union would attempt to undermine Britain's established position in Europe while encouraging so-called 'national liberation movements' in the wider world.[17]

In 1946, Roberts could not foresee that the new Great Game's major adversaries would be the USA and USSR, with Britain playing a smaller part as its empire disintegrated. Nor did the views of the future given by Kennan and Novikov turn out to be accurate. As far as the past was concerned, Kennan and Roberts both found it useful to look there for an explanation of Soviet behaviour. Varga and Novikov, on the other hand, made little or no attempt to look for the roots of Western imperialism. All three telegrams, however, indicated clearly that the international situation in 1946 already seemed more dangerous than that in 1945.

To Czechoslovakia and Vietnam (–1968)

Turning from evaluation in the late 1940s to what we can perceive fifty years later, let us note again that one of the basic qualifications for superpower, the ability to destroy the world, was not acquired before the 1960s. The USA acquired the ability to produce the A-bomb in 1945, and then the H-bomb – appropriately known as the 'super' – in 1952. Nuclear calculations rose from the equivalent of thousands of tons of TNT to millions, from kilotons to megatons. The equivalent years for the USSR were 1949 and 1953 respectively. In 1953, the USA possessed 1,000 nuclear warheads, and by 1961, there were 18,000 – the number having tripled in a bare two years, with the Pentagon increasing its number of Soviet targets from less than thirty to more than 2,500. By now, rockets were beginning to replace bombers as the principal means of delivery, and the USSR was doing what it could to equal its rival in all respects.[18]

In the days of their early youth, the superpowers had to depend mostly on conventional arms. Images of the Russian troops with snow on their boots stretching back to the Napoleonic wars returned, along with the fear that they might march all over Western Europe. But, as the US Navy Department knew early in 1946 and we should now more widely realise, their large-scale presence in Eastern Europe was the consequence not only of a desire to dominate but also of the need for subsistence. Meanwhile, to quote Paterson again, the USA had become 'a military giant' and 'a global power'.

The full terror of nuclear weapons was most keenly felt in the initial period when they were actually used and before familiarity, if not quite breeding contempt, did lead to acceptance. For example, before the Soviet bomb was exploded in the same year, Vannevar Bush, president of the Carnegie Institution in Washington and government scientific adviser, was complaining in 1949 of 'the prophets of doom' crying that almost any alternative to war was preferable. Afterwards, as is well known, many authorities even learned to stop worrying and love the bomb, praising it for having created a balance of terror. Without doubt, in general, as Nikolai Krementsov has observed, 'The Cold War gave defining form to two systems of Big Science, two mutually isolated but interdependent creatures, each almost unthinkable without the other.'[19]

Another point to reiterate from our vantage point at the end of the 1990s is that the first focus of the superpower relationship fifty years ago was Europe. Thus, in 1947, although the Truman Doctrine announced on 12 March was global in its observations that the moment in world history was one in which 'nearly every nation must choose between alternative ways of life', the almost exclusive emphasis was on Greece and Turkey. Then, the Marshall Plan as set out on 5 June made reference to the serious world situation but gave its major consideration to 'the requirements for the rehabilitation of Europe'. A response with the same focus came on 18 September at the United Nations from the Soviet representative Andrei Vyshinsky (formerly Stalin's 'hanging judge' in the 'show trials' of the 1930s). As well as alleging that 'The so-called Truman Doctrine and the Marshall Plan are particularly glaring examples of the manner in which the principles of the United Nations are violated, of the way in which the Organization is ignored', he also claimed that the USA was counting on making European countries directly dependent on 'the interests of American monopolies' and attempting 'to split Europe into two camps'.[20]

As a sequel, the USSR was to consolidate the takeover of Hungary and Czechoslovakia, while the USA did all it could to make sure that communist parties did not come to power in Italy and France. At the centre, the importance of Berlin stood out. Thus, the first crisis in the superpower relationship was indeed over the partitioned former capital city of the Second and Third Reich. Western currency reform led to Soviet closedown of the surface access routes in the summer of 1948 and the famous Berlin Airlift ensued until the spring of 1949.[21]

Almost from the beginning, the US administration harboured thoughts of rolling back and undermining communism more completely. NATO was formed in 1949 under the sponsorship of the USA with an emphasis on the self-defence of Europe and North America along with the development of free institutions, particularly through the encouragement of economic collaboration. Equally, while not abandoning hope for ultimate world revolution, the Soviet Union showed through its own uncompromising intervention that it wanted to make the area it had occupied in 1945 its own, sponsoring the Warsaw Pact in 1955 to give its continued occupation a veneer of legality. But history showed that Central and Eastern Europe had always been a problem for Russia and its Soviet successor. Before the First World War, Austria and Germany were effective counterweights. Afterwards, the successor states created at the Paris Peace Conference were strong enough with fitful Western support to maintain their independence. This was largely because the heir to the Tsarist empire, the nascent Soviet Union, had been pushed back from its predecessor's frontiers during the Civil War and Allied intervention following the Russian Revolution. Now that most of these frontiers had been recovered and some of them even extended, dissidence and civil disturbance in the 'socialist camp' showed that all was far from well.

Soviet aspirations in Eastern and Central Europe were most clearly mirrored in US intentions in Latin America, which was much more its own preserve, so much so that it is virtually omitted from some histories of the Cold War. Yet it must not be omitted from any consideration of the global relationship of the superpowers. After all, the Monroe Doctrine was not ordained by the Almighty, and the treatment meted out to some opponents of US domination of Latin America, often with the covert connivance or even the open encouragement of the US government, was in no way preferable to that inflicted upon dissidents in the European Soviet sphere of influence. For example, in 1954, a constitutionally elected government in Guatemala was overthrown by a CIA-backed invasion of exiles after attempting to expropriate some of the unused holdings of the United Fruit Company. The US ambassador complained that President Arbenz 'thought like a communist and talked like a communist and if not actually one would do until one came along', while President Eisenhower dubbed him 'a puppet manipulated by the communists'.[22]

The Middle East was a significant area where spheres of interest, if not of influence, overlapped. Although recognised by both superpowers soon after its foundation in 1948, Israel acted for the most part as a partner in Western, particularly US policies, after 1950. Thenceforth, the USSR attempted to align itself with some of the Arab states, with limited success. In this region too, the situation was complicated by the fact that the old imperial powers, Britain and France, still believed that they rather than the USA and USSR should predominate. As D.K. Fieldhouse has observed, Labour Foreign Secretary Ernest Bevin was 'at least as Churchillian as Churchill in his defence of the Empire'.[23]

At first, Africa, the old focus for imperial competition, was not a continent of great interest to either superpower. Asia certainly was, but Soviet withdrawal from the Far East and then from Iran by the end of 1946 made it appear safer to the USA than Europe. India received its independence along with partition in 1947 without any great fear of communist infiltration. But the Chinese Revolution of 1949 changed the US attitude to Asia quickly and completely. For too long, successive administrations had clung to the belief that the Kuomintang (Guomindang) led by Chiang Kai-shek could hold out against Mao Zedong and his followers, and the final collapse was difficult indeed to accept. Since most of the US experts on China had been dismissed for their defeatism, or worse, there were few left to argue against the acceptance of the idea of a Moscow–Peking monolithic Communist bloc. Hence, to a considerable extent, the increasing involvement in Vietnam.

At first, we should recall, the model for Vietnamese nationalism had been the American and French Revolutions. This was made clear by Ho Chi Minh and his followers in the Declaration of Independence of the Republic of Vietnam of 2 September 1945, which interpreted the 'immortal statement' of 4 July 1776 as 'All the peoples on the earth are equal from birth, all the peoples have a right to live, be happy and free', and accused 'the French imperialists' of 'deceitfully raising the standard of Liberty, Equality and Fraternity'. [24] Already, partly because of the wish to appease the French Government striving to assert its grip at home against the opposition of domestic communists, the Truman administration was moving away from FDR's idea of allowing Indochina to be placed under trusteeship. In December 1946, when war began between France and the Viet Minh, Secretary of State Dean Acheson wired the American consul in Saigon a message beginning: 'Keep in mind Ho's clear record as agent international communism.' More generally, at the end of 1949, National Security Council Report NSC 48/2 extended the Truman Doctrine to Asia:

> Now and for the foreseeable future it is the USSR which threatens to dominate Asia through the complementary instruments of communist conspiracy and diplomatic pressure supported by military strength. For the foreseeable future therefore, our immediate objective must be to contain and where feasible to reduce the power and influence of the USSR in Asia to such a degree that the Soviet Union is not capable of threatening the security of the United States from that area.

In fact, Stalin had been surprised almost as much as Truman by the Chinese Revolution, which upset his hopes for a Soviet security zone in Manchuria and Sinkiang (Xinjiang) and complicated his view of the Soviet relationship with the

USA and the West. Moreover, as Donald Zagoria pointed out, in the years immediately following the Chinese Revolution, 'Mao's claims to ideological autonomy and the persistent Chinese insistence that they had discovered a model to be followed in other colonial and semi-colonial countries was the cause of considerable friction with Stalin.' Ideology apart, the longer historical perspective indicated keen rivalry between the predecessors of the USSR and PRC in the nineteenth century and before. In January 1950, then, the almost simultaneous recognition of Ho's government by both the Soviet Union and the People's Republic of China was far from the 'communism conspiracy', the belief in which influenced the US government in its decision to include Vietnam more explicitly in its plans for security in Asia.[25]

Soon after this, in April 1950, the National Security Council approved NSC 68 declaring that: 'The Soviet Union, unlike previous aspirants to hegemony, is animated by a new fanatic faith, antithetical to our own, and seeks to impose its absolute authority over the rest of the world.' Denouncing the 'totalitarian dictatorship' with its 'institutionalized crimes' and the 'concentration camp' as the prototype of the society which its policies are designed to achieve, the paper also saw the USSR as 'inescapably militant' with a 'fundamental design' of the destruction of the USA. Here, ironically, was a clear boost to the national security state, itself not a little militant and aiming at the destruction of the USSR. All this was before the outbreak of the Korean War in June 1950, appearing to confirm the National Security Council's worst fears, although in fact Stalin was at first less than enthusiastic about the North Korean invasion of South. And the war as it ensued was a great reverse for him, making him anxious about the strength of the USA and suspicious about the reliability of the PRC.[26]

After the death of Stalin, the Soviet Union did indeed begin to look further outwards, but the threat posed to South-East Asia was never as great as successive US administrations feared. Furthermore, the notorious Moscow–Peking axis, whose monolithic solidity had been vastly exaggerated, fell fully apart. One reason for this was the meeting of non-aligned states in April 1955 held in Bandung, Indonesia. This Conference confirmed the Five Principles of Peaceful Coexistence previously agreed by India and China. As Zhou Enlai put it in his speech:

> If we follow the principles of mutual respect for sovereignty and territorial integrity, non-aggression, non-interference in each other's internal affairs, equality, and mutual benefit, the peaceful coexistence of countries with different social systems can be realized. When these principles are ensured of implementation, there is no reason why international disputes cannot be settled through negotiation.

In the short run, it is true, the Soviet Union demonstrated support for China by accepting the Bandung principles and by stressing that the post-Stalinist line of the two-camp division of the world had been replaced by a more varied approach allowing for the collaboration between communists and nationalists in the struggle against Western imperialism. Soviet–Chinese solidarity appeared stronger than ever; but appearances were deceptive, with the PRC considerably less enthusiastic than the USSR for the policy of 'peaceful coexistence'.[27]

Again, at the beginning of 1956, the USSR and the PRC seemed to be pulling in the same direction. Khrushchev made his famous 'Destalinisation' speech, at about the same time that Mao appeared to be encouraging a hundred flowers to bloom. However, both leaders soon revealed that there were to be strict limits on any moves towards communist pluralism. Alarmed by their reception in Warsaw, where they were denied an invitation to a meeting of the Polish Central Committee, Khrushchev and his comrades decided that they would have to draw the line when the Hungarian Communist Part showed signs of straying too far from the straight and narrow path. Hence, the Hungarian Revolution and Soviet tanks in the streets of Budapest. Meanwhile, Mao made moves to suppress the 'Chinese Hungary' in Wuhan province, and suggested that Khrushchev was going soft on counter-revolution.[28]

Western governments made no move in support of the Hungarian revolution-aries, even though some of the media sponsored by them encouraged the revolutionaries to believe that such support would be forthcoming. President Eisenhower had in any case decided that rollback was no longer possible. Moreover, Western governments were preoccupied by the Suez crisis, which showed that there were divisions in their camp as well. While the British and French governments maintained that their action was at least in part against the encroachment of communism, Vice-President Richard M. Nixon put the US administration's point clearly in a speech of 2 November 1956:

> In the past the nations of Asia and Africa have always felt we would, when the pressure was on, side with the policies of the British and French Govern-ments in relation to the once colonial areas. For the first time in history we have shown independence of Anglo-French policies towards Asia and Africa which seemed to us to reflect the colonial tradition. That declaration of independence has had an electrifying effect throughout the world.[29]

Late in 1956, Eisenhower was re-elected as most voters decided that they liked Ike. Hoping for a quiet second term, he very nearly got it. On the other hand, by the time that he handed over the office of president of the USA to John F. Kennedy at the beginning of 1961, the seeds of crisis were already sprouting all over the world.

In Europe, the collapse of the summit scheduled for May 1960 in Paris, after an American U-2 spy plane had been shot down while overflying the Soviet Union, helped to provoke more trouble. And in Asia, from Dien Bien Phu of May 1954 onwards, the USA was becoming more involved in Vietnam. A month before, Eisenhower enunciated the 'falling domino' principle, expressing the fear that Japan might have to make an accommodation with a South-East Asia turned completely communist and even Australia and New Zealand put under threat when the whole row of dominoes had been knocked over.[30]

On the Soviet side, the split with China emerged ever more clearly. In November 1957 in Moscow, Mao observed that 'the international situation has reached a new turning point. There are two winds in the world today; the East wind and the West wind. ... I think the characteristic of the situation today is the East wind prevailing over the West wind.' The East did not have to be too closely defined, perhaps, as Mao and Khrushchev would locate it differently. Mao probably had in mind the bid for leadership over the Third World already indicated at the Bandung Conference in 1955, as he now talked of support for 'wars of liberation'. Khrushchev saw this as irresponsibility, although he was soon to become involved in a gamble that was reckless indeed.[31]

In June 1961, the Soviet leader met the new US President, John F. Kennedy, in Vienna. Khrushchev's insistence that the USSR, like the PRC, would continue to support 'wars of liberation' led to a vigorous debate which led Kennedy to conclude that 'a long winter' was about to follow. In August, the Berlin Wall was hastily erected, allegedly to stop pernicious capitalist influences penetrating eastward, but in fact to stop disaffected emigrants moving west. The arms race moved into a higher gear, with the USA in the lead.

The story goes that Khrushchev used to speculate about the US rockets aimed at his Black Sea holiday home from Turkey. Certainly he complained that, while the Soviet Union was surrounded by US bases, there were no Soviet bases near the USA. By mid-1962, giving as a reason the threat to the Castro regime evidenced by the abortive US-backed invasion at the Bay of Pigs, he moved to make up the deficiency by sending medium-range missiles to Cuba which had been expelled from the Organization of American States and subjected to an economic embargo earlier in the year. In October, Kennedy announced a naval 'quarantine' of Cuba and demanded the removal of the missiles. Strategic Air Command went onto red alert, which meant some of its bombers were continually in the air loaded with nuclear bombs. The 'long winter' threatened to become a short, final fall. Even if we may now see that both Khrushchev and Kennedy were anxious to go to considerable lengths to avoid war, nobody perceived the crisis in that way at the time.[32]

Realising that their means of communication had been less than adequate during the crisis, the superpowers established the 'hot line' direct from Moscow to Washington as a consequence. This served also to underline the fact that there were now only two major players in the new Great Game, and that the UK and France, the old imperial powers, now played minor roles, or were even spectators. Then, the two leaders made their exits, as Kennedy was shot in November 1963 and Khrushchev ousted in October 1964.

Lyndon Baines Johnson and Leonid Brezhnev (at first accompanied by Alexei Kosygin) moved into centre stage. LBJ's greatest ambition was to build a Great Society at home, but he found himself increasingly drawn into counter-productive action abroad. He enunciated a Johnson Doctrine, that the USA could use military force whenever communism appeared to offer a threat to the Western hemisphere, and went on to help instal right-wing leaders in Brazil, Peru and the Dominican Republic. But this was little or nothing in comparison with increasing intervention in South-East Asia. From July 1965 to December 1967, the USA dropped more tons of bombs on Vietnam, Laos and Cambodia than the Allies had dropped on Europe throughout the Second World War.[33]

In another incendiary region of the world, in the Six Day War of June 1967, Israel destroyed most of the armed forces of its main opponent, Egypt. The Soviet Union was unable to do much about such reverses to its own policies, and in any case became preoccupied with its own major sphere of influence when the 'Prague Spring' blossomed in 1968. The Soviet leader was soon to devise his own Brezhnev Doctrine – that the USSR could use force whenever the cause of communism appeared to be under threat in Eastern Europe – a mirror image of the Johnson Doctrine in the Western Hemisphere. Although the superpowers had signed a non-proliferation treaty in 1967, and fifty-seven other states joined them in 1968, a projected Moscow summit was called off when the Warsaw Pact countries, led by the Soviet Union, invaded Czechoslovakia in August 1968. Was this a mirror image of US action in South-East Asia?[34]

The dollar versus the ruble

In the years following the Second World War, there was just one economic superpower, as indicated most succinctly by the global significance of the dollar as opposed to the much narrower meaning of the ruble. The USA went from strength to strength as the dominant force in world capitalism, while the USSR could aspire to little more than leadership of the socialist camp. Even then, as was often observed, economic progress was less marked in the Russian metropolis than in some of the other Soviet republics and satellite states. To some extent, this gap was the consequence of the Soviet attempt to keep up in the emerging arms race. It was also partly the result of historic differences between the rate of development in Russia and other parts of Europe immediately to its west. But, to a significant extent, the cause of the USSR's relative economic backwardness is to be found in the destruction inflicted upon it during the Second World War.

Let us imagine a role reversal between the superpowers. From 1941 to 1945, New York and most other Eastern cities were reduced to ruins, while industry and communications were almost totally destroyed up to the Mississippi and beyond, where there was no California. Tens of millions of armed forces personnel and civilians were killed, and many more injured. Homelessness, starvation and disease had become widespread. In any international economic relations, obviously, a power with such weaknesses would find it extremely difficult to bargain on equal terms with any prospective partners, especially if none of them was well-disposed towards it.

In fact, the USSR had lost 27 million (some say 40 million) service people and civilians. Livestock had been killed, farm buildings and machinery destroyed, and all branches of industry ruined on a gigantic scale in the areas which had been occupied, where over half of the urban living space had also been lost. 65,000 kilometres of railway track and 15,800 locomotives were no longer at the disposal of the communications network. Survivors managed to continue in appalling circumstances, often living hand to mouth in holes in the ground.[35]

The USA, on the contrary, was emerging from the war with less than half a million dead, nearly all men and women in the services, and with both agriculture and industry booming. Nevertheless, the government realised that economic prosperity had been produced by the war, and that the only way to keep it going was by restoration of the Open Door and a world made safe for capitalism. As far as US policy towards the Soviet Union was concerned, good economic relations, that is to say on American terms, would make for good relations in general as well as benefiting business in particular.

From the other side, as Philip Moseley observed at the war's end, 'when the Soviet leaders look at America, they think primarily of its great economic power'. Thus, when the Bretton Woods agreement of July 1944 appeared to be offering 'equal opportunity' in foreign trade and investment, Molotov was justified in asking what this could mean when the United States had no peers. Moreover, participation in the agreement would mean the Soviet Union revealing to the Western world the state of its gold reserves and other information which, following tradition as well as embarrassing immediate circumstances, it was determined to keep to itself. But in April 1945, Molotov was warned by Truman that no reconstruction aid would be given to the USSR unless it accepted his government's interpretation of the Yalta agreements. Afterwards, the President commented: 'I gave it to him straight "one-two to the jaw".' Quite possibly, he was moved by the spirit of muscular Christianity which he had expressed during his vice-presidential campaign in October 1944: 'I think Almighty God intends for this nation to assume leadership in world affairs to preserve the peace.'[36]

Generally, however, as Thomas G. Paterson has observed:

> The United States was no more evil or more noble in its relations with international organizations than Britain or Russia; each major power attempted to employ them for its own national purposes. But there was a difference; the United States held a distinct advantage in the International Bank for Reconstruction and Development and the International Monetary Fund and so added them to its arsenal of Cold War weapons.

So, of the IBRD and IMF conference in March 1946, their erstwhile defender Lord Keynes complained: 'I went to Savannah expecting to meet the world and all I met was a tyrant.'[37]

Of course, there were differences of leading American opinion. Thus, while Secretary of the Treasury Henry Morgenthau was in favour of a loan to the USSR of $10 billion which would involve delivery of some Soviet raw materials and thus guarantee the jobs of 60 million workers in the USA, the US Ambassador in Moscow Averell Harriman supported aid to the USSR via the United Nations Relief and Rehabilitation Administration (UNRRA) only if the Soviet Union collaborated in the restoration of normal commercial relations throughout Europe. And the State Department's chief adviser on Soviet affairs, George Kennan, argued in a memorandum that the USSR would use any loans extended to it exclusively to strengthen its military power.[38] A clear illustration of differing attitudes was the problem of Lend-Lease: although acknowledging the importance of military and economic supplies during the war, the Soviet government was shocked by the abrupt termination of Lend-Lease in August 1945. By the middle of 1946, the Soviet request for a loan was finally rejected after much delay. And the problem was compounded by disagreements over reparations and concessions, from Europe through Iran to Manchuria.[39]

As the USA's reservations became greater, so did the USSR's stubbornness. If there was not yet an Iron Curtain, there was already no prospect of an open Soviet door. But this was not because of some unhelpful personality trait of Stalin or his henchmen. Certainly, Stalin himself remained suspicious of the outside world, while giving his own people far from his complete trust as he called on them to make even more sacrifices for the restoration of communications, heavy industry and agriculture. Molotov was expressing deep-seated and widespread anxiety when he observed that the USA was so economically powerful that the dollar threatened the independent existence of all other currencies.[40] Again, in order to pursue greater understanding, let us reverse the superpower roles. Having suffered huge damage, the USA is confronted with requests, even demands, for equal economic opportunities from a USSR which has been barely touched by the war. It holds back increasingly from exposing its weakness in the face of a challenge from a much stronger power. However ridiculous this role reversal might seem, it helps us to understand the attitude of Stalin, Molotov and other advisers in 1945 and after; although, of course, the weight of the centuries was also, as always, of great significance.

While a pattern had been set in the dollar–ruble relationship soon after the conclusion of the Second World War, extremely important developments took place in later years. In 1947, following the Truman Doctrine which directed millions of dollars towards Greece and Turkey in particular, the Marshall Plan held out the prospect of billions for Europe in general. The USSR and its neighbours were invited to participate, but the principles of entry including open accounts and joint resources were too much for Stalin, who understood all too well the relative weakness of the ruble and the meagre contribution that the Soviet Union could have made to the common pool. No doubt too, the US Congress might have been less enthusiastic about this means of combating communism if the USSR had said 'da' rather than 'nyet'. As a partial substitute for the Marshall Plan, the Soviet Leader introduced in October 1948 his own grandiose 'Stalin plan for the transformation of nature', intending that rivers and trees would obey his orders for irrigation and shelter-belts. In 1949, the beleaguered socialist camp moved under Soviet control towards the formation of the Council for Mutual Economic Aid, or Comecon, as Western Europe began the movement in the direction of its own common market with the encourage-ment of the USA. But, to quote Alec Nove, 'Comecon in fact led a sleepy and inactive existence until well after Stalin's death, and the USSR's relations with its satellites were conducted, at this period, almost exclusively on a bilateral basis'. There was little trade and no aid outside the socialist camp during the same period, although large credits were extended to China after the revolution of 1949.[41]

In 1949 too, the explosion of the Soviet A-bomb combined with Mao's Red Revolution to overcome any lingering doubts in the USA that more federal expenditure was necessary on armaments. Early in 1950, NSC-68 (National Security Council Paper 68) argued that since the Soviet Union spent 13.8 per cent of its GNP (gross national product) on its armed forces while the USA spent no more than 6–7 per cent, the US defence budget needed to be increased, even up to 20 per cent. A considerable part of the new funds would be used to develop the 'thermonuclear' bomb, much more powerful than the atomic predecessor. In support of the actual rise proposed, from less than $15 billion per year to between $35 and $50 billion, Secretary of State Dean Acheson and others argued that the US economy was in danger of depression if left to itself – a new kind of pump priming in a military New Deal. There was no recognition in the paper that the Soviet GNP was much smaller than that of the USA, and that an arms race was bound to ensue, moving towards thermonuclear weapons and beyond. In any case, it remained secret for more than a quarter of a century, up to 1975, and could not be debated until too late. And in the short run, most doubts among those in the know were removed by the outbreak of the Korean War and the apprehension, however unfounded, that Mao and Stalin were plotting together to overthrow world capitalism. Billions of dollars were poured into Asia, and especially into Japan, to counter the communist conspiracy.[42]

The inauguration of Eisenhower followed by the death of Stalin in early 1953 produced less change than continuity. However, his farewell warning about the 'military-industrial' complex was preceded by other observations that poverty and starvation needed to be overcome in the struggle against communism, and that an economy based too largely on armaments could lead to some kind of dictatorial government bent upon war. Moreover, his insistence on 'more bang for the buck' meant reducing conventional weapons and increasing the number of nuclear warheads throughout his presidency from 1,000 to 18,000 in a strategic policy of 'massive retaliation'.[43] Meanwhile, Khrushchev was concerned about what we might call 'more roar for the ruble'. While conscious of the need to feed the Soviet population and to develop the consumer sector at the same time, he gave heavy emphasis to the arms industry. Comecon was revived, while aid went to India and elsewhere in the Third World; trade with the West increased too. The launching of the first earth satellite in October 1957 through a series of space successes to the first manned orbital flight by Yuri Gagarin in April 1961 appeared to give some substance to Khrushchev's proud boast that the USSR was catching up with and overtaking the USA as the sun of communism was rising over his country. Soon, however, Khrushchev was to become too confident, and overambitious economic schemes as well as an adventurous foreign policy were to bring him down by 1964.

The impact of the Sputnik on the USA was considerable nevertheless, and persuaded John F. Kennedy to talk of the need for the USA to enter the space race more energetically at the same time as closing an alleged 'missile gap'. From his inauguration in 1961 until his assassination in late 1963, JFK strove mightily to make sure that his New Frontier was protected by a mighty fortress, urged on by the challenges in Berlin, Cuba and Vietnam. New technologies would help the USA to develop a more scientific global strategy at the same time as reaching for the moon. In the process, trusted allies could be given, or better, sold war supplies ranging from bullets to rockets. Meanwhile, the Alliance for Progress, begun in 1961, proposed the injection of billions of dollars into the Latin American economy to make for peaceful rather than revolutionary change.

Then, during the presidency of Lyndon Baines Johnson from 1963 onwards, while the threats to peace in Europe and Latin America had died down, war in South-East Asia looked as it if might flare up from brushfire to conflagration of the whole forest. By 1967, the Vietnam War cost more than $20 billion per annum, and LBJ feared that his dream of the Great Society might not come true.

And as far as the overall Cold War was concerned, the USA now had more than 1,000 ICBMs (intercontinental ballistic missiles), at its disposal while the Soviet Union's total was not far off 900. In 1967, the two superpowers managed to agree a non-proliferation treaty, which was signed by nearly sixty other powers in 1968. But the Soviet invasion of Czechoslovakia in August 1968 brought an abrupt end to hopes of reductions in expenditure on the arms race, and the ensuing presidential election included the by now ritual mutual recriminations from Democrats and Republicans about not spending enough on defence.[44]

While the USA was neglecting its arms expenditure, the argument ran, the USSR was paying much more attention to all kinds of weaponry. Generally speaking, at least some authorities asserted, the ruble was catching up with the dollar, while at least one of them believed that 'as a result of the record of performance of the economies during the fifties and early sixties, the USSR was able to reduce the gap separating the magnitude of its industrial output from the American one from about 16 years in 1955 to about 5 years by 1967'. Was the process of industrialisation tending towards convergence?[45]

The war of words

Unlike that of 'superpower', the first use of the term 'Cold War' is difficult to locate. It was certainly used by a Spanish writer Don Juan Manuel in the fourteenth century to describe the struggle between Christians and Moslems in the following manner: 'War that is very strong and very hot ends either with death or peace, whereas cold war neither brings peace nor gives honour to the one who makes it.' Even then, the conflict was largely ideological. Moreover, the roots of our own Cold War may be found at about the same time, according to some observers. For example, while A.J.P. Taylor wrote in 1981 that the clash between East and West 'goes back at least to the great schism which long ago divided the Orthodox and Roman Catholic churches', Arnold Toynbee suggested in 1948 that 'the Soviet Union of today, like the Grand Duchy of Moscow in the fourteenth century, reproduces the salient features of the mediaeval East Roman Empire'. In Chapter 1 above, we have examined aspects of this theme at some length.[46]

As the national, imperial and interwar stages of international rivalry were succeeded by the process of decolonisation and the superpower confrontation, the great debate at the heart of our own Cold War differed from its predecessors in its intensity and its comprehensiveness. To a considerable extent, the contrast was the consequence of developments in mass communication, the newspaper, radio and cinema augmented increasingly by television, overtaken indeed by television by the end of the 1960s. But, more profoundly, not only have fundamental questions about the individual and society been answered in a starkly different manner, the argument has also been reinforced by the threat of a hot war of total annihilation.

Such huge themes may be conveniently approached from the point of view of one individual, the poet and critic Archibald MacLeish. A New Deal supporter, and a member of government information agencies during the Second World War before becoming Assistant Secretary of State from 1944–5, he was not very optimistic about what would transpire after the war was over, writing during it that, 'as things are now going, the peace we will make, the peace we seem to be making, will be a peace of oil, a peace of gold, a peace of shipping, a peace, in brief, without moral purpose or human interest'.[47] Nevertheless, as a founder member of the United Nations Educational, Scientific and Cultural Organisation (UNESCO) from 1945–6, MacLeish believed that the best hope for postwar peace was to be found in the United Nations in general. He was sceptical about the Truman Doctrine, but in favour of the Marshall Plan. Above all, he seems to have been concerned with the conformist climate arising in the USA during the late 1940s, believing that the American revolutionary spirit was in danger of being crushed in a witch hunt. In 1947, he wrote:

> Both Capitalism and Communism are products of the thinking and the prac-
> tice of earlier times before the great modern revolutions in physics, in
> chemistry and in engineering had taken place. ... The problem for our
> generation is not to take sides in an old, stale and more or less irrelevant
> quarrel, but to find and find quickly the new and unrealized means of living
> in a world never before inhabited by mankind.

As Professor of Rhetoric and Oratory at Harvard from 1949–62, MacLeish wrote several essays expressing this anxiety, and the manner in which the new debate had been overtaken by a fixation on the Soviet Union: 'left-wing movements attacked right-wing movements not on American issues but on Russian issues and right-wing movements replied with the same arguments turned about'. American education and intellectual life were subject to the same domination, and even religious dogma was affected: 'the first duty of a good Christian in the United States in those years was not to love his enemies but to hate the Communists.'

All this happened at a time when the USA had become the greatest world power ever. The true spirit of revolution was American and Jeffersonian, MacLeish believed, but perhaps people should ask themselves: 'Are they still the young champions of freedom in the west who warned the Holy Alliance to let the fires of revolutionary freedom burn as they might on this continent, or have they joined with those who put the fire out?' And they should remember that: 'The true test of freedom is in its *use*.'[48]

By June 1955, MacLeish compared the stain of McCarthyism to 'the snail's corrosive track on a clean leaf'. Lamenting the most disturbing fact about the whole experience that a 'sane, decent majority of Americans' were outraged yet tolerated the Senator's 'debasement of morality, his betrayal of principles', he went on to cite Walter Lippmann's *The Public Philosophy* as stating the real issues: whether individual freedom and effective community were compatible.[49] Some of us at the beginning of the twenty-first century would think that MacLeish's interpretation of history could be one-sided, for example on the part played by 'the young champions of freedom in the west' in the making of the Monroe Doctrine. Generally speaking, we might find the style of the Professor of Rhetoric and Oratory somewhat over the top. Nevertheless, as well as catching the spirit of the 1940s and 1950s, MacLeish also correctly sensed a crisis of transition. We can agree wholeheartedly with him that Walter Lippmann had caught the dilemma of our times.

Back in the 1940s, the onset of the Cold War in the USA was caught by a Soviet visitor, the journalist and novelist Ilya Ehrenburg. In Knoxville, Tennessee, in the spring of 1946, Ehrenburg glanced through a newspaper calling attention to the fact that in Psalm 120 there is a reference to a place called Mesech where lived 'him that hateth peace', while the prophet Ezekiel in Chapter 38 had denounced Gog and Magog, to whom obeisance was made in the place called Meshech. Mesech and Meshcech were one and the same place, none other than Moscow. This was just a provincial newspaper, but Ehrenburg also found himself denounced more widely in the Hearst press as 'a disguised agitator', 'comrade-cynic' and 'Ilya of the Comintern'. The new harsh mood was described to Ehrenburg by 'a friend of Roosevelt', whom he quotes as saying:

> Truman doesn't have a war in mind. He believes that Communism threatens certain Western European countries and could triumph if the Soviet Union were to recover economically and forge ahead. An implacable American policy and atom tests will force Russia to spend all her strength and her resources on modernising her armaments. The supporters of the hard line talk about the threat of Soviet tanks, but what they're doing in fact is to declare war on Soviet saucepans.[50]

Whatever the truth of Ehrenburg's reportage on the falling temperature in the USA, it is a matter of regret that he says less about the Soviet counterpart. However, as is well known, the implacability of American newsmen and politicians was no match for that of Stalin and his adherents. The combination of a more difficult situation both internal and external, a more recent revolution and a widely different tradition led to some distinctive attitudes rather than a simple mirror image of the picture presented by Archibald MacLeish. To start at the top, in his 'election' speech of 9 February 1946, Stalin talked of the inevitability of war as long as capitalism existed and the formation of two hostile camps led by the USA and UK in the Western world owing to the uneven development of capitalism. Although there was no overt reference to hostilities between the communist and capitalist powers, at least some commentators in the West saw this speech as the beginning of the Third World War.[51] In the Soviet Union itself, Stalin's wise words and actions were given the most positive reception in the authorised version of the Leader's life as produced in 1947:

> In conjunction with the tried and tested Leninists who are his immediate associates, and at the head of the Bolshevik Party, Stalin guides the destinies of a multinational Socialist State, a state of workers and peasants of which there is no precedent in history. His advice is a guide to action in all fields of Socialist construction. His work is extraordinary for its variety; his energy truly amazing.[52]

To turn to the most notorious name after Stalin's, that of A.A. Zhdanov, we may briefly note his characterisation of the period following the Second World War:

> Today the centre of the struggle against Marxism has shifted to America and Britain. All the forces of obscurantism and reaction have today been placed at the service of the struggle against Marxism. Brought out anew and placed at the service of bourgeois philosophy are the instruments of atom-dollar democracy, the outworn armour of obscurantism and clericalism: the Vatican and racist theory, rabid nationalism and decayed idealist philosophy, the mercenary yellow press, and depraved bourgeois art. But apparently all these are not enough. Today, under the banner of ideological struggle against Marxism, large reserves are being mobilised. Gangsters, pimps, spies and criminal elements are recruited.

An editorial accompanying Zhdanov's essay on 'The International Situation' in 1947 complained of 'the path of betrayal of the national interests and rejection of the sovereignty of their countries' by the bourgeoisie of Europe, while 'the working class, headed by the Communist Parties, is the most consistent leader of all the patriotic and democratic forces who defend the sovereignty and independence of their country'. Karl Marx, who had argued that the working class has no country and must above all devote itself to the cause of internationalism, would have turned in his grave.[53]

The international situation in popular culture was summed up by V.M. Molotov in a speech turning to the results of 'equal opportunity' for small states which had been ruined by the great conflict:

> Given such a situation, we would probably live to see the day when in your own country, on switching on the radio, you would be hearing not so much your own language as one American gramophone record after another or

some piece or other of British propaganda. The time might come when in your own country, on going to the cinema, you would be seeing American films sold for foreign consumption – and not those of better quality, but those manufactured in greater quantity, and circulated and imposed abroad by agents of powerful firms and cinema companies which have grown particularly rich during the war.[54]

Molotov had heard and seen nothing yet. But he and his comrades did all they could not only to stop the spread of this alien culture but also to disseminate their own. Both directly and through 'front' organisations, a concerted attempt was made to spread the message of all aspects of Soviet communism from politics to the arts.

In October 1947, at the first meeting of the Communist Information Bureau (Cominform) in Belgrade, Zhdanov claimed that more and more intellectuals were being won over to the cause of Communism. Later that month, after a dissenting intervention at an East German Writers' Congress which earned for him the title 'Father of the Cold War in Berlin', Melvin J. Lasky wrote to his fellow intellectual Dwight Macdonald comparing that city to:

what a frontier-town must have been like in the States in the middle of the 19th century – Indians on the horizon, and you've simply got to have that rifle handy or [if] not your scalp is gone. But in those days a frontier-town was full of Indian-fighters. ... Here very few people have any guts, and if they do they usually don't know in which direction to point their rifle.

Both Lasky and Macdonald were to become associated with the US cultural offensive in the Cold War, including the Congress for Cultural Freedom and its creation, the journal *Encounter*. A Jew from the Bronx, Lasky was among the outsiders to the establishment group from which the Congress sprang. In the beginning, the dominant influence in the CIA was the 'aristocracy' of the east coast Ivy League, 'a *Bruderbund* of Anglophile sophisticates who found powerful justification for their actions in the tradition of the enlightenment and the principles enshrined in the Declaration of Independence', remembered by one of them as inspired by 'the atmosphere of an order of Knights Templars ... to save western freedom from Communist darkness'.[55]

But Anglophilia soon turned out to be not enough. By 1952, there was recognition by the editors of the journal *Partisan Review* running a symposium entitled 'Our Country and Our Culture' that

the kind of democracy which exists in America has an intrinsic and positive value: it is not merely a capitalist myth but a reality which must be defended against Russian totalitarianism. ... Europe is no longer regarded as a sanctuary; it no longer assures that rich experience of culture which inspired and justified a criticism of American life. The wheel has come full circle, and now America has become the protector of western civilization.

And this was not only American self-assertion: in 1951, a leading French intellectual, Raymond Aron, had already pronounced himself 'entirely convinced that for an anti-Stalinist there is no escape from the acceptance of American leadership'. However, Aron did not necessarily approve of the onslaught against his colleagues Sartre, de Beauvoir and other leading lights of the Left Bank in Paris.[56]

In 1953, the first number of *Encounter* came out. Before then, the cultural offensive had included US government support of other publications. These included Arthur Koestler's novel *Darkness at Noon*, depicting the evils of Soviet repression and first published in 1948, and three works of non-fiction all appearing in 1949: Arthur Schlesinger's *The Vital Center*, arguing for 'the restoration of the radical nerve' with 'no lamp in the window for the Communists'; the collection of essays by former Communists entitled *The God That Failed*; and George Orwell's *Nineteen Eighty-Four*.[57] Among those who joined the struggle was Conyers Read, who gave a Presidential Address to the American Historical Association in which he argued that:

> Discipline is the essential prerequisite of every effective army whether it march under the Stars and Stripes or under the Hammer and Sickle. We have to fight an enemy whose value system is deliberately simplified in order to achieve quick decisions. And atomic bombs make quick decisions imperative. The liberal neutral attitude, the approach to social evolution in terms of dispassionate behaviorism will no longer suffice. Dusty answers will not satisfy our demands for positive assurances. Total war, whether it be hot or cold, enlists everyone and calls upon everyone to assume his part. The historian is no freer from this obligation than the physicist.

Conyers Read declared: 'This sounds like the advocacy of one form of social control against another. In short, it is. But I see no alternative in a divided world.'[58] In a sense, the pleading of Read and his colleagues had already been overtaken by Arnold Toynbee in *A Study of History*, which *Time* magazine hailed in 1947 as transforming the subject from Ptolemaic to Copernican as it 'shattered the frozen patterns of historical determinism and materialism by again asserting God as an active force in history.'[59]

As the years rolled by, the cultural offensive enlisted 'high culture' including literature, music and art to the cause, as well as Hollywood and religion. The CIA probably supported the publication of more than a thousand 'quality' books, including Boris Pasternak's *Doctor Zhivago* and Bertrand de Jouvenel's *The Art of*

Conjecture (and even commissioning the air-drop into the Soviet Union of a translation of T.S. Eliot's *Four Quartets*). While Dwight Macdonald saw this kind of operation as a counter to 'the spreading ooze of Mass Culture', Jason Epstein asserted that the CIA and its associates 'were not moved by a disinterested love of the intellect or by deep aesthetic convictions, they were interested in protecting and extending American power'. Patronage in music included that of the avant-garde outlawed in the Soviet Union and appealing to the élite minority in the West, although Susan Sontag made the wry comment that 'we knew we were supposed to appreciate ugly music'. Similarly, in art, Abstract Expressionism received considerable CIA support. Irrespective of his actual talent, Jackson Pollock received particular attention as a 'real American, not a transplanted European ... if he is a cowboy, so much the better'. Another 'cowboy' of even greater service to the cause was John Wayne, along with his favourite director John Ford, embodying quintessential American values in such movies as *They Were Expendable* and *The Quiet Man*. Hollywood had no difficulty at all in making the transition from the pro-Soviet *Mission to Moscow* with its idealised portrait of Stalin to such productions as *The Red Nightmare* and *The Red Menace*.[60] Meanwhile, the CIA establishment's favourite theologian was Reinhold Niebuhr, who argued for an approach to international relations along the following lines:

> we cannot win the ideological struggle on the Continents where technical civilization is in its infancy if we equate democracy with extravagant forms of individualism, which may be regarded as a luxury which only the richest of all nations, our own, can afford. The rest of mankind must try to develop equilibria of power and a tolerable justice within the framework of freedom on the base of domestic stability and foreign prestige.

Niebuhr was given a widespread pulpit in the *Time-Life* publications of the devout Henry Luce, and was praised by Sidney Hook for making 'God an instrument of national policy'.[61]

Main Street USA fell into line by 1950, when, *inter alia*, a mock-Communist takeover of Mosinee, Wisconsin, was staged by members of the American Legion donning appropriate armbands, 'arresting' the mayor and 'executing' the town police chief. The soil was well prepared for the junior senator from the same state, Joseph McCarthy, who caused embarrassment to some members of the establishment but by no means to all. For, as Joel Kovel emphasises, as well as being an opportunist, McCarthy drew 'the enthusiastic support of right-wing Republicans' and 'was actively abetted by the mastermind of repression, J. Edgar Hoover', while finding 'allies among businessmen hostile to government'. At the intellectual level, *Encounter* published an article in 1954 arguing that McCarthy should be seen in the context of the USA's 'insistent search for new national security, for a world, indeed, made safe for democracy', in profound contrast to 'European weariness, and scepticism of any such achievement'.[62]

The Hungarian Rising of 1956 appeared at first to be a vindication of the anti-Communist crusade, with the eloquent testimony of many defectors from the Red ranks, especially Jean-Paul Sartre. Yet there were two considerable problems: what to do in Hungary and how to accommodate the almost simultaneous Anglo-French invasion of Suez.[63] The launching of Sputnik – the first satellite – in 1957 appeared for a short time to suggest that communism was far from completely barren of ideas and expertise. Then came the even greater setback of Vietnam, which meant a cultural break which will be investigated in the next chapter.

The culture of the Cold War could be at a high intellectual level, as for example Karl Popper's *The Open Society and Its Enemies*. Moreover, by no means all the arguments advanced during the period of the Cold War concerned the conflict itself. Such works as David Riesman's *The Lonely Crowd* (1950) and J.K. Galbraith's *The Affluent Society* (1958) criticised aspects of advanced capitalist society rather than communism. Meanwhile, in the Soviet Union, the great interest aroused by V.D. Dudintsev's novel *Not by Bread Alone* (1956) stemmed from the everyday experience of the struggle against internal bureaucracy rather than external imperialism. Relating the difficulties experienced by a young engineer and inventor with an obscurantist factory director, it also touched on a theme which could be considered more universal, the advantages and disadvantages of advances in science, represented most significantly perhaps in the debate about the uses in war and peace of nuclear energy. To take an individual example of how the argument developed in one eminent mind, Bertrand Russell, who had advocated in 1948 that threat of the use of the A-bomb should be made against the Soviet Union to bring it into line, was to become one of the ultimate weapon's most passionate opponents. Meanwhile, groups of scientists from the USA, USSR and elsewhere came to a series of Pugwash conferences to calculate how close the doomsday clock was to midnight.[64]

The shadow of the great mushroom cloud hung over humankind in general, yet the image did not take over from the word until towards 1968. Television, at first looked upon in comparison with the press and radio as a fad that could not last, was to outshine the others in a manner suggested by Marshall McLuhan in *The Gutenberg Galaxy: The Making of Typographical Man* (1962) and other works. Even in the USSR, where there were no more than 10,000 sets in 1950, the number had grown by the end of the decade to 4.8 millions, enabling television to play a not inconsiderable part in the cultural 'thaw'.[65] Was there to be a cultural as well as economic convergence?

The years from 1945 to 1968 completed the decline of European empires and brought to the fore two new superpowers. In 1945, this emergence was already discerned by several commentators on world affairs, yet it took several years to gain more general acceptance.

As the USA and USSR expanded their spheres of interest, those of the former great powers contracted. Thus, the first phase of the Cold War was so intimately connected to the process of Decolonisation that, in a global context, it was often difficult to separate them. Looking back from the vantage point of half a century later, we can more clearly see that the youth of the superpowers was accompanied by the demise of the empires that had preceded them.

5 Maturity

Cold War and the Third World, 1968–91

The 'Revolution' of 1968

By 1968, as the Soviet Union crushed the 'Prague Spring' and the United States was deeply enmired in Vietnam, the Cold War had lost the crusading element that had been present on both sides in some of the years after 1945, while the process of decolonisation had, in the formal sense at least, neared completion, having created an 'independent' Third World. And so the superpower relationship had reached a kind of maturity in détente.

By this time, President Lyndon B. Johnson had given six reasons for US involvement in the Far East. According to Walter LaFeber, who has assembled these reasons and commented on them, they 'tell us much about the entire course of post-1945 US foreign policy':

1   Every President since Roosevelt had promised Vietnam protection. To break this promise would undermine American 'credibility'.
2   As Theodore Roosevelt had pointed out, Americans believed that they now lived in the 'Pacific era'. In this context, as Johnson himself put it, 'the deepening shadow of China' lay over all Asia. Moreover, strengthened since 1964 by its possession of the hydrogen bomb, China was 'helping the forces of violence in almost every continent'. Containment was provided by the American action in Vietnam.
3   Like Anthony Eden at the time of the Suez crisis and almost every other Western politician involved in conflict since 1945, the President declared that: 'We learned from Hitler at Munich that success only feeds the appetite of aggression.' (What, incidentally, if the opposition had learned the same lesson?)
4   Johnson pointed out the links between his domestic policy and the Vietnam War. In his considered view, the difficulties with Senator McCarthy after the fall of China to communism in 1949 'were chickenshit compared with what might happen if we lost Vietnam'.

5 LBJ had absolute confidence in the American 'can do', 'no problem' approach. Advanced technology, such as the defoliation of whole forests and jungles by spray-spreading helicopters, would prove more than a match for the backward Vietcong.

6 Public support would be maintained if escalation of the war effort were kept slow and moderate. In other words, a strong president standing up to communism would be popular as long as he did not demand any painful sacrifices.[1]

The next president, the Republican Richard M. Nixon, suggested in a bipartisan manner that the Democrat Woodrow Wilson was 'our greatest President of this century' with 'the greatest vision of America's world role', but 'wasn't practical enough'. By implication, Nixon would lead a more realistic collective effort to make the world safe for democracy. In Asia, the USA would collaborate with Japan to build 'a Pacific community', a process which could be joined by China once it had made more changes to its system. As for his National Security Council director, who was to become Secretary of State in September 1973, Henry Kissinger observed that the American frontier experience had created an expansive sense that 'America was not itself unless it had a meaning beyond itself.' The former Harvard Professor cited 'the great historian' Frederick Jackson Turner, but would not be unaware of John F. Kennedy's proclamation of a New Frontier.[2]

In sum, then, US foreign policy since 1945 had the same foundations as before 1945: from the Pilgrim Fathers through to the Founding Fathers to Woodrow Wilson via the Monroe Doctrine and the frontier. Now, however, there were key differences: 'entangling alliances' in Europe and beyond, especially in the Far East, and the possession of nuclear weapons. However, while the ideology of US foreign policy was far from flexible, it was by no means as rigid as its Soviet counterpart.

On 5 May 1968, Theses for the 150th Anniversary of the Birth of Karl Marx were set out in *Pravda*. From 1964 onwards, this document asserted, 'The Communist Party of the Soviet Union, guided by the directions of Marx and Lenin, is seeking the most efficient utilization of the economic laws of socialism in the building of communism'. As far as the relationship with Eastern Europe was concerned, 'the construction of communism in the USSR and the consolidation of socialism in the countries of the socialist commonwealth are a most important part of the world revolutionary process'. In the wider world, 'as a result of the revolutionary victories of the international proletariat and the implementation of the ideas of Marxism-Leninism, the era of the liberation of peoples from the colonial yoke has begun'. On the other side in the great class struggle, 'in the present epoch the workers' movement in the capitalist countries has grown immeasurably', as 'state-monopoly capitalism operates in the interests of enriching the monopolies, robbing the working people, suppressing the workers' movement and the national-liberation struggle and unleashing aggressive wars, thus exacerbating all the contradictions of capitalism'. But problems were to be found not only in the capitalist camp, for 'disruption of the internal unity of the Communists is a grave crime against the world working class'. Therefore: 'The Marxist-Leninists are resolutely rejecting the attempts of the Peking leaders to replace scientific communism with anti-Marxist "ideas of Mao Tse-tung".' In their own way, then, and no doubt with their own recollections of Russian and Soviet experiences of that part of the world, Soviet ideologists, like their US counterparts, were becoming increasingly conscious of the Far East.[3]

There was little or no specific hint in these Theses of the dissidence to be found in other quarters of the socialist camp, especially in Czechoslovakia, where in the 'Prague Spring' a new government led by the Slovak Alexander Dubcek appeared to be undermining the control of the Communist Party by lifting censorship and paying too much attention to the rights of national minorities. Fearing a 'domino' effect throughout Central and Eastern Europe, the Soviet government made several attempts to dissuade Dubcek and his associates from their bold new initiatives, and then sent in Warsaw Pact forces. On 22 August 1968, a special correspondent of *Pravda* reported that on the day before, 'at sunrise, ancient Prague with its characteristic skyline appeared before our eyes'. He claimed that: 'The Soviet troops entered the city in an organized manner. They had come as true friends in response to an appeal from brothers, and their purpose was to remove a present threat to the socialist system and to constitutionally established government in Czechoslovakia.' On 26 September, *Pravda* declared that:

> There is no doubt that the actions taken in Czechoslovakia ... aimed at defending the fundamental interests of the socialist commonwealth and primarily at defending Czechoslovakia's independence and sovereignty as a socialist state, will be increasingly supported by all who really value the interests of the present-day revolutionary movement, the peace and security of peoples, democracy and socialism.

On 29 September, *Pravda* recalled the Munich agreement, pointing out that in 1938, 'only the Soviet Union remained faithful to its commitments, and it was not to blame that the assistance it had offered was refused'.[4]

On Munich, *Pravda* scored a point: the USSR had indeed expressed its willingness to come to the assistance of Czechoslovakia. But, thirty years later, the hollowness of its latter-day offer to defend Czechoslovakia was clear for all to see. And what had once been a cogent analysis of world development had degenerated into a 'Marxism-Leninism' that neither Marx nor Lenin would have recognised. Indeed, more generally, what had been something like a genuine debate for many intellectuals in earlier years had degenerated by now into empty rhetoric for a considerable number of them. Not only in the USSR but for students and teachers on US campuses in particular, the explanations of Johnson and Nixon for the war in Vietnam rang almost as hollow as those of Brezhnev and company for the invasion of Czechoslovakia.

In an essay first published in the spring of 1989 and entitled '1968, Revolution in the World-System', Immanuel Wallerstein put forward six theses:

1   *The year 1968 brought a revolution in and of the world system.* It was a single revolution, a great, formative, watershed event.

2   *The primary protest of 1968 was against US hegemony in the world system (and Soviet acquiescence in that hegemony).* From 1945 to 1967 the USA had been in control, translating its economic advantage into wide political and cultural domination, supported by Western Europe and Japan and 'a stylized Cold War relationship with the USSR based on reserving to the USSR a small but important zone of political domination (Eastern Europe)' – the 'so-called Yalta arrangement'. Meanwhile, the USA had striven for a moderate decolonisation, that is to say without new nations having strong links to the USSR and communism, but with their participation in 'the existing set of international economic arrangements'. Moreover, at home, the US government had sought to avoid internal conflict based on class or race. In 1968, there were threats to this hegemony as well as protests against it.

3   *The secondary, but ultimately more passionate protest of 1968 was against the 'old left' systemic movements (for example, against Stalinism).* Old solutions to the world's ills, not only Soviet but also moderate socialist and national liberation, were now looked upon as 'part of the problem', which would have to be solved by various kinds of 'Maoisms'.

4   *Counterculture was part of revolutionary euphoria, but was not politically central to 1968.* What came to be known as life-style (sexuality, drugs, dress) could be accommodated without difficulty by a consumption-oriented economy.

5   *Revolutionary movements representing 'minority' or underdog strata need no longer, and no longer do, take second place to revolutionary movements representing presumed 'majority' groups.* Minorities, whether based on sex or race, or on some set of beliefs such as the ecological refusal to accept without question the imperatives of increased global production, would never again accept the legitimacy of waiting for some other revolution, but would agitate for settlement of their claims either by themselves or in 'rainbow coalition'.

6   *The debate on the fundamental strategy of social transformation has been reopened among the antisystemic movements, and will be the key debate of the coming twenty years.* Six potentially antisystemic movements – the 'old left' and minorities in the West, traditional Communist parties and emergent extra-party organisations in the Soviet bloc, traditional national liberation movements and

newer 'indigenist', often religious, forms of protest in the Third World – had at least begun to debate about the strategy of social transformation.

In 1989, Wallerstein added to his six theses on 1968 a series of six queries addressed in turn to: (1) the possibility of achieving significant political change without taking state power; (2) forms of social power worth conquering other than political power; (3) forms of organisation for anti-systemic movements; (4) the political basis of any trans-zonal co-operation involving the West, the Soviet bloc and the Third World; (5) the real, updated meaning of the French Revolution's 'liberty, equality, fraternity'; and (6) the achievement of plenty (or even enough) without productivism. Two years after the publication of his six theses, in 1991 – the year that the Soviet Union collapsed – Wallerstein wrote: 'The regime changes of 1989 were ... the outcome of the latent, continuing revolt of 1968.'[5]

Today, at the beginning of a new century and a new millennium, with a longer perspective at our disposal, we can at least agree that 1968 marked a watershed. Another reason for this is that the Vietnam War still raging in that year marked the greatest loss of human life inflicted by either superpower during the years of the Cold War. Before that war was brought to a conclusion, moreover, Neil Armstrong took his first short step on to the moon, emphasising the USA's technological superiority but also marking indeed a giant leap for humankind. Nobody who first witnessed the television images of July 1969, blurred though they were, could avoid thinking in a different way than before about the world, as a fragile small particle of a boundless universe.

Here, however, is one of the problems of recent history, the parallax in the viewpoint of the generations that were in their prime at the end of the 1960s. To take those of the superpowers in particular, by no means all citizens of the USA were at Woodstock, or experimenting with drugs, sex and the further reaches of loud music. Nevertheless, the period was one which had a considerable effect not only on Immanuel Wallerstein but also on his academic colleagues in other fields including history. As far as the USSR was concerned, there emerged a comparable group of intellectuals, the *shestidesiatniki*, or people of the 1960s, influenced first by the Khrushchev 'thaw' in the earlier part of the decade and then by the events of 1968 and after at the decade's end. This group also, although more restricted than their counterparts in the USA, made a considerable impact on the interpretation of history, even on its making. We shall investigate these generations and their later influence below.[6]

Vietnam and détente (–1979)

Back in 1968, the Soviet leader enunciated the 'Brezhnev Doctrine', justifying intervention in the 'Prague Spring' on the basis that the socialist states had the right to save their fellows from 'world imperialism' and thus preserve the 'indivisible' socialist system. Here was an echo of the 'Johnson Doctrine' announced by the American President in 1965: 'American nations, cannot, must not, and will not permit the establishment of another Communist government in the Western Hemisphere.' Any change 'should come through peaceful process', while the US would defend 'every free country of this hemisphere'.[7] But any comparison of the two doctrines must make allowance for the circumstance that, while Brezhnev remained in power from 1968 to 1979 and beyond, Nixon was succeeded in 1974 by Ford, who was followed by Carter. Both Nixon and Carter were to announce their own doctrines reflecting their own preoccupations. (To be facetious, a Ford Doctrine might have sounded like a new policy for selling automobiles in the wake of the resignation of 'Tricky Dicky' Nixon, labelled by some satirists as an unsuccessful second-hand car salesman. More seriously, Ford carried less authority, perhaps, as an unelected president.)

On the Soviet side, the intervention in Czechoslovakia in 1968 helped to deter East and Central Europeans from attempting to emulate the 'Prague Spring'. Meanwhile, under the new leadership of Willy Brandt and the SPD (Social Democrats), the introduction of West Germany's *Ostpolitik* led to the recognition of East Germany in 1969–70. The emergence of a more flexible 'Eurocommunism' in Western Europe aroused some hopes that there could be a peaceful transition to more fluid interchange between the two halves of the continent. These were reflected in the Helsinki Final Act of 1975, which ratified existing frontiers throughout Europe. However, disagreements at a later meeting in Belgrade (1977–8) concerning lack of cultural contacts and of implementation of human rights indicated that the barriers exemplified by the Berlin Wall were still there. And the USA's predominance in NATO continued to demonstrate that the continent remained one where superpower rivalry was clearly posed.

The strongest continuity in US policy was in the Western Hemisphere, where something like the Doctrine enunciated by the Democratic President Lyndon B. Johnson was implemented by his Republican successor Richard M. Nixon in Chile from 1970 onwards. This was partly because the Johnson Doctrine was in the tradition of the Monroe Doctrine, an update perhaps of Teddy Roosevelt's Corollary, speaking softly while brandishing the thermonuclear bomb. Having ordered the CIA to spend millions of dollars to prevent a victory for the socialist presidential candidate Salvador Allende, Nixon then ordered that Allende's democratic victory should be reversed. An economic squeeze having failed to dislodge him, Allende perished in 1973 during a right-wing counter-revolution from which General Augusto Pinochet emerged as dictator. Secretary of State Henry Kissinger was quoted as commenting: 'I don't see why we have to let a country go Marxist just because its people are irresponsible.'[8] The fear persisted that the Soviet threat was posed in every country of Latin America, although in fact Soviet influence was much smaller than the apprehension and the status quo could be maintained in the Western hemisphere without too much difficulty. The

President and his Secretary of State could thus devote their major energies to other pressing problems.

A few months after his inauguration, the President enunciated his own Nixon Doctrine. In Guam in mid-1969, he proclaimed that the USA 'cannot – and will not – conceive all the plans, design all the programs, execute all the decisions and undertake all the defense of the free nations of the world'. So while 'allies and friends' would continue to receive help for their defence and development, they would also be encouraged to help themselves. US troop reductions would be implemented wherever possible, while further commitments of combat forces would not be made unless a major power intervened in a Third World conflict. As far as the war in South-East Asia was concerned, this meant Vietnamization, a policy which rested on two foundations: allowing the 'good Asians' in the South to assume as much responsibility as possible, and bombing the 'bad Asians' in the North into acceptance of withdrawal.[9] For the second aim to be fulfilled, supply trails and hostile bases in Laos and Cambodia would also have to feel the weight of US air strikes. While pressure at home was relieved by the announcement of the end of the draft from 1973, Secretary of State Henry Kissinger finally arrived at an agreement with North Vietnamese negotiators at the beginning of that year. The provision of the 'unity and territorial integrity' of the whole country was implemented more than that allowing the South 'the right to self-determination'. Arguably the longest and most disastrous war in US history came to an end with the fall of Saigon in April 1975 some months after Nixon's resignation.[10]

Before then, Nixon, who had made his name by denouncing those showing any sympathy for, even any serious interest in, the major Communist powers, decided to achieve a major reputation by opening a new era in US dealings with them both. To begin with, he took advantage of tension between the USSR and the People's Republic of China. China's denunciation of Soviet 'social imperialism' had met with impassioned rejoinders not only ideological but also historical. For example, the Soviet government maintained in a statement issued on 13 June 1969 that, if the principle put forward by the PRC were accepted that 'the state identity of territories is determined not by the people inhabiting them, but by memories of past campaigns', then 'Latin America should revert to the Spanish crown and the United States to the British fold'. Heated words had almost led to open conflict in March 1969 when there were fatal casualties on both sides along the disputed frontier of the Ussuri River, and further outbreaks of violence threatened. The Soviet Union put out feelers for US support, but Nixon decided that he would go to China first, Kissinger preparing the way through some tortuous preliminary negotiations.

Richard M. Nixon became the first US President to alight on Chinese soil in February 1972. This was a moment of high drama (it was indeed soon to become the subject of a grand opera), providing excellent photo opportunities in meetings with Chairman Mao Zedong and Premier Zhou Enlai. It also led to some significant agreements concerning economic and cultural exchange, although official diplomatic recognition was not to come until 1979. A joint US–Chinese declaration that no power should be allowed to establish hegemony in the Pacific and Asia was tacitly directed at the Soviet Union, even if it was less capable of achieving such an ambition than either of its rivals.[11]

Three months after his visit to China, Nixon went to the USSR in May 1972. The times were not propitious. At the end of March, the North Vietnamese had attacked the demilitarised zone (DMZ) separating them from their Southern compatriots. In retaliation, the Americans had bombed Hanoi and Haiphong, hitting four Soviet ships in Haiphong harbour. However, although their first meeting was cool, Brezhnev and Nixon later warmed to each other and established an easier intimacy. There was little agreement on Vietnam, while on China, according to one account, Brezhnev tried to convince Nixon that 'we the whites' should collaborate in restraining their common rival before it became 'a superpower'.[12] The US president would not be drawn, since China was an important bargaining counter in his dealings with the USSR as well as an important element in his world outlook in general.

Nevertheless, the first Brezhnev–Nixon summit produced no less than four significant agreements: two on armaments and two on other aspects of the superpower relationship. SALT I (Strategic Arms Limitation Talks) restricted the number of ICBMs (intercontinental ballistic missiles). Under the same heading, ABMs (antiballistic missile systems) were to be limited to Moscow and Washington DC, and to another designated area on each side. 'Basic Principles of US–Soviet Relations' consisted of a joint commitment to peaceful coexistence along with the promise of renunciation of regional privileges (without specific mention of the Monroe, Brezhnev or other Doctrines).[13] An agreement on trade and technology was very welcome to the Soviet side, which actually was to benefit most from the import of cheap American grain. But the agreement soon foundered on the questions of Jewish emigration and human rights in general. SALT I was ratified by the US Senate, but the armed forces on both sides did not cease their clamour for more and better weapons.

During the Nixon and Ford years, there were ample reminders that the superpowers could not command the unswerving loyalty of their friends in the wider world. In October 1973, Egypt and Syria attacked Israel with the aim of regaining what they had lost in the Six-Day War of 1967. Israel fought back, and was poised to take more territory than before, in what became known as the Yom Kippur War. Attempts made by the superpowers to restore peace as well as relations between them were complicated by the fact that the USA had replaced the USSR as Egypt's chief patron.

Having failed to regain the losses of 1967 in armed struggle, the Arab states attempted to attain their aim through an embargo on oil. The war itself had already increased the price of this indispensable commodity several times over, and it continued to rise afterwards. There were significant consequences flowing from the search for alternative sources of supply. In particular, the USA was drawn closer to Iran, paying a high price for the privilege. Help in the hour of need came also from the Soviet Union, but again at a price. Mutual suspicion over intentions in Iran, recalling those of the immediate post-Second World War period, as well as regarding policies before and during the Yom Kippur War, helped to sink good relations between the superpowers, as well as leading to a huge rise in world debt.[14]

While President Ford did what he could to hold the fort at a time when the USA felt beleaguered, it was left to President Carter to provide a new positive view out to the wider world. At first he stressed global issues: human rights, the environment and development. However, all too soon he found himself preoccupied by the principal concern of his predecessors: anti-communism. Moreover, having promised at the beginning to cut defence spending by over a third, he soon found himself increasing it. Meanwhile, his National Security Council director Zbigniew Brzezinski, passionately anti-Soviet, gave emphasis to the approach of the Trilateral Commission, which since its creation in 1973 had been attempting to create a coherent approach to global problems on the part of the USA, Europe and Japan. But this approach soon faltered: tensions developed on the one hand because of the massive Japanese trade surplus, and on the other because of Europe's apprehension that it was increasingly exposed to the first line of Soviet nuclear fire. Both Europe and Japan took a more open view than the USA on the question of trade with the USSR and on the question of relations with the anti-Israeli Middle East. In the latter area, Carter could claim some success in the shape of the Camp David Accords of September 1978 (confirmed in March 1979), the first agreements between Israel and Egypt.[15]

In Latin America, the USA's primary sphere of interest, Carter managed to regularise relations with Panama over the canal in 1978, but failed to stop the reformist Sandinistas from taking power in Nicaragua in 1979, and was unable to prevent the intensification of a horrendous civil war in El Salvador.[16]

While Africa also remained to a considerable extent a surrogate battlefield for the superpowers, their greatest clash was to come in Central Asia. However, although the two key states of Iran and Afghanistan were adjacent, the reasons for superpower involvement in them differed. As we have seen, the USA came to depend on Iran more than before during the oil crisis of 1974–5. The Shah's corrupt regime was propped up by regular supplies of military equipment, while US intelligence agencies for the most part followed the Shah's advice not to involve themselves with the opposition. When demonstrations and strikes reached new levels of intensity in 1978, nobody on the government side appeared to understand why. Most blame was attributed to the communists, while the greater threat was in fact posed by a force too readily dismissed as outdated and insubstantial: Moslem fundamentalism. The unrest interfered with oil production and provoked another oil crisis. The opposition became so strong that in February 1979 the army accepted the rule of the Ayatollah Khomeini returning from exile, while the ailing Shah fled. His admission into the USA for cancer treatment provoked the seizure of the US Embassy into Tehran, where fifty-three US citizens were held hostage. Carter's presidency came to an ignominious end after the disastrous failure in April 1980 of an attempt at the rescue of the Embassy hostages by helicopter.[17]

Before then, however, the second superpower had also become embroiled in a Central Asian crisis. On 1 January 1979, the USA formally recognised the People's Republic of China, extending to China economic privileges withheld from the Soviet Union. Already unhappy about US support for Soviet dissidents (at the same time as US neglect of their Chinese counterparts), Brezhnev nevertheless met Carter in Vienna in June 1979 and made a further SALT agreement with him, while allowing more Soviet Jews to emigrate. But before SALT II could be ratified by the US Senate, the Soviet armed forces invaded Afghanistan in late December 1979.

Afghanistan had known little peace since the days of the Great Game in the nineteenth century, when the forward policies of the British and Russian empires had involved carving out spheres of influence for themselves and sowing seeds of dissension in the spheres of influence of their rivals. Updated infiltration from both sides in the Cold War did not promote stability, although there was plenty of feuding of a domestic nature as well. The Soviet client government was undermined by coups in 1973 and 1978. During the latter turmoil the US ambassador was kidnapped by insurgents, and then killed during an attempt to free him by a pro-government group, which included Soviet advisers. Brezhnev and his advisers decided that they must restore order, and secured an invitation for this purpose from the Afghan government. Soon, they found themselves embroiled in a long struggle all too reminiscent of that of the USA in Vietnam.[18]

The Moslem affiliation of many of the belligerents, in particular of the insurgents, was exploited by the CIA with the connivance and support of Pakistan, while China was also interested in embarrassing the Soviet Union. But in any case, the fire of fundamentalism needed little stoking, either in Afghanistan where it was mostly anti-Soviet, or in neighbouring Iran where it was primarily anti-American. Confident of the efficacy either of communist or capitalist modernisation, the superpowers now found themselves up against a powerful force which neither of them had anticipated.[19]

Afghanistan and collapse (–1991)

In October 1979, a Soviet spokesman divided the world into four zones consisting of 'developed socialism' (the USSR itself); 'fraternal countries' (in Eastern Europe and beyond); 'progressive regimes' such as Nicaragua; and the capitalist camp. The Soviet invasion of Afghanistan in December 1979 was aimed at maintaining the power of the communist party in a 'progressive regime' which could be helped to enter the ranks of the 'fraternal countries'. Fear of Chinese or other intervention contributed to the fateful decision, which had echoes not only of the Great Game of empire of the nineteenth century but also of the more recent American action in Vietnam. Certainly, like its fellow superpower, the Soviet Union was to discover that to begin an intervention was easier than to bring it to a successful conclusion.[20]

In the same year, 1979, an essay was published by an American university professor making a distinction between 'authoritarian' governments (as in Latin America and the Philippines) and 'totalitarian' regimes (such as the USSR and the PRC). While 'authoritarians' undoubtedly clamped down upon political freedom, she argued, they not only retained stability but were also capable of becoming more democratic. Moreover, their economies were open to foreign investors, and they were usually on the side of the USA in the Cold War. On the other hand, 'totalitarians' were opposed to the USA and to 'Open Door' capitalism, and as communist (or fascist) regimes were determined to keep their political system closed, too. Had Jimmy Carter appreciated the distinction, the essayist considered, he could have maintained the Shah of Iran in power (and thus avoided the Soviet intervention in neighbouring Afghanistan?). But instead, the President had stressed human rights irrespective of regime, and thus pursued a policy which had not advanced the interests of the USA but even reversed them.[21]

Such suggestions were hardly original, and indeed might be said to have been common currency among conservatives in the Cold War period. Nevertheless, the author of the essay, Jeane J. Kirkpatrick, came to the attention of the winner of the 1980 presidential election, Ronald Reagan, and he appointed her US ambassador to the United Nations in 1981. However, at the same time as recognising the 'authoritarian'–'totalitarian' distinction, the incoming President also accepted the need for a new Wilsonianism. For him, this appears to have meant making the world safe for democracy by increasing the USA's military strength and being prepared to use it against 'revolutionary' movements in Latin America and elsewhere. This part of his policy was certainly in the tradition of Woodrow Wilson. He went further than his illustrious predecessor in his opposition to the headquarters of Leninism, however, most famously talking of the Soviet Union as 'the focus of evil in the modern world' and 'an evil empire', and even entertaining the prospect of Armageddon. He also insisted that a Soviet conspiracy was responsible for all the unrest in the world, suggesting that 'if they weren't engaged in this game of dominoes, there wouldn't be any hotspots in the world.'[22]

Meanwhile, the prince of darkness, alias the General Secretary of the CPSU and Marshal of the Soviet Union with sixty decorations, Leonid Brezhnev, was still using the language of Leninism in public, although allegedly holding no allegiance to it in private, and was in any case in poor health. His collected works were widely on sale, but rarely bought; a clear indication that Soviet society, like its leader, had lost much of its faith and energy. The implication of terminal decline was reinforced after Brezhnev's death in 1982 by two ailing successors, Iurii Andropov and Konstantin Chernenko. But then, in March 1985, the Soviet system appeared to gain a new lease of life with the emergence of a younger, fitter General Secretary, Mikhail Gorbachev. According to some observers, his significance was more than personal, since he represented the arrival to a position of influence in Soviet society of a whole generation 'increasingly urbanized and educated, professionally differentiated, and politically, ideologically and culturally diversified'.[23]

These were the heady days of a 'Moscow Spring' when the words *perestroika* and *glasnost* (reconstruction and openness) sent a thrill around not only the Soviet Union but also the USA and much of the rest of the world. Unlike his predecessors, Gorbachev actually met the people, talking and smiling his way through many impromptu meetings as well as more formal speeches. In retrospect, however, the message that he was trying to put across seems without clear focus: he appears to have been advocating sweeping changes without actually making them. To take the most important example as far as ideology was concerned, in 1987 Gorbachev talked about 'socialist pluralism', but in 1988, he declared that Marxism-Leninism was 'the scientific basis of the party's approach to an understanding of social development and the practice of Communist construction'. While underlining the importance of the Communist Party of the Soviet Union, he also gave new emphasis to the part that could be played by other 'social organisations' and even proposed that the Soviet Constitution's reference to the 'leading and guiding' role of the party be reformulated.[24]

As a leading authority, Archie Brown, has indicated, Gorbachev 'saw more clearly than any of his predecessors the links between domestic and foreign policy'.[25] For example, to downgrade the heavy emphasis on defence would help to reduce the power of the Soviet military–industrial complex and remove imbalance in the economy at the same time as promoting a greater element of free enterprise. And so the nine summit meetings with US Presidents (five with Ronald Reagan and four with George Bush) in the less than seven years of Gorbachev's leadership paved the way for later developments while providing a boost for his own authority and a cover-up for a failing superpower. But they also promoted world peace, and Gorbachev's personal contribution here was significant. For Ronald Reagan, who had increased defence spending from $1.1 trillion to $1.5 trillion and then introduced SDI (the Strategic Defense Initiative or 'Star Wars') in a thinly veiled further challenge to the 'evil empire', was partly persuaded by the 'man-to-man' chemistry between himself and Gorbachev to go further than his predecessors towards reconciliation. Moreover, Jeane Kirk-patrick's arguments had worn more than a little thin by the time of the first

Reagan–Gorbachev summit meeting in November 1985: support for the racist government in South Africa as well as for some of the more disagreeable dictatorships in Latin America was turning out to be unprofitable, while the boom in US trade with China had called for another presidential visit in 1984 and more handshakes.

In 1987, an Intermediate-Range Nuclear Forces (INF) Treaty was signed in Washington DC at 1.45 p.m. on 8 December. This time, allegedly set by Nancy Reagan's astrologer and therefore constituting a 'Star Peace', has been deemed by some observers, for example the former German Chancellor Helmut Schmidt, to mark the end of the Cold War.[26] Certainly, it achieved the elimination from Europe of a whole class of nuclear weapons, the Soviet SS-20s along with the Western cruise and Pershing missiles. Possibly, the INF Treaty also helped to promote the even more dramatic developments of 1989, the collapse of the 'evil empire' in Eastern Europe and the Soviet withdrawal from Afghanistan. In 1989 too, Gorbachev went to China, declaring that Sino–Soviet relations were entering a 'qualitatively new stage'. Certainly, demonstrations in support of his *glasnost* and *perestroika* formed part of an upsurge of dissidence reaching a climax in the bloody crushing of a student sit-in in Tiananmen Square. However, the leaders managed to establish the normalisation of relations between the USSR and China themselves, their parties and their countries, and a return visit by President Jiang Zemin to Moscow in the spring of 1991 took the process a stage further.

Also in 1991, Gorbachev worked on the improvement of relations with Japan, but the big problem of the nearby Kurile Islands, occupied by the Soviet Union since the end of Second World War, made close agreement difficult. The Soviet leader seemed ready for compromise, but succeeded only in provoking suspicion and even opposition back in the USSR, where his hold on power was already losing strength, without being able to conclude a deal. On the Pacific Rim, Gorbachev was able to improve relations with South Korea, and, in the wider Third World, to assist the withdrawal of the Soviet Union from its overextended presence. But there were charges that he had gone too far and too quickly here, and in his ready compliance with the United Nations resolutions leading to the Gulf War early in 1991. At Gorbachev's final summit, in July 1991 in Moscow with President Bush, a Strategic Arms Reduction Treaty (START) to the order of 30 per cent on both sides was drawn up. This increased the suspicion of too much deference to the USA.

In the Soviet Union, new directions in international relations needed ideological explanation. Therefore, Gorbachev moved from insistence on worldwide class war towards 'humanistic universalism'. He emphasised that Lenin himself had spoken about 'the priority of interests common to all humanity over class interests'.[27] Here, not for the first time but nearly the last, Gorbachev upset inflexible traditionalists, while there was a more general concern that he was making too many concessions to the West in his pursuit of world peace and personal popularity. His foreign policy, therefore, helped bring about the decision of the State Emergency Committee to make its abortive bid for power in August 1991, stridently announcing that now was the time for all good men and women to come to the aid of the party. For Gorbachev had been tampering with Marxism-Leninism at home too, let us recall, especially as far as the leading and guiding role of the CPSU was concerned. And so, in his decline and fall as well as in his rise, there were close links between his foreign and domestic policy.

The failed coup of August 1991 gave an opportunity to the President of the Russian Republic, Boris Yeltsin, to seize the initiative and bring about the end of the Soviet Union. Now Marxism-Leninism was abandoned completely in favour of a simpler nationalism. For Yeltsin had realised that:

> Russia never had its own voice and it did not argue or disagree with the centre. ... It was clear to me that the vertical bureaucratic pivot on which the country rests had to be destroyed, and we had to begin a transition to horizontal ties with greater independence of the republic states. The mood of the people, the democratization of society, and the growth of people's national self-awareness led directly to this.[28]

Certainly, the new independence of Russia was to a considerable extent a consequence of neither internal nor international circumstances but of developments in what was soon to be known as the 'near abroad', that is the other former Soviet republics. The Baltics – Estonia, Latvia and Lithuania – had spoken up for themselves soon after 1985 and, after a considerable amount of pressure and a little violence from the Soviet side, were allowed to depart in peace by September 1991. In Transcaucasia too, there was a considerable amount of dissatisfaction, and here more than a little violence. Armenia, Azerbaidzhan and Georgia all had problems among themselves and with their own national minorities as well as with Moscow, but came to believe that independence provided them with the best chance of a comprehensive solution to their problems. Georgia made the first formal declaration on 9 April 1991. By the end of that year, no republic wanted to maintain the integrity of the Soviet Union, although all of them, with the permanent exception of the three Baltics and the temporary exception of Georgia (until 1994), had joined a looser association, the Commonwealth of Independent States.

Meanwhile, back on his ranch, and in the White House, President Reagan had been following his own doctrine before handing the reins of power over to President Bush at the beginning of 1989. Previously as anti-communist as his predecessor, the new president found it no easy task to adjust his outlook to the developments taking place in the Soviet 'empire' and then in the Soviet Union itself. On the other hand, he seemed to have no difficulty in overcoming reservations about the Tiananmen Square massacre to accord 'most-favoured-nation' status to the PRC while withholding it from the USSR. He appeared somewhat bemused by the speed of the emergence of a new Central and Eastern Europe, although more than ready on 21 November 1990 to sign the treaty on the final regulation of the German question with the powers that had joined with the USA in posing it in 1945, Great Britain and France as well as the USSR. For some observers, this treaty marked the end of the Cold War more than had the conclusion of the INF Treaty on 8 December 1987. Then, although finding Gorbachev congenial company and welcoming his new friend's support for the Gulf War, Bush gave a clear impression on television of accepting the August 'coup' without objection as a *fait accompli*. While welcoming Gorbachev's return, he soon exchanged warm handshakes with Boris Yeltsin.

Overstretch and breakdown

We have already seen that the dollar versus ruble contest during the Cold War was almost over before it started, occasional appearances to the contrary notwithstanding. Even before the Second World War, the USSR's oft-announced intention of catching up and overtaking the USA was far from realisation. With the destruction brought about by the war, the prospect receded further: the gap was never really closed, and by 1991 the strain on the Soviet Union brought complete breakdown. Meanwhile, from time to time even the US economy experienced serious difficulties, and some experts feared that the 'imperial overstretch' brought about by the Cold War could lead to another 1929, or worse. Was the victory of capitalism over socialism permanent and complete?

The Vietnam War contributed to inflation and to debt. Dollars were flowing overseas through military expenditure and private investment. Imports exceeded exports for the first time in many years. By 1971 the annual deficit in the balance of payments approached $50 billion, and the Nixon administration had to take drastic action. The dollar was devalued and put on a par with other currencies in what Europeans complained was a Marshall Plan in reverse: its hegemony as asserted in the Bretton Woods agreements of 1944 was now over. The relative decline in US economic power was further reflected in the oil crises of 1973–4 and 1979.

However, as far as the superpowers are concerned, 'relative' was the operative word. In its great struggle to catch up with the USA, the USSR was actually falling further behind. The shortfall of the Eighth and Ninth Five-Year Plans from 1965 to 1975 showed that the technological gap with the capitalist West was widening. For all the vast sums poured into agriculture, grain had to be imported from the USA. Emphasis, as ever, was also given to the Soviet armed forces, throwing the economy further off balance. Moreover, in 1973, the average Soviet salary was little more than a quarter of its US equivalent; to some extent, perhaps, a reflection of Soviet industrial productivity amounting to about one-half, and agricultural productivity about one-quarter, of that of the USA. In any case, it was difficult for Soviet citizens standing in queues and all too conscious of shortages not to be envious of their American counterparts.

In the late 1970s, with the return of Cold War, the strain on Soviet citizens and their economy grew worse. Ironically, if millions of tons of grain had not been imported from the USA, the USSR might have been obliged to sue for peace, since its own agriculture was failing to provide a sufficient amount of the basic necessities. While some of the indices for heavy industry were impressive enough, there was a great emphasis on the extracting and processing of raw materials and fuel. No up-to-date economy could measure its success by coal and oil, cement and steel production. And while the technological gap was growing wider, the Soviet standard of living was falling further behind. Birth rates fell and death rates rose, with infant mortality much higher than elsewhere in the developed world. Moreover, as in so many other areas, disparities were indicated by the situation at the top. Brezhnev owned a fleet of mainly foreign cars when nearly all Soviet citizens could aspire to no more than ownership one day of an automobile of domestic manufacture, considered inferior even by patriots. Like many of his fellow countrymen, he drank and smoked far too much and was overweight, but while others survived as best they could, the best medical resources were devoted to keeping him alive, even on one occasion allegedly bringing him back from the dead.[29]

On the US side, after the arrival and departure of the puritan Jimmy Carter, a new age of prosperity was symbolised by his successor. Surpassing Franklin Roosevelt's admonition that all Americans had to fear was fear itself, Ronald Reagan found success in the radiation of complete confidence, cutting taxes and promising to balance the budget while increasing military expenditure by 40 per cent. By the mid-1980s, the US arms budget neared $300 billion a year (while the Soviet equivalent neared $250 billion, but at a much higher percentage of GNP). But the President asked for more, not only to be able if necessary to destroy the 'evil empire' but also to make the USA invulnerable to attack through the Strategic Defense Initiative, or 'Star Wars' as it became popularly, and appropriately, known. Certainly the budget deficit became astronomical, growing by more than $1 trillion to about $3 trillion, while the trade deficit exceeded $170 billion officially, and was almost certainly more than $200 billion when the huge profits from the illegal commerce in drugs were included. More than 20 per cent of US banking assets were held by foreigners, who also owned a considerable part of US industry. But somehow, as long as the President kept smiling through his well-rehearsed optimistic speeches, Mr and Ms average American appeared content.[30]

By this time, surprisingly, an almost equally engaging smile as well as similarly reassuring words were coming from the new leader of the rival superpower, Mikhail Sergeevich Gorbachev. Promising far-reaching economic reforms, he held out the prospect of the prosperity that had for so long been denied Soviet citizens. Unfortunately, however, he could not cajole the Soviet people into changing the habits of many lifetimes, nor persuade the IMF and World Bank to advance the loan which he considered necessary for the reconstruction of the Soviet economy.

In the same year that Gorbachev succeeded a series of geriatrics as General Secretary of the CPSU, the Soviet government brought out *Guidelines for the Economic and Social Development of the USSR for 1986–1990 and for the Period ending in 2000*. It proclaimed that 'The next fifteen years will be a historic period for our country on the road towards perfecting socialism and building communism.' The next fifteen years would indeed be 'a historic period for our country' (although that would come to depend on which country you belonged to after the collapse of the USSR, and the road would be away from socialism and communism rather than towards them). The basic aim of the Twelfth (and last) Five-Year Plan was:

> to increase the growth rates and efficiency of the economy on the basis of accelerating scientific and technological progress, the technical modernisation and re-equipment of production, intensive utilisation of the created production potential, perfecting the system of management and the economic mechanism and achieving on this basis a further rise of the Soviet people's well-being.[31]

Fine words, but there had been all too many of those before. Already the Tenth and Eleventh Plans, heralded with grandiose announcements, had fallen all too far short in the attempt to adapt to the technological revolution and introduce appropriate management.

The drift away from the plan to the market may be followed through two main stages, before and after 1989. From 1985 to 1989, there was an attempt at reform of the Soviet system; that is, to improve its efficiency with 'profit' and 'incentive' but without the wholesale introduction of the market or the overall lowering of living standards. At the same time, Gorbachev made unacceptable demands on his people as part of an attempt to continue control of the economy from above. Most seriously, he called for the abandonment of the time-honoured thirst for strong drink. Flouting age-old tradition, and thus making a contribution to the downfall of his government, Nicholas II had introduced prohibition at the outbreak of the First World War. After the Revolution of 1917, an abstinent tendency in the first Soviet government was soon reversed, and by the late Soviet era, during the years of the Eleventh Five-Year Plan from 1981 to 1985, the turnover tax on alcoholic beverages brought in nearly 170 billion rubles! Then in 1988, Gorbachev had to admit that if the income from sales at home of such liquids and sales abroad of another liquid, oil, were deducted from the Soviet budget, there had been little significant economic growth for about twenty years, and even from 1981 onwards, some decline. Nevertheless now, through personal example and public restriction, he hoped to improve the health and work-rate of the people and thus reverse the more general downward direction in the economy. But, as the next years went by, an increasing number of his fellow citizens would drink to his demotion.

During those years, from 1989 to 1991, there followed a number of reforms leading towards the end of the Soviet system: for example, in 1990, the encouragement of small private businesses in August of that year and the reduction of state controls in October, followed in July 1991 by further denationalisation and privatisation. Dissatisfaction was reflected in widespread strikes, for which not the least cause was the anti-alcohol campaign, which one opponent likened to 'the castration of the working class'. Gradually the campaign was relaxed, and by the early 1990s the Russians were catching up and even overtaking the world's other leading drinkers. Meanwhile, all kinds of advisers came in from the capitalist West, offering all kinds of solutions for the Soviet Union's economic problems: generally speaking, the lower the level of under-standing of the ailments, the higher the level of optimism concerning the efficacy of the treatment.[32]

By late 1991, the exchange rate was more than 90 to the dollar as opposed to 0.6 in 1985, while gold reserves were nearly exhausted. Russian experts drew little comfort from the news that the sale of Big Macs had increased from zero to 15 million while growing increasingly annoyed at the often condescending recommendation to them of policies drawn, not from the actual practice of capitalism, but from models that were largely idealised. For they well knew that, while the Soviet economy was collapsing, there were still signs of overstretch in the American economy as well.[33]

In the USA in 1988, as politicians vied for the succession to President Reagan, an extraordinary event occurred: a history book entered the best seller lists, and even became the subject of in-flight entertainment in transatlantic air crossings. 'Presidential candidates don't have time to read, but aspirants for the White House would surely benefit from pondering Yale historian Paul Kennedy's new book', observed *Time*, (although not explaining how they could ponder a book without reading it). The basic argument of *The Rise and Fall of the Great Powers: Economic Change and Military Conflict from 1500 to 2000* is simple enough: 'The historical record suggests that there is a very clear connection *in the long run* between an individual Great Power's economic rise and fall and its growth and decline as an important military power (or world empire).' These two develop-ments do not occur in parallel, the argument continues, but there is a tendency for military overspending to accelerate a Great Power's relative loss of status. A second general observation of the book is that 'there is a very strong correlation between the eventual outcome of the *major coalition wars* for European or global mastery, and the amount of productive resources mobilized by each side'.[34] What attracted so much attention was not the rise and fall of the Habsburg empire in the sixteenth and seventeenth centuries nor the rise and fall of the British empire in the nineteenth and twentieth centuries but the implications for the USA with the approach of the year 2000. What was pondered most was the final chapter, 'To the Twenty-First Century'.

In this chapter, as well as underestimating the difficulties of the USSR, Kennedy overestimated the problems of the USA, at least *in the short run*. Discussing 'The United States: The Problem of Number One in Relative Decline', he argued that 'imperial overstretch' threatened the USA, and that 'decision-makers in Washington must face the awkward and enduring fact that the sum total of the United States' global interests and obligations is nowadays far larger than the country's power to defend them all simultaneously', that 'the United States today has roughly the same massive array of military obligations across the globe as it had a quarter-century ago, when its shares of world GNP, manufacturing production, military spending, and armed forces personnel were so much larger than they are now'. Relative decline showed not only in agriculture and older manufactures but also in industrial-technological output. There were also 'unprecedented turbulences in the nation's finances'.[35]

Whatever they read and pondered in their campaign, neither presidential candidate used rhetoric noticeably different from their predecessors throughout the Cold War. The unsuccessful Democratic candidate Michael Dukakis was reduced to demonstrating his potential for bellicosity by riding around in a tank, while the successful Republican President George Bush continued to assert the USA's willingness to intervene militarily wherever and whenever necessary. Hence, the unleashing of 'Operation Desert Storm' on 27 February 1991 and the consequent deaths of about 100,000 Iraqis, paying for the errors of their leader Saddam Hussein. The readiness to accept the departure of Gorbachev and the Soviet Union at the end of the same year appeared to show the advantages of not being soft on communism right up to the end. But had the kind of loans been advanced before 1991 that were extended afterwards, the outcome might have been different.

At the end, Alec Nove was struck by 'a paradox, or dilemma'. To carry out reform needed strong government, but such government was being dismantled: 'So by the time the reform programme was radicalised, the means to enforce it no longer existed.' However, in the view of R.W. Davies, it was that self-same strong government, or at least the one-party state, and the 'new ruling élite' that, in the absence of other parties and the presence of a rigid censorship, 'hindered the emergence of innovative ideas and encouraged the stagnation of the élite'. In other words, there were internal social reasons for the collapse of a superpower as well as imperial overstretch.[36]

While the costs to the victor were not disproving the power of Kennedy's case *in the long run*, the defeated superpower was soon showing its wounds to the world. Already indeed, the Chernobyl disaster of 1986 had shown that the nuclear threat was by no means confined to military confrontation. Now the ecological disaster brought about by the race to keep up with the USA could be found all over the USSR. Far from giving emphasis to the victory of capitalism over socialism, however, the insidious poison was making an impact everywhere. Moreover, if far from the point of collapse, the USA was grievously wounded by problems of race and poverty, which were making some cities extremely difficult to live in. As we shall argue in the final chapter, these comparatively unnoticed by-products of the Cold War marked a defeat for the whole world. The contest between true blue and would-be red had been to the neglect of the necessary green.

The war of images

During 1968 and after, one of the books most in evidence among revolutionary youth was the *Little Red Book* of Chairman Mao. Apparently, China had replaced the Soviet Union as the ideal. At least partly, this was owing to the circumstance that enough was known now about the USSR during the Stalin period for it to be replaced by China, about which very little was known. However, for Western society the *Little Red Book* had little to say, and in any case more people brandished than read it. Rather more pertinent was a work which allegedly outsold Mao's thoughts in France, and did quite well elsewhere. This was *One Dimensional Man: The Ideology of Industrial Society*, by Herbert Marcuse, a seventy-year-old philosopher teaching at the University of California. First published in 1964, this book achieved its greatest popularity during and after the events of 1968.

One Dimensional Man intentionally vacillates between two contradictory hypotheses: '(1) that advanced industrial society is capable of containing qualitative change for the foreseeable future; (2) that forces and tendencies exist which may break this containment and explode the society'. In advanced industrial society, the distinction between private and public is obliterated as technology creates more effective forms of social control and cohesion which are also more pleasant. The consequent totalitarian tendency stretches throughout the world, even to pre-industrial areas, and creates similarities in the development of capitalism and communism. This neo-totalitarianism is not a specific form of political control but a specific form of production and distribution which could be compatible with a 'pluralism' of parties and media. However, it does not mean the 'end of ideology': on the contrary, it means more, for the ideology is now in the process of production and distribution itself. Higher culture becomes part of the material culture too, and thus loses the greater part of its truth, whereas traditional bourgeois culture found rich representation, for example in seventeenth-century Dutch painting or in the English-language novel of the nineteenth century. Sex is integrated into work and public relations and is thus made more susceptible to controlled satisfaction.[37]

Equally, 'the fact that the prevailing mode of freedom is servitude and that the prevailing mode of equality is superimposed inequality is barred from expression by the closed definition of the concepts in terms of the powers which shape the respective universe of discourse'. Orwellian definitions approaching 'war is peace' creep into the language of nuclear strategy such as the 'clean bomb' and 'harmless fall-out'. Moreover, a 'universe of discourse' in which 'the categories of freedom have become interchangeable and even identical with their opposites' ignores 'historical reality':

> If a bureaucratic dictatorship rules and defines communist society, if fascist regimes are functioning as partners of the Free World, if the welfare pro-gramme of enlightened capitalism is successfully defeated by labelling it 'socialism', if the foundations of democracy are harmoniously abrogated in democracy, then the old historical concepts are invalidated by up-to-date operational redefinitions. The redefinitions are falsifications which, imposed by the powers that be and the powers of fact, serve to transform falsehood into truth.[38]

This does not mean that history disappears from the universe of discourse, since the past is evoked often enough, whether as 'the Founding Fathers' or 'Marx-Engels-Lenin', but these references are 'ritualized invocations' which do not allow 'development of the content recalled'. A whole range of activities – labour relations (where 'personal discontent is isolated from the general unhappiness') and the conduct of elections (where 'the range of judgement is confined within a context of facts which excludes judging the context in which the facts are made'), scientific thought (where the world tends to become 'the stuff of total administration, which absorbs even the administrators') and philosophy (tending to become 'an endless language game with building stones') – are all accommodated in the totalitarian, closed operational universe of advanced industrial civilisation.[39]

Marcuse suggests that:

> In the contemporary period, all historical projects tend to be polarized on the two conflicting totalities – capitalism and communism, and the outcome seems to depend on two antagonistic series of factors: (1) the greater force of destruction; (2) the greater productivity without destruction. In other words, the higher historical truth would pertain to the system which offers the greater chance of pacification.

He draws a gloomy picture of Western 'man' in particular:

> While the people can support the continuous creation of nuclear weapons, radioactive fallout, and questionable foodstuffs, they cannot (for this very reason!) tolerate being deprived of the entertainment and education which make them capable of reproducing the arrangements for their defence and/or destruction. The non-functioning of television and the allied media might thus begin to achieve what the inherent contradictions of capitalism did not achieve – the disintegration of the system. The creation of repressive needs has long since become part of socially necessary labour – necessary in the sense that without it, the established mode of production could not be sustained. Neither problems of psychology nor of aesthetics are at stake, but the material base of domination.

In his conclusion, Marcuse observes that, within the advancing one-dimensional society: 'The aesthetic dimension still retains a freedom of expression which enables the writer and the artist to call men and things by their name – to name the otherwise unnameable.' For him, the work of Samuel Beckett shows the 'real face of our time' and that of Rolf Hochhuth 'its real history'. Meanwhile:

> The totalitarian tendencies of the one-dimensional society render the traditional ways and means of protest ineffective – perhaps even dangerous because they preserve the illusion of popular sovereignty. ... However, underneath the conservative popular base is the substratum of the outcasts and outsiders, the exploited and persecuted of other races and other colours, the unemployed and the unemployable. They exist outside the democratic process; their life is the most immediate and the most real need for ending intolerable conditions and institutions. Thus their opposition is revolutionary even if their consciousness is not. ... But the chance is that, in this period, the historical extremes may meet again: the most advanced consciousness of humanity, and its most exploited force.[40]

Marcuse's heavy concentration on the fragmentation of society left him very little opportunity to discuss the widest setting, the biosphere (although he did imagine a pertinent 'unbearable nightmare'). However, at least some of his disciples, while thinking about how they should behave in order to remain red, were beginning to consider whether or not they should become green. For an ecological moment was arriving, after nearly a century of preparation. In 1875, Eduard Seuss coined the term 'biosphere' in his book *The Face of the Earth*. In 1926, Vladimir Vernadsky widened this vision in a book entitled *The Biosphere*, combining ecology with Darwinism in the suggestion that the earth's surface was the product of biological activity. He went further in his belief that the human race would transform the biosphere into the 'noosphere' – the sphere of the mind – while a new world view – 'cosmism' – would involve the reduction of chaos on earth and in space through united human effort.[41]

The Second World War submerged ecological awareness everywhere, but soon afterwards, in 1948, William Vogt produced *Road to Survival*, including a 'bio-equation': CB:E. Here, C indicates the *carrying capacity* of any given area of land, that is its ability to afford food, drink and shelter. B stands for *biotic potential*, or the ability of that land to produce plants, especially for food, but also for shelter and clothing. E indicates *environmental resistance*, or limitations imposed by the environment. So, the carrying capacity is the resultant of the ratio between the other two factors. In 1962, Rachel Carson made a huge impact with her *Silent Spring*, holding out the frightening prospect of the death of wildlife through the overuse of agrichemicals and pesticides.[42] And now, with the application of defoliants and other pollutants to the war in Vietnam, the time was ripe for the emergence of the green movement in the USA from 1968 onwards. The May 1970 number of the radical journal *Ramparts* was an 'Ecology Special', catching the spirit of the time with an incendiary cover exclaiming: 'The students who burned the Bank of America in Santa Barbara may have done more towards saving the environment than all the Teach-ins put together.'

In the USA, undoubtedly, 1968 had unleashed a new great debate accompanied, as many campuses as well as some other buildings clearly demonstrated, by a considerable degree of violence. In the USSR the process was muted, both passively and actively, so to speak; that is to say, anybody who dared to speak out publicly against the party line was silenced. Nevertheless, from 1968 onwards a 'Chronicle of Current Events' attempted to record infringements of human rights. There was some disturbance even in academic circles, for example in the field of history where P.V. Volobuev was dismissed from his post as Director of the Institute of History of the Academy of Sciences for a suspect interpretation of the Russian Revolution. Back in the USA, political activists narrowly failed to gain acceptance of a motion deploring and condemning the Vietnam War at the AGM of the American Historical Association at the end of 1969. One of the radicals, Jesse Lemisch, who had been dismissed from the University of Chicago because his 'political concerns interfered with his scholarship', argued that it was not so much a political position as dissent from established views that cost him his job and aroused objections to radical history.[43]

Perhaps the most famous dissident of the post-1968 period, however, was Alexander Solzhenitsyn, who was forced into emigration in 1974. At first widely hailed as a great prophet, compared indeed by *The Times* of London to none other than Jesus Christ, he lost much of his popularity when he began to attack the West for its materialism, even to predict its collapse from within, and to assert the supremacy of the Russian national spirit as expressed in Orthodoxy. Almost as well-known was the dissident physicist Andrei Sakharov, who had helped to construct the Soviet atomic bomb but now argued in favour of intellectual freedom and even believed in convergence. By no means every free thinker in the Soviet Union considered Solzhenitsyn and Sakharov the best voices for their aspirations. Many preferred poets and 'guitar poets', while the villagers writing about traditional life and its decline in the provinces were also widely popular. There was also a hankering for the 'pop' culture of the West, for example, for the Beatles.

The Communist Party did all it could to stem the tide of foreign influence, arguing against convergence in culture as in the economy, and continuing to deny religion and assert materialism. But, after a holding action throughout the later 1970s and early 1980s, the celebrated arrival of *perestroika* and *glasnost* after 1985 began to open the floodgates. As the Soviet Union moved towards a state of collapse, dissidence gained recognition, and previously prohibited literature achieved publication. Solzhenitsyn and Sakharov could now be read openly. But from an over-rich diet of liberated reading matter, indigestion soon ensued, and then a loss of appetite. Neither opponent of the old system found much favour in the new. But both retained honoured places in distinctive Russian traditions: Solzhenitsyn as the Slavophile, pre-Petrine, calling for the spiritual renewal of the Orthodox universal outlook; Sakharov as the Westerner, post-Petrine, the advocate of a 'Union of Soviet Republics of Europe and Asia' and of a political convergence leading towards world government.[44]

A curious paradox does indeed emerge after 1991. However celebrated in their time, the political writings of Solzhenitsyn and Sakharov do not make much of an intellectual impact now that the milieu in which they were produced no longer exists. As an example, let us take Sakharov's four-stage plan for co-operation coming towards the end of his most substantial essay 'Progress, Coexistence and Intellectual Freedom', composed in the summer of 1968:

1   In the USSR and other socialist countries, a reformist multiparty system will necessarily emerge from 1968 to 1980, not because it is an essential stage in the socialist system's development, nor even less a cure for all ills, but because 'a ruling Communist Party refuses for one reason or another to rule by the scientific democratic method required by history.'

2   The pressure exerted in the USA and other capitalist countries by internal progressive forces (the working class and the intelligentsia) making persistent demands for social progress and peaceful coexistence will lead to the victory between 1972 and 1985 of leftist reformists who will begin to put into effect a programme of rapprochement or convergence with socialism, while attacking racism and militarism.

3   From 1972 to 1990, as they overcome their alienation from each other, the USA and USSR will collaborate in solving the problem of world poverty,

with a 20 per cent tax on the national income of developed countries, construction of gigantic fertiliser factories and atomic-powered irrigation systems in the developing world. The resources of the sea will be used much
more than before, and the process of disarmament will continue.

4   From 1980 to 2000, 'the socialist convergence will reduce differences in
social structure, promote intellectual freedom, science, and economic progress, and lead to the creation of a world government and the smoothing of
national contradictions'. More progress will be made in the field of nuclear
power, while 'the expansion of space exploration will require thousands of
people to work and live continuously on other planets and on the moon, on
artificial satellites and on asteroids whose orbits will have been changed by
nuclear explosions'.

This ambitious programme presumed a worldwide interest, especially from
the intelligentsia, the expectation that modifications of both capitalism and
socialism would reduce contradictions and differences, and appropriate economic
development in both systems. Of course, nothing like Sakharov's programme was
to ensue, and the idea of socialist convergence disappeared with the collapse of
the Soviet Union. Moreover, Sakharov himself was to change his mind in later
years.[45]

The decline and fall of the Soviet empire brought a strong note of triumphalism into intellectual discussion in the USA. Ironically, as pointed out above, this
note was struck just as one of the principal Western weapons in the intellectual
struggle, *Encounter*, was failing. Yet many of the questions posed in 1968 were still
unanswered, as we shall see when we look at some post-1991 publications in the
concluding chapter. For the moment, let us do no more than give simple emphasis
to the point that Marcuse made in a more complicated fashion, that from about
1968 onwards, images did indeed appear to be overtaking words, first in the USA
and the West, then in the USSR and the rest of the world.

Let us begin with some simple figures. In 1950, as already noted, there were
10,000 television sets in the Soviet Union; by 1960 there were 4.8 million. By
1976, about 7 million sets were being produced every year, and in 1986 it was
estimated that more than 90 per cent of the population had private access to
television. During the 1960s, radio and the press remained more important than
television as providers of information, but by the middle of the 1980s they had
been overtaken by the upstart medium, which also led to a decline in the
importance and popularity of cinema. Needless to say, this process had occurred
considerably earlier in the USA.

Even in such an age of transition, 'steam radio' played an important part, for
between them, Voice of America, Radio Free Europe and the BBC did much to
encourage dissidence, both active and passive, in the USSR. Nor should it be
forgotten that Soviet radio was even more active than its rivals, sending out just

over 2,000 hours of broadcast in 80 different languages every week. In 1979, a conference in Tashkent discussed a New World Order of Information to counter the 'cultural imperialism' of Western media throughout the Third World. However, it would seem that the Soviet message made less of an impact than its rival.

Even in the USSR itself, propaganda often fell on deaf ears or unseeing eyes, with as much as a quarter of the population in the 1970s being unaware of the meaning of the word 'colonialism'. Such ignorance was to be found throughout both superpowers as 'current affairs' were followed in soap opera more than in news programmes. Especially popular during the last years of the Soviet Union (and perhaps making a small contribution to its downfall) was the Mexican *The Rich Also Cry*, with more than its fair share of adultery and divorce, murder and suicide, simple escapism at its most tear-jerking and responsible for both absenteeism from work and decline in crime rates at the time of transmission.[46]

Against such a background, it is difficult to calculate how far the media were responsible for the collapse of the Soviet Union in 1991 and the events leading up to it in Eastern Europe. But the contrast between the almost sepulchral solemnity of Soviet newscasters and the much more telegenic informality of CNN journalists surely indicated some of the reason for the great changeover. Even towards the end, however, ingenuity brought 'Aesopian' moments to admire. For example, after the major Soviet news broadcast *Vremia* (Time) it was the custom to play music along with the weather forecast. On the day of the announcement of the 'coup' of August 1991, one heard an orchestral version of the Beatles' *Yesterday*, reminding viewers that their troubles had indeed been far away before the introduction of curfew and other draconian measures by the State Emergency Committee. More seriously, Yeltsin's appearance on a tank outside the Moscow White House gave a pointer towards a shift of power even before Gorbachev was publicly humiliated by his supplanter for all the world to see.

CNN was joined as an insidious influence by information technology, as Frank Ellis pointed out in 1998:

> If television played a crucial role in undermining Soviet values, the final blow to the Soviet system's ability to insulate itself from Western influences was struck in the 1970s and 1980s with the rapid spread of information technology (IT). IT permeated and revolutionized every facet of Western society from videos to combat aircraft. ... IT deployed two potent weapons against the Soviet media structure: speed and volume. ... The ability of the new electronic media to seep through just about any barrier, and, no less important, their ability to impose a new *modus operandi* on the dissemination of news, meant that the Soviet Union had, whether the Party liked it or not, had been drawn into a global media structure, in which the West was setting the agenda.[47]

Already apparent before 1985, this new cultural circumstance became overwhelming after 1991. Moreover, in a whole range of questions, Soviet experts had been isolated from the Western mainstream. For example, as late as 1988, the Soviet Minister of Health Yevgeny Chazov insisted that Slavic genetic superiority had rendered the populace untouchable by HIV and AIDS. But could Russia and the other former republics of the USSR switch on to the globalising culture centred on the USA and maintain their traditional distinctive characteristics at the same time? This was a major problem for Soviet superpower in its maturity.[48]

6 The legacy

Death or rebirth? 1991–

The end of the Cold War?

In the late 1980s, the Cold War came to an end. Or did it? The former German Chancellor Helmut Schmidt had no doubt, observing that 'the INF [Intermediate Range Forces] treaty *was* the end of the Cold War'. This was signed in Washington, DC at 1.45 p.m. on 8 December 1987.[1] Another popular suggestion would be the destruction of the Berlin Wall in 1989. At least two other possibilities have been put forward, both from 1990: Gorbachev's acceptance of reunified Germany's membership of NATO, and the signing of the Paris Charter for a New Europe. And so, the Cold War was not like the other major conflicts of the twentieth century, the First and Second World Wars. There is no unanimous acceptance of 8 December 1987 as a conclusion as there is of 11 November 1918, the Armistice, and 14 August 1945, the Japanese surrender. Moreover, why should there be general agreement about when the Cold War came to an end while, as we have seen, there is no general agreement about when it began?

A further consideration is: can such a conflict be deemed to be over when there is no general disarmament, when some 35,000 nuclear weapons remain in existence?[2] Has the Cold War really come to an end, or are we living through no more than another period of détente? Another intriguing question about the Cold War, yet again reflecting its peculiar nature, is: who won, and who lost? At least, appearances might turn out to be deceptive concerning the obvious victor, the USA, and the obvious loser, the USSR. Arguably, as we will see in this concluding chapter, nobody won and the whole world lost.

First, let us look at the present state of the historiography of the Cold War, bearing in mind that our major purpose has been to view that conflict in a broader context including not only the twentieth century but earlier centuries as well. In the USA, the dominant argument in the late 1940s came to be known as the 'orthodox' view. This consisted basically of the belief that the Soviet Union under Stalin broke many agreements made during the Second World War, culminating in those at Yalta, and used as many opportunities as possible to realise expansionist ambitions in Eastern Europe and elsewhere. The USA and its allies responded to Soviet aggression rather than provoking it or launching any aggression of their own. Major revisionist schools then emerged, first from the right and then from the left. From the early 1950s to the early 1960s, conservative 'realists' argued that Roosevelt and other Western statesmen had trusted Stalin too much, motivated as they were by moralistic and idealistic considerations rather than by the world as it actually was and national interests as they should have been. Then, in the mid-1960s, a 'New Left' revisionism arose to give a negative verdict on the policies of Roosevelt's successor. Harry S. Truman was accused of adopting the policy of containment too readily and completely and thus reinforcing Soviet totalitarianism. Throughout the years of the Vietnam War, a passionate debate raged about the nature of the USA's involvement in earlier conflicts, especially the Second World War and the Cold War. The common ground of scholarly standards, and even of some measure of interpretative agreement, was largely abandoned. However, from the end of the 1970s until the beginning of the 1990s, academic arguments largely resumed traditions of restraint and mutual respect, and the realist and New Left schools in particular realised more completely than before an area of agreement which has been called post-revisionist.[3]

Meanwhile, in the Soviet Union, there was far less variation in interpretation, and severe criticism meted out to those deemed to have deviated from the acceptable line. To give one example, L.I. Zubok's *The Imperialistic Policy of the USA in the Countries of the Caribbean Basin, 1930–1939* was criticised in 1949 for elucidating 'the nature and policy of American imperialism from a cosmopolitan standpoint' and referring to 'the open idealisation of the policy of American imperialism in the period of the presidency of Franklin Roosevelt'. A more 'correct' view had been put forward in 1947 by D. Voblikov:

> The Truman Doctrine concerning the world domination of the USA supplemented and made concrete in the so-called Marshall Plan, places that country in the forefront of world imperialism and reaction. American monopolistic capital, enriched by the excess profits of the war years and emboldened to that extreme, has led an offensive against the popular masses within the country and against the progressive forces of the whole world. ... The new addition to the Monroe Doctrine combines hypocrisy and brutal coercion, the policy of the dollar, and the policeman's club, spreading this policy throughout the world.[4]

After the death of Stalin, a limited 'thaw' set in, but the room for manoeuvre of Soviet historians remained severely limited, and individual scholars were disciplined for what appeared from outside to be no more than minor deviations. It was not until after the arrival of Gorbachev, *glasnost* and *perestroika* that Soviet historians found it possible to enter into a freer dialogue among themselves and with Western colleagues.

A few years before then, in 1983, John Lewis Gaddis suggested a convergence of views along the following lines:

1   'Full attention to the use by the United States of economic instruments to achieve political ends.'
2   A tendency 'to stress the absence of any ideological blueprint for world revolution in Stalin's mind. ... Stalin is now seen as a cagey but insecure opportunist.'
3   Confirmation 'that the [US] government from time to time, did exaggerate external dangers for the purpose of achieving certain internal goals.'
4   Acceptance of the argument that 'there was in fact an American "empire".'[5]

Not everybody subscribed to these tenets, and at least some analysts dismissed post-revisionism as 'orthodoxy plus archives'. Interpretations continued to evolve through the 1980s and the early 1990s, into the post-Soviet years.[6]

In his book *We Now Know: Rethinking Cold War History*, published in 1997, Gaddis points out that by 'we' he means post-Cold War scholars as he has interpreted their findings, while 'now' is at a particular time when the Cold War may be viewed more clearly than when it was actually going on and 'know' is necessarily contingent but nevertheless the consequence of an approach to new evidence with an open mind. Admitting his linguistic limitations, he overcomes them as much as possible through the use of translated work. He follows the example of Louis Halle's 'classic but premature book' *The Cold War as History* by treating his subject 'through a certain cycle with a beginning, a middle, and an end'. Here, then, is an academic treatment especially welcome for present purposes.

Where is the beginning? Juxtaposing the famous observation of Alexis de Tocqueville in 1835 that each of the 'two great nations' seemed 'called by some secret design of Providence one day to hold in its hands the destinies of half the world' with the valedictory remark of Adolf Hitler in 1945 that the 'laws of both history and geography will compel these two Powers to a trial of strength', Gaddis suggests that the post-1945 conflict could also be 'improbable accident' but was most likely 'something in between'. He then sets about locating this elusive middle ground between the supernatural and the natural in the period before 1917. At the time Tocqueville wrote, he observes, 'the world's most democratic republic' and 'the most prominent example of monarchical authoritarianism' had 'about as many connections as exist now, say, between Paraguay and Mongolia'. American diplomats and merchants would have been among those surprised by the second assertion, while Native Americans and Afro-Americans would question the first. The description of Russia is less exceptionable, but to assert that after 1825 it played 'only an occasional role in the maintenance of a European order that seemed stable enough in any event' is astonishing, given, for example, the suppression of Poland and the invasion of Hungary in the context of the continent-wide revolutions of 1830 and 1848 respectively. Even more seriously, the pages taking the story up to 1945 give little or no indication of a vital aspect of the pre-1917 relationship intensified by the comparative experience of the First and Second World Wars: Russian, then Soviet backwardness. In any appraisal approaching objectivity, the scene for the great drama has to be set accurately and fully.[7]

The middle of the cycle, the Cold War itself, has been the primary focus of most of the previous publications of John Lewis Gaddis and is competently handled in *We Now Know*. There are illuminating chapters on, among other subjects, the spheres of influence of the superpowers in Europe and Asia, and a number of more particular questions from the German problem centred on Berlin to the Cuban missile crisis of 1962 and beyond. Unfortunately, however, Gaddis finds it difficult to make the sympathetic leap which would enable him to see the Cold War from the Soviet point of view, which to a considerable extent remains the Russian point of view. For example, it would still be widely agreed in Russia that so great was the loss of life and destruction suffered by the Soviet Union, in what is still often called 'The Great Patriotic War', that socio-economic recovery was at least as high a priority as political expansion in the immediate aftermath. As Melvin P. Leffler points out: 'Soviet losses during World War II are mentioned in a sentence and then passed over.' Continuing his comment on the approach of Gaddis, Leffler comments:

> Interestingly, he argues that Pearl Harbor had a lasting impact on U.S. na-
> tional security policy. At Pearl Harbor, 2,400 Americans died. During the
> entirety of World War II, 425,000 American servicemen were killed. It is
> interesting that, for Gaddis, the Japanese attack left an indelible imprint on
> postwar American conceptions of national security, but the war had little
> impact on the Kremlin.

Leffler goes on to quote Elena Zubkova, who gives the figure for Soviet human losses, civilian as well as military, as 26.6 million. For Zubkova, the war years 'shaped all of postwar life. Without an understanding of the phenomenon of the war as it entered the flesh and blood of that generation, postwar history and social behavior are incomprehensible.'[8]

The USA's abrupt termination of Lend-Lease and negative response to re-quests for further assistance were among other circumstances leading towards the great schism, a point given insufficient emphasis by Gaddis. Coming on to the end, he puts forward some mostly unexceptionable hypotheses while concluding, as noted above, that the responsibility for the Cold War was shared by 'authori-tarianism in general, and Stalin in particular'. The first resulting from 'the laws of both history and geography', and the second from 'some secret design of Providence'? Certainly, hardly anybody would want to absolve Stalin from his many sins. Nevertheless, many of the policies pursued by him were dictated by circumstances rather than by himself. Arguably, therefore, Cold War interpretation will not reach full maturity before it goes beyond such exclusive attribution of responsibility, or at least the realisation that we were all in it together. On the other hand, to blame Stalin for what went wrong in the relationship of the wartime allies is conveniently to let everybody else off the hook. The 'democratic republic' is absolved completely, it would seem: Latin America, except for Cuba, goes unmentioned, while the US intervention in Vietnam is appraised as no more than 'foolish and tragic' and such events as the bombing of Vietnam, Laos and Cambodia – the heaviest in history – pass unmentioned. Leffler writes in general of *We Now Know* that it 'is likely to set the parameters for a whole new generation of scholarship'. Nevertheless, he criticises Gaddis for unequivocally blaming the Cold War 'on Stalin's personality, on authoritarian government, and on Communist ideology' while exonerating the USA from all responsibility.[9]

As a Russian counterweight to the arguments put forward by John Lewis Gaddis, let us turn to the article of A.O. Chubarian on 'The New History of the "Cold War"', published at the end of 1997. Welcoming the development of oral history and the opening up of archives in the former Soviet bloc, he acknowledges that Russian publication lags behind that of the West. Taking the example of Gaddis in particular, Chubarian notes that his American colleague's view of the twentieth century includes the comparison of the communist revolutions in Russia, China and elsewhere to earthquakes. Responding to these great upsets, the USA sought to save humanity through a policy of Wilsonian emphasis on moral norms and human rights. Yet Gaddis also considers that Soviet society collapsed from within according to the working out of Marxist law. Chubarian finds another inconsistency in the equation by Gaddis of Stalin with Hitler, which by analogy made it impossible for the West to collaborate with the Soviet dictator after 1945. If this indeed were the case, it would render difficult the evaluation of all the documents emerging from Soviet archives.[10]

As a counterbalance to the interpretation of John Lewis Gaddis, Chubarian cites that of Leffler, who continues to take a realist position, suggesting that the opening up of Soviet archives confirms that Stalin had no preconceived plans for expansion but reacted in Europe and Asia to developing circumstances. Meanwhile, Richard Pipes has argued that 'The Hard-Liners Had it Right', in his view correctly opposing every liberal attempt to deal with the Soviet Union and supporting all measures to restrain and then to crush the USSR.[11]

Returning to the exposition of Gaddis, Chubarian approves of his attempt to place the Cold War in the context of the twentieth century as a whole, noting that from immediately after the October Revolution of 1917 there was a certain dualism in Soviet foreign policy. That is to say, Lenin's government was faced from the first by the interconnections and the contradictions between the process of the world revolution and the defence of Russian national interests. And thus it was after 1945, too, when Stalin had not forgotten the world revolution but feared more imminent developments such as the revival of Germany and Japan. While the idea was developed in the Cominform of two camps – socialist and capitalist – struggling for world mastery, the Soviet government was most concerned with what was going on in its immediate sphere of influence in Eastern Europe. However, Chubarian believes that Russian historians should join their American colleagues in ongoing discussions considering the ideologies and the policies of both sides in the Cold War, making four specific suggestions:

1   To what extent did US estimates of Soviet strength correlate with the actual position? Was there some exaggeration of the Soviet threat promoting a spiral of confrontation?
2   What were the perceptions of the Soviet government regarding American intentions? Enough documentation is now available to calculate the strength of anti-Americanism in the USSR and its allies and the degree of Soviet fear of the actions which the USA might take.
3   How close was the correlation of ideology and policy on both sides?
4   What was the strength, structure and influence of the two military–industrial complexes?[12]

Taking up the specific question of the sources of information available to the Soviet government, Chubarian notes that they almost invariably adhered to ideological stereotypes and established doctrines. Deviations from the line in 'fraternal' countries were therefore greeted with alarm, from Tito onwards. Nevertheless, some differences of emphasis may be perceived, for example between the intransigent Ministry of Foreign Affairs and the international section of the Central Committee of the CPSU, which was more flexible. Thus, there were alternatives put forward at such times of crisis as Cuba, Czechoslovakia and Afghanistan. Even in Stalin's time, there could be disagreement. Although decisions were normally announced as unanimous and without alternatives, several of them, such as the proposal for elections throughout all Germany in March 1952, deserve closer scrutiny.

Here as elsewhere, not only does the clash of world revolution and national interest reveals itself but so also does the weight of history. And so, it seems that Stalin and Molotov continued to look upon Germany and Eastern Europe as their greatest problem. They did not see the partition of Germany as permanent, but were concerned not to allow the erection of an anti-Soviet *cordon sanitaire*. In the Near and Middle East, they believed that it was possible to agree with the West on spheres of influence in a traditional manner. Stalin himself appears to have believed in the power of the 'Big Three' to settle global problems, to have been deeply shocked by the death of Roosevelt and the electoral defeat of Churchill. There may have been an element of wishful thinking in the contact between Stalin and Churchill via the Soviet ambassador in London in 1947 and 1948. Certainly, the Soviet leader experienced considerable difficulty in adjusting himself to the necessity of dealing with Truman and Attlee. The reception of the Marshall Plan was also complicated by memories of the Genoa conference in 1922, when the Bolsheviks vacillated between their wish to receive Western credits and loans on the one hand and their fear of dependence on the countries of the West on the other. Having made the decision for themselves not to participate, Stalin and his advisers leant heavily on such countries as Czechoslovakia and Finland to do likewise.[13]

Thus, like Melvin P. Leffler, A.O. Chubarian argues against the attribution of the major responsibility for the Cold War to Stalin, as made by John Lewis Gaddis. This attribution also clashes with the recommendation by Gaddis of the approach made by Louis Halle in *The Cold War as History* 'through a certain cycle with a beginning, a middle and an end'. However, if while endorsing that recommendation we also recall the definition of history as a dialogue between the past and the present, we need to consider at some length what the present consists of. And we also need to fit the dialogue into a wider context of world views.

Let us take the second of these two desiderata first.

World process or civilisations?

As Leffler has observed, *We Now Know* 'resonates with the triumphalism that runs through our contemporary culture, and in many ways it is the scholarly diplomatic counterpart of Francis Fukuyama's *The End of History*'.[14] The decline and fall of the USSR did indeed bring about a triumphalist reaction in the USA, exemplified by Fukuyama's *The End of History and The Last Man* (to give its full title), first published in 1992. Appropriately enough, the work is addressed primarily to American readers. Beginning with the observation that the twentieth century 'has made all of us into deep historical pessimists', Fukuyama goes on to make clear what he means by 'all of us': 'As individuals, we can of course be optimistic concerning our personal prospects for health and happiness. By long-standing tradition, Americans as a people are said to be continually hopeful about the future.' Having made some acknowledgement of widespread fear and apprehension, Fukuyama proceeds to adhere to that long-standing tradition, announcing that 'good news has come' in the shape of victory for liberalism, that is democracy and the free market. In this manner, his book is indeed infused with the same spirit that we have detected above in some of latter-day historiography in the USA on the Cold War.

By history, as we need to understand from the beginning, Fukuyama means 'a single, coherent, evolutionary process, when taking into account the experience of all peoples in all times'. Here he follows Hegel, who found the end of that process in the liberal state, rather than Marx, who asserted that it would be found in a communist society. For Hegel, man emerged from the master–slave relationship with the French Revolution, to which Fukuyama adds the American Revolution. Later:

> Though the Bolshevik and Chinese revolutions seemed like monumental events at the time, their only lasting effect would be to spread the already established principles of liberty and equality to formerly backward and oppressed peoples, and to force those countries of the developed world already living in acordance with those principles to implement them more completely.[15]

Four years after the appearance of Francis Fukuyama's *The End of History and the Last Man*, there was published an almost equally celebrated book taking a different approach, Samuel P. Huntington's *The Clash of Civilizations and the Remaking of World Order*. No doubt it would be an over-simplification to say that Fukuyama's triumphalist global interpretation of 1992 had been replaced by an apprehensive fragmented approach by Huntington in 1996. Nevertheless, there is a marked difference of mood from one book to the other, noted by Huntington himself. For him, Fukuyama's basic assumption was that 'the end of the Cold War meant the end of significant conflict in global politics and the emergence of one relatively harmonious world'. But this was put forward in a 'moment of euphoria', which could not last any more than similar moments after the end of the First and Second World Wars. And so, observes Huntington, 'the one harmonious world paradigm is clearly too divorced from reality to be a useful guide to the post-Cold War world'.

In its place, Huntington offers the central theme 'that culture and cultural identities, which at the broadest level are civilization identities, are shaping the patterns of cohesion, disintegration, and conflict in the post-Cold War world'. For Huntington, the West is in decline, while Asian civilisations are on the rise economically, politically and militarily, and Muslim civilisations are expanding demographically. In an emergent world order based on civilisations:

> The survival of the West depends on Americans reaffirming their Western identity and Westerners accepting their civilization as unique not universal and uniting to renew and preserve it against challenges from non-Western societies. Avoidance of a global war of civilizations depends on world leaders accepting and cooperating to maintain the multicivilizational character of global politics.

At the end, Huntington is not a million miles away from Fukuyama's beginning in paying special attention to the USA, accepting Richard Hofstadter's observation that 'It has been our fate as a nation not to have ideologies but to be one'. Arguably, his remarks are addressed primarily to his fellow Americans, even though they have not made such an impact as Fukyama's on the historiography of the Cold War. Certainly, in a list of the interests of the USA and Europe serving the cause of Western civilisation, the former principal Cold War adversary finds itself in a subordinate position. The recommendation is 'to accept Russia as the core state of Orthodoxy and a major regional power with legitimate interests in the security of its southern borders'. Elsewhere, Huntington suggests: 'While the Soviet Union was a superpower with global interests, Russia is a major power with regional and civilizational interests.' Understandably enough, this relegation has not been readily accepted by the Russians, especially those who look upon themselves as leading the struggle for the preservation of Europe, even of the West as a whole, from the advance of Asia.[16]

Late twentieth-century publications bear ample testimony to the continued liveliness of the debate among Russian historians about directions to be taken after the collapse of the Soviet Union and Marxism-Leninism. Interpretations of the present predicament and its origins abound, so many indeed that it is difficult for the outsider to keep up with them all. But we will consider some examples, under two headings represented above by Huntington and Fukuyama respectively, 'civilisation' and 'world process'. First let us take 'Russia – A Collapsed Civilisation?', a discussion initiated by A. S. Akhiezer. Suggesting that there are two kinds of basic civilisation or 'supercivilisation', the traditional and the liberal, Akhiezer goes on to observe:

> Russia possesses evident enough attributes of both the traditional civilisation (for example, the mass influence of collectivism giving rise to the creation of historically complicated relationships not conducive to a rise in the effectiveness of human activity) and the liberal (for example, the existence of the liberal movement including the assumption of power by liberal governments in February 1917 and August 1991, the development of the demand for the growth of effectiveness in human activity).

Therefore, to contrast a traditional East with a liberal West is no longer appropriate in any typification of Russia since it occupies a special position between the two supercivilisations. Hence a great schism, which can be expressed in a number of ways, most simply between extremes of society and government. Other countries have not suffered a schism as great as Russia's, Akhiezer insists, but he also asserts that there is more to the specificity of Russia than the schism alone, and that dialogue and analysis may combine to overcome it.[17]

Among other civilisationist paths has been the Eurasian, described in an idiosyncratic manner by the self-proclaimed genius, Lev Gumilëv, who put forward a basic idea of 'impassionedness', possibly better rendered as *élan vital* or life force. Coupled with the concept of the 'noosphere' – that is, the biosphere modified by human ingenuity, adopted from Vladimir Vernadsky – 'impassioned-ness' led on to Gumilëv's theory of the ethnos, a group distinguishable from another by a typical pattern of behaviour, and sometimes combining with other such groups in a superethnos such as the Graeco-Roman, the Byzantine, the Arab, the Ottoman, the West European, the Chinese, the Old Turkish, the Mongol and the Great Russian. While the affinity that could be found within the superethnos was lacking in the relations between one superethnos and another, Great Russia was able to prosper because it could move away from the Byzantine superethnos and resist the West European because of its long symbiosis with the nomads of the steppe. Far from constituting a yoke, the connection with the Mongols prevented Russia from domination by a succession of Western enemies, beginning with the Varangians and continuing through to the Germans and Poles.[18]

While Russia remains 'pluralist', the views put forward by Akhiezer, Gumilëv and their critics, will flourish along with others. *Alternativistika, globalistika, konfliktologiia, refleksologiia, sinergetika* and *virtualistika* have arrived as new sciences, while approaches such as *bikhevioristskie metodiki* [behaviouristic methods] and *keinsianstvo* [Keynesianism] have been considered in an atmosphere that remains volatile. Meanwhile, a considerable number of colleagues in Moscow, St Petersburg and elsewhere have welcomed the opportunity to remain aloof from all grand schemes, to concentrate on 'concrete' problems in the Anglo-American empiricist, pragmatic manner. They too must be recognised.

But by no means all Russian analysts believe that world process or what they call 'formation' has given way to 'civilisation'. Those of such persuasion give emphasis to universal processes, often in the tradition of Marx, but also with suggestions that he was wrong about a number of problems, for example that of the commune, and that all of his doctrine that is still valid was taken from other sources, including Adam Smith and Adam Ferguson of the Scottish Enlighten-ment. Equally, there has been the suggestion that Marx was far too Eurocentric in his approach, which was saved from parochialism by Lenin. Some say drop Marxism but not materialism; others argue that Marxism should be purified and improved. Generally, 'formation' accepts that there are stages through which human development as a whole must pass.[19]

Certainly, through the later nineteenth century to V.O. Kliuchevskii, the modern 'Russian historical tradition' is far from Anglo-American empiricism, although it does bear closer comparison with the French *science* and the German *Wissenschaft* and can broadly be deemed European. Moreover, a close comparison can be made between the 'historical sociology' expounded by Kliuchevskii and the Marxist-Leninism of his Soviet successors: the common aim has been an approach characterised by its *zakonomernost*, or 'regularity of law'. A famous debate in the early 1960s between an American scholar and two Soviet colleagues centred around this concept, which still governs the work of many post-Soviet scholars today.[20]

As a representative of the 'formation' school, let us first take the sociologist Vsevolod Vilchek, who sets out to demonstrate the 'logical *zakonomernost*' of the development of 'non-classical' societies (in the sense of not following normal lines of development), one of them – Russia – in particular. He posits five stages of of production – primitive, slave, feudal, industrial (capitalist) and post-industrial (communist) – parallelled by five kinds of knowledge – pre-mythological, mythological, canonical ('collective-subjective'), scientific (individual and objective) and post-scientific (problematic). He adds a further series of five modes of social communication – pre-oral, oral, written, printed and post-printed – combining with the others to constitute the bare bones of his formation theory. Within this framework, Vilchek assigns a special place to Russia, rejecting analogies ranging through Pinochet's Chile, post-Second World War West Germany, the countries of Eastern Europe and China, because of the failure to take advantage of appropriate opportunities presented in 1987–8. Gorbachev drew back from the brink, fearing a chaos and collapse which his hesitation only made more certain. Here (without suggesting Nero or any other personal counterpart to Gorbachev), Vilchek finds a resemblance solely to a literally classical society – ancient Rome – which might grow if the Commonwealth of Independent States develops into the States of Eurasia.[21]

To turn to another example of the 'formation' approach, Igor M. Diakonoff considers that the 'process of the history of mankind can best be likened to the flow of a river', with its own laws and regularities, although he entitles his book *The Paths of History*. Marxism, 'one of the great doctrines of the nineteenth century', can now be seen to have several limitations, he believes, especially regarding the first and the last of its five 'formations': neither pre-class nor communist society can be shown to have the 'motive contradictions' that are central to Marx's dialectic of history. (The middle three 'formations', all with class antagonisms, are slaveholding, feudal and capitalist.) Diakonoff substitutes his own eight phases of the historical process, each of them with its own system of social values or ideology and a characteristic level of military development: primitive, primitive communal, early antiquity, imperial antiquity, middle ages, stable absolutist post-medieval, capitalist and post-capitalist. He asserts that 'The unity of the laws of the historical process is made apparent also because they can be identified in Europe as well as on the other extremity of Eurasia', in Japan and also in South America. But he insists that process does not mean progress, since there is regress too: 'there is no progress without loss, and the more one progresses, the more one loses.'

Here, we shall concentrate on the eighth, post-capitalist phase as expounded by Diakonoff, who finds its first signs in the 1930s, arising from the recurring problem of capitalist overproduction. Keynesian solutions to this problem, such as the New Deal's governmental 'pump priming', showed the way forward, although even today they have yet to spread throughout the whole world. The features of the eighth phase include: freedom of opinion and religion; nuclear and other destructive weapons capable of destroying humanity; mechanisation and electronisation of information and of everyday life; increasing replacement of books and cinema by television and computers. But, perhaps most important of all, there is the obsolescence of old classes and the impact of the rise of a 'new social class' drawn from the service sector and the intelligentsia along with the growth of large international firms in industry and a 'green' labour-saving revolution in agriculture. A sharp fall in child and general mortality means that 'family-planning on a universal scale becomes a life-and-death necessity for the human race'.

The eighth phase actually begins along with the emergence of its most important diagnostic features, which coincided with the arrival of the hydrogen bomb accompanied by the Cold War and decolonisation. A loss of identity stimulates local nationalisms, although no minor independent states can arise or survive. The most negative prospects are the contamination and pollution brought about by nuclear armaments as well as through other branches of industrial activity. The possibility remains of large-scale wars involving not only nuclear but also bacteriological and chemical weapons. Even without wars, humanity is nevertheless threatened by the arrival of plagues which could upset Earth's biological balance. There are two most likely scenarios: either humankind will die out by the twenty-second century along with most of the biosphere as we know it; or it will reverse population growth while controlling and directing scientific advance.[22]

Diakonoff first published his book in 1994, and all of the work reviewed in this section has been produced in the 1990s. It will certainly have to be taken into consideration in any future comprehensive consideration of the Cold War, and of the relationship between the superpowers too. But history continues to move on in a manner which continues to surprise and shock. Let us attempt to analyse its trajectory at the end of the millennium before moving on to evaluate the past in summary and consider the future in conclusion.

The end of the millennium

Returning to our central concern with superpower, we must first ask the question: is there only one left? Not so, according to the former German Chancellor Helmut Schmidt:

The Americans now think they are the only superpower in the world. This is a misunderstanding of their real situation. Russia will stay weak for at least another twenty-five years, maybe fifty, two generations. Nobody really knows. It's a country in turmoil. Yet they are still a superpower.

Among those of the opposite persuasion, certain that only one superpower remains, is Zbigniew Brzezinski, whom I quote with his own italics:

> *America stands supreme in the four decisive domains of global power*: militarily, it has an unmatched global reach; economically, it remains the main locomotive of global growth, even if challenged in some aspects by Japan and Germany (neither of which enjoys the other attributes of global might); technologically, it retains the overall lead in the cutting-edge areas of innovation; and culturally, despite some crassness, it enjoys an appeal that is unrivaled, especially among the world's youth – all of which gives the United States a political clout that no other state comes close to matching. *It is the combination of all four that makes America the only comprehensive global superpower.*

Making little or no reference to the USA's internal problems or to global problems such as the environment, Brzezinski concentrates on how to secure what he considers to be 'the chief geopolitical prize', Eurasia. Here, Europe constitutes a democratic bridgehead into the 'black hole' of the former Soviet Union, where Russia 'remains a major strategic player, in spite of its weakened state and probably prolonged malaise'.[23]

Let us subject these observations to some scrutiny. First, recall the definition given at the beginning of Chapter 1: 'A "superpower" must be able to conduct a global strategy including the possibility of destroying the world; to command vast economic potential and performance; and to present a universal ideology.' Let us accept that the USA retains in full all three characteristics, while there is considerable doubt, to put it mildly, concerning those of its erstwhile rival. But the present situation is by no means completely clearcut. Looking at Brzezinski's definition geopolitically, we have to agree that, even after the collapse of the Soviet Union, that Russia 'remains a major strategic player' as the largest country in the world. That vast amount of Eurasian real estate simply cannot be omitted from global strategic calculations, even if most of it remains empty; indeed, even as it becomes emptier, for while the world's population has risen from 3 billion in the 1960s to 6 billion in the 1990s, the number of Russians has been falling and threatens to fall even more steeply to 140 millions and below. The possibility of such demographic decline has implications of catastrophe, especially when the millions in the most populous neighbour are taken into consideration. A nightmare scenario is indicated in the following sardonic riddle:

Question: what will be the greatest problem of international relations in the
   twenty-first century?
Answer: the frontier between Finland and China.

In spite of this and other evidence of frailty, however, Russia retains the power to
annihilate humankind. And in unstable political conditions, the possibility that
some reckless finger might set off the Russian trigger is an even greater nightmare
than than the comparatively customary, and therefore comfortable, Soviet threat.
Meanwhile, Russia retains vast economic potential even at a time of disastrous
economic performance, while, as we have seen above, carrying on the search for a
new ideology.

   Could there be another superpower? A revived unified Europe is one possibility, but another, more likely, is China. Consider one individual's view taken in
1988 of the world as it would be in 1999. Richard Nixon had made China one of
the centrepieces of his foreign policy. Drawn together in the early 1970s by what
he saw as the imperatives of national security, China and the USA should in his
estimation continue their close military and economic co-operation to counter
the threat from the USSR, which he considered to be aiming at world domination, persistently infringing human rights along the way. He said little or nothing
about the Chinese infringement of human rights, or any ambition that the PRC
might have for world domination. Like nearly everybody else in 1988, Nixon did
not foresee the collapse of the Soviet Union, warning of the superficial charms of
Mikhail Gorbachev without any suggestion that here was the last Soviet leader.[24]
Much of what Nixon said in 1988 turned out to be inaccurate in 1999, and any of
our own forecasts about the twenty-first century will probably turn out the same.
However, it seems probable that, as far as superpower is concerned, what we
might call the fateful triangle of the USA, Russia and the PRC is likely to play an
important part in the foreseeable future.

   A further, somewhat fanciful consideration is that you cannot have one superpower without the other, that the two of them have been inseparable Siamese
twins, especially as far as ideology is concerned. That is to say, they have been the
embodiments and advocates of the two most powerful sets of ideas devised so far,
capitalism and socialism. This thesis and antithesis could be continued by the USA
and a new partner, the PRC, still governed by a self-styled communist regime in
spite of many appearances to the contrary. Alternatively, the argument could be
put forward that both capitalism and socialism are becoming increasingly
inappropriate under the pressure of new imperatives. That is to say, we have not
reached the end of history, since the arguments put forward by Adam Smith in the
eighteenth century and Karl Marx in the nineteenth century can no longer carry
complete conviction in the late twentieth century. The principal stumbling block
for both capitalism and socialism is the impending exhaustion of the earth's
natural resources and the associated pollution of the environment already too

much under way. In other words, the blue and the red must give way to the green. Moreover, could it be that what we have called 'superpower' is a twentieth-century phenomenon, and that the process of globalisation changes the nature of the game? Or has 'superpower' been just part of a sequence of the rise and fall of great powers in some huge cycle of civilisations? In this book, we have used as a basic metaphor the course of a human life. However, in this chapter, we are confronting the question: death or rebirth? In other words, we are admitting the possibility that history is not at an end.

We will return to such general considerations after a retrospective analysis of the years 1998–9, when the world might be said to have been suffering from what we could call Post-Cold War syndrome. But an analysis by whom? It is high time that the use of the term 'we' in this book is subjected to some fuller scrutiny. The first point to make is that it is not always exclusively authorial, but often includes you, the reader. It carries the assumption that we are all interested in history as a means of understanding at least some aspects of the world around us and, possibly, as a path to more complete comprehension. But such aspiration, whether of the more modest or more ambitious variety, needs to be tempered by the realisation that we, that is you and I, are limited in our vision by many considerations, including the position that we occupy in time as well as place. For example, as we have amply seen, Russians and Americans tend to view the world differently. Veterans of the First World War will have a different outlook to those of us who came to maturity during the Second World War and the Cold War. Whoever we are, none of us has a mature memory of the year 1898, to which we gave some emphasis at the beginning of Chapter 2. Almost certainly, few or none of us will be in a position to experience the vicissitudes of the year 2098, and will probably have even more varied ideas about circumstances and perceptions likely to prevail then. Needless to say, beyond place and time, we all have a personal philosophy. So did the politicians and other individuals included in this study who have also been subject to what we might call 'historical parallax', the apparent change of position of an event according to place and time as well as beliefs and values. For example, some emphasis has been given above to the outlooks of the 'Big Three' – Churchill, Roosevelt and Stalin – at the end of the Second World War, and even more to the outlooks of Lenin and Wilson at the end of the First World War after the Russian Revolution. More recently, those of us who have experienced the elation and disappointment of 1968, or of 1989 and 1991, must have different outlooks to those who have not.

This phenomenon will be of influence as we give emphasis to developments at the end of the twentieth century first in the USA and Russia, and then in the wider world. Let us begin at the top, with the two presidents and their outlooks. Is it possible to see Clinton and Yeltsin in any way as the successors to the progenitors of superpower, Wilson and Lenin? The second case is the easier to consider, since the Russian president explicitly rejected the world outlook in which he was brought up and began his career. Whatever Yeltsinism is, it has nothing to do with Marxism-Leninism. Throughout the year 1999 up to his resignation on its last day, the ailing Russian President maintained a nominal hold on the reins of power by hiring and firing prime ministers and other advisers, but otherwise cut rather a sorry spectacle as he did so, making little reference to the principles on which he was operating. Twice, he became bogged down in the war in Chechnya, motives for the action ranging from the search for electoral advantage to the preservation of the Russian state. As for Clintonism, in the context of the most publicised events of 1998, some definitions could be ribald. But, as far as the public policies that the US President attempted to pursue were concerned, there were indeed some distinct echoes of those inaugurated by President Wilson. These encouraged him to support NATO intervention in Kosovo, for example.

The political process excited little interest in either the USA or Russia. More American citizens attended church every week than could be bothered to vote every two or four years, while an even deeper cynicism was rampant among their Russian counterparts. The assertion that democracy is the worst form of government except for all the others came under great strain when its participants showed little interest in the major issues of our time. Nobody would want the Cold War to return, but it could be argued that its constraints nevertheless imposed a certain discipline and seriousness of purpose.

As far as the economy is concerned, the USA appeared to be going from strength to strength, while Russia went from bad to worse. At the meeting of the World Trade Organisation in November 1999, however, some US citizens protested about the manner in which their country's leading participation threatened the development of the world's poorer countries at a time when Russia looked as if it was becoming one of the latter. And there were still a few voices warning of the possibility of another American, or even global recession.

Culturally, the world seemed to be unified by the new information technology catching everybody in the Net, with the consequence of a more complete US domination of the ether. On the other hand, there were arguments that the impact of IT was superficial, and that Russian and other national cultures would continue to survive within the framework of their nation-states.

Overriding all other considerations are, or should be, what we might call green imperatives. In September 1999, a UN report entitled *Global Environment Outlook 2000* indicated that there were two main trends. First, the ecosystem was under threat from serious imbalances in productivity and in distribution of goods and services. Second, the international co-ordination of care for the environment was lagging behind developments in economy and society. In the late 1990s, carbon dioxide emissions were nearly four times more voluminous than half a century previously. Meanwhile, many experts were agreeing that with the use of agrichemicals in intensive farming, the combustion of fossil fuel and the cultivation of leguminous crops, the nitrogen cycle might be disrupted in a manner as threatening to the environment as the disruption of the carbon cycle. Moreover, the increasing use of pesticides, heavy metals, small particulates and other substances posed further threats. Natural disasters and unusual weather conditions were both on the increase. Forests and grasslands were being destroyed. As a consequence of rapid population growth, about a fifth of the world's people could not use safe drinking water and a half lacked a safe sanitation system. Seas and cities were subject to pollution, as was the atmosphere in general. Human intervention was disrupting the ecology of disease agents and upsetting the balance of health. Both the USA and Russia contributed more than their fair share to the worsening situation, the former through the extremely high per capita use of natural resources with large amounts of post-consumer and industrial wastes, the latter through land and water pollution as well as forest depletion. The picture was not all doom and gloom, since there were possibilities of a worldwide reduction of CFCs (chlorofluorocarbons) en route to the closure of the hole in the ozone layer, and Europe's reduction by 75 per cent of sulphur dioxide emissions to eradicate the menace of acid rain.[25]

But the question remains as to why more action has not been taken. Will we go on as we are until the only people able to survive are those who can afford to buy space helmets and suits along with clean air and pure water, walking the earth (or rather fenced-off enclaves) like Neil Armstrong and his successors walked on the moon? At least part of the answer, I would suggest, is the aforesaid Post-Cold War syndrome, in other words, the consequence of triumphalism throughout the West, especially in the USA. Now that liberal democracy and the free market have swept all before them, there appears to be more of a case for celebration than for complaint. However, even as the Cold War was beginning, the larger problem was certainly discerned. In 1949, in his book *The Vital Center: The Politics of Freedom*, Arthur M. Schlesinger, Jr wrote:

> The human race may shortly be confronted by an entirely new range of problems – problems of naked subsistence whose solution will require the combined efforts of all people if the race is to survive. We have raped the earth too long, and we are paying the price today in the decline of fertility. Industrial society has disturbed the balance of nature, and no one can estimate the consequences. ... In the light of this epic struggle to restore man to his foundations in nature, the political conflicts which obsess us today seem puny and flickering. Unless we are soon able to make the world safe for democracy, we may commit ourselves too late to the great and final struggle to make the world safe for humanity.[26]

Still adhering to the Wilsonian dream, Schlesinger also had intimations more than half a century ago of the nightmare of ecological disaster that confronts us all too clearly today.

From the past: summary

What Schlesinger wrote in 1949 makes a bigger impact half a century and more on: the political conflicts which obsessed us throughout the years of the Cold War do indeed appear puny and flickering in the light of the epic struggle to restore humanity to its foundations in nature. Another way in which to place those Cold War years in perspective is to take the long view stretching back over half the second millennium and more. That has been the basic purpose of this book, the approach being analogous to other avenues of human enquiry. For example, meteorologists improve long-term forecasts by studying as much of past weather patterns as possible, assisted by dendrochronologists examining tree-rings and geologists examining deep core samples.

As part of the exercise, we have to realise that the present barely exists, since it is over in an instant. To some extent, it can be defined not only as the end of the past but also as the beginning of the future, or even as the past becoming the future. However, in that complicated process, there are new elements, some not immediately apparent, as well as old, which can be viewed with somewhat more confidence. To put the point another way, and specifically, the American–Russian relationship can be understood only if it is scrutinised in full. And the most accessible aspect of that relationship is its past.[27]

This has been the implicit argument of the preceding five chapters, which we will now summarise. First, a few words about the basic metaphor. To describe the rise and fall of the superpowers, we have used the analogy of a human life, taken through five phases each comprising a chapter: inheritance, conception, gestation, youth and maturity. In such a manner, we have given emphasis to the temporary nature of the phenomenon. We have also opened ourselves up to all kinds of discussion about the nature of life itself as well as the employment of the basic metaphor. In this chapter, we have posed the even more difficult question of their legacy: death or rebirth? But let us leave that question until we have considered the five phases, approaching them thematically, that is to say, politically, economically and culturally.

The political inheritance of the USA goes back to classical times, most evident in the architecture of Washington, DC, but also to be found everywhere in the discourse of the Founding Fathers. Likewise, Catherine the Great, Empress of Russia in the later eighteenth century, both commissioned buildings and produced writings drawing on the traditions of Greece and Rome. Diplomatic conventions at this time had similar roots. Simultaneously, both future superpowers were evolving political systems adapted to actual local conditions as well as assimilating the theoretical inheritance, both classical and more recent: federal union and enlightened absolutism respectively.

The period of the French Revolution and Napoleon updated and supplemented both the language and the practice of politics. While the USA made a certain contribution here, the Russian Empire added little. Nevertheless, both powers were singled out for future dominance by one of Catherine the Great's enlightened correspondents, Baron Melchior von Grimm, nearly half a century before the more famous prediction of Alexis de Tocqueville. More immediately, Russia's contribution to the defeat of Napoleon and to the settlement of Europe afterwards was outstanding at a time when the USA was fighting a second war for independence against Britain and then going on to push back the frontier in North America while showing a protective interest in the Western hemisphere – Central and South as well as North America – in the enunciation of the Monroe Doctrine.

However, as the nineteenth century wore on, the British and other empires of Western Europe constituted the great world powers until towards the century's end, when first Germany and then the USA announced their arrival. Russia was always there, looming over the continent of Europe at the same time as occupying large parts of Central and Northern Asia. The fear of Cossacks returning to Paris with snow on their boots never completely disappeared, while apprehension about the safety of the Middle East and India led to the Crimean War and then to the Great Game of empire between Russia and Britain. But the shock defeat of the Tsar's forces in the war against Japan in 1904–5 lowered the rating of the power of Nicholas II abroad and helped to provoke a revolution at home. While the USA was vigorously asserting its presence in Latin America and the Pacific at the same time as proclaiming the superiority of its democratic system of government, the last Tsar was making a belated and half-hearted attempt to make his absolutism constitutional at the same time as attempting to ensure that defeat in Asia would not be followed by reverses in Europe.

The conception of superpower took place as a consequence of the imperial showdown that came to be known as the First World War. It was marked by the clash between Wilsonism and Leninism in the immediate aftermath of two of the most momentous consequences of the global conflict, the entry of the USA into what had hitherto been a largely European affair, and the Russian Revolution, both Nicholas II's autocracy and Kerensky's democratic republic falling in their turn before the seizure of power by the Bolsheviks. From this very beginning, however, one salient point needs to be made. Woodrow Wilson spoke out on behalf of the world's greatest power, with maximum publicity; Vladimir Lenin tried to make the voice heard of one of its weakest, and was almost totally ignored. As a consequence of the First World War, the USA went from strength to strength. The Soviet Russian Republic was virtually crippled by the reverses inflicted by Germany and its allies, then by a horrendous civil war compounded by foreign intervention. In such circumstances, so to speak, the less Lenin was heard, the louder he shouted. Then, after the World War and Russian Civil War came to an end, and the frenzied improvisation of War Communism was given up, he was obliged to make the great compromise of the New Economic Policy with the peasant majority within what was soon to become the Union of Soviet Socialist Republics, while coming to terms with the capitalist powers which he had previously been denouncing. By the time of Lenin's collapse early in 1923, the Soviet Union was set on a new course. In some respects, the last years of Woodrow Wilson are more misleading, giving the impression that the USA's failure to become a member of the League of Nations meant a withdrawal of its world power. But the ups and downs of US domestic politics, extremely significant though they are, must not blind us to wider realities. The League could be defeated by the Senate, but the USA remained the major victor of the First World War. Wilson might collapse before the end of his administration in 1921, but his successor Harding was soon to issue invitations to the other major powers to a Conference on the Limitation of Armaments in Washington, where the major influence was the host nation. Soviet Russia wanted to be invited, but was ignored.

The Washington Conference indicated the nature of the gestation of super-power. The USA called, and the other major powers responded. At the same time, the Soviet aim of world revolution was kept alive by the Communist International, which exerted little or no global influence apart from causing alarm. As the international situation deteriorated again, the Soviet Union sought agreements with its new neighbours in East and Central Europe and with the Western European states, while the United States could hold back from such entanglements. Both the USSR and USA entered the Second World War as a consequence of surprise attacks, but the similarity ends there. One future superpower was almost mortally wounded, while the other suffered a painful scratch. At the end of the second global conflict, the USA became a more complete world power than at the end of the first, while the USSR was devastated a second time.

And so, the Cold War during the youth of the superpowers was not a struggle between equals. Yet the major players in the great poker game, the super two taking over from the big three, could not always be absolutely sure of which cards their opponents held. Now that the Cold War is rightly or wrongly thought to be over, we are in danger of forgetting what it was like to live through. There was bluff and counterbluff and the stakes were often raised, even very nearly to the point of the final call. Traditional geopolitical considerations gave the advantage to the dominant force in the Eurasian heartland, the USSR, especially during the period after the Chinese Revolution when a Moscow–Peking communist monolith appeared to exist. But appearances were deceptive. That monolith never existed, and the USSR was scarcely strong enough in the first phase of the Cold War to achieve the ambitions ascribed to it.

This heartland meant less in the second phase of the Cold War, post-1968, which took in all the world's continents more completely than before and was also characterised by the People's Republic of China emerging as a third potential superpower. Moreover, strategists were becoming more aware that concepts such as the heartland were becoming redundant in an age of intercontinental ballistic missiles. In retrospect, both they and other analysts should have seen what was coming, but hardly anybody did. We were all becoming too accustomed to the idea of a mature phase in the relationship between the two superpowers, especially after Gorbachev seemed to be putting new life into the Soviet system. And so, the collapse of the Eastern bloc and then of the Soviet Union came almost as a complete surprise. But then, if the Cold War was over, the relationship between the superpowers, both the victorious and the defeated, had to continue in some shape or form, as the prospect of a third superpower loomed ever larger. Would there be death or rebirth?

In this brief survey of the political development, we have given more attention to inheritance and conception than to gestation, youth and maturity. This reflects a view of life itself but more particularly of history, agreeing with Marx that the tradition of dead generations weighs on us like a nightmare, although also insisting that there is to be found in this tradition a tiny element of unfulfilled dream.

Let us turn to a sphere of human activity where Marx's determinism has been most celebrated; the economic. At the end of Chapter 1, far less space was devoted to Karl Marx than to Colin White. This was mostly because of the belief that the circumstances of today are very different to those in which not only Karl Marx but also his predecessor Adam Smith put forward their views, and also because of the belief that Marx's class conflict and Smith's competition might well be superseded as the engine of history by the more universal wish for security. Less important overall, but more so in this specific instance, neither Marx nor Smith devoted central attention to the subject of this book, the relationship of the USA and Russia, both concentrating on Britain and to some extent Europe in their major work.

White hits the nail on the head when he gives emphasis to the very different conditions in which America and Russia developed throughout the years of imperialism and beyond. These conditions largely determined the nature and pace of the two processes of industrialisation, capitalist and socialist, and are still with us to a considerable extent even now. They also constituted the background to the economic rivalry between the USA and the USSR, to which we will now turn before returning to the present predicament.

Many skilled and energetic economists, both Soviet and Western, devoted much of their time to comparisons of the economic performance of the two superpowers up to the point of the USSR's collapse. Their methods, arguments and findings cannot be analysed, or even summarised here. But one earnest, reflective post-Soviet study has come to the following conclusions:

1   'The former Soviet Union was especially active (and not without success!) in building up resources for catching up with the USA': employment in the economy was 1.5 times more, in industry 1.4 times more, capital formation was three times greater. More iron and steel was produced in the Soviet Union, to name but two items. All of this was the consequence of 'huge investment and accumulation, faster rates of growth of means of production, the presence of gigantic natural and human resources and the operation of extensive factors in economic development'.

2   But Soviet gross output in industry was less impressive than American: the former was no more than 51 per cent of the latter.

3   'The Soviet Union had very weak results in the field of high-tech output, personal consumption and efficiency of production.' The USA produced five times more plastic, ten times more PCs and ten times more durable consumer goods. American ratios were higher in labour productivity, material and capital output as well.

4   In general: 'The totalitarian command non-market economy could not be competitive with a developed market economy.'

Given the different economic goals of capitalism in the USA and socialism in the USSR, then, the Soviet economy had its periods of success but failed disastrously in the end. During the period of gestation of superpower, there was considerable recovery in the 1920s, fast heavy industrial growth in the 1930s, and a remarkable performance in the difficult conditions of the Second World War. Nevertheless, in spite of the reverses of the Great Depression and the no more than partial success of the New Deal, the USA was far in front by 1945 and maintained that lead afterwards, even if there were some appearances to the contrary during the youth of the superpowers in the late 1950s and early 1960s. From about the middle of the 1960s, however, in the period of maturity, there was a deceleration in the growth of Soviet heavy industry, 'traditionally the main engine of relatively high rates of growth in the past', and also in light industry and transportation and, worst of all, in agriculture. Moreover, the USSR was far behind in the technological revolution. Calculations on the eve of the collapse of the Soviet Union in 1990 indicated that its GNP was approximately no more than one-third of that of the USA, and at least one expert suggested that the figure was as low as 14 per cent. The post-Soviet performance has been even worse, prompting at least some doubts about the suitability for the Russian Federation of 'a developed market economy'. In other words, there is continued divergence rather than convergence.[28]

Convergence is a cultural as well as economic concept. As noted in Chapter 1, Alexander Herzen observed in 1865 that 'The North American States and Russia represent two solutions which are opposite but incomplete, and therefore complement rather than exclude each other.' He hoped for the reconciliation of American individuality and Russian collectivism in a higher form of existence. But here I shall use the pH 'universal indicator' test employed more extensively elsewhere, defining Europe in the first instance as the 'neutral', America as 'alkali' turning blue and Russia as 'acid' turning red. To take one example of how the two frontiers were influenced by the continent in between, Montesquieu's Eurocentric *The Spirit of the Laws* was used by the American Founding Fathers in their creation of a federal republic, while the Russian Empress Catherine the Great adapted it for the purposes of her 'enlightened absolutism'. But this was not so much a personal choice as, on the one hand, the inbuilt tendency in the USA towards representative government, ultimately democracy, the individualistic political culture formed by the immigrants from Europe in their new setting, and on the other hand, the Russian communal spirit, the authoritarian, collectivist political culture forming in Russia over the centuries in *its* particular environment.

This is the inheritance of the superpowers, the given at the beginning of the twentieth century on the eve of conception. But this moment brings the pH test to an end, or at least changes its nature, since the predominance of European culture is no more. Through the years of gestation, a challenge is offered to traditional European liberalism in the shape of two kinds of internationalism both of European origin and constituting the old pH test's last application: Wilsonism and Leninism. Through the years of youth and maturity, the centre is cut out, so to speak, and the peripheries take over. As John Gould Fletcher put it at the end of the 1920s, the situation of Europe had been both 'grotesque and tragic' throughout the decade, the continent having become 'like a patient suffering from shell-shock who acts irresponsibly and has no coherent purpose in life'. Of the 'two new world-philosophies' on offer, Europe had chosen neither. But it had played a major part in producing them both, and therefore already contained something of each in its make-up.

There were now two pH tests so to speak, but more self-conscious than their predecessor. European predominance evolved over a long period of time, and was taken for granted by such figures as Lord Bryce on the eve of its collapse. Wilsonism and Leninism actively strove for global reaction, to turn the world blue or red. Attempting to help these processes along the way, there were 'fellow-travellers' or even communists in the USA, dissident admirers of the USA in the USSR. But from the very beginning, the USA held a distinct advantage, at a time when the first, written media of mass communication were being overtaken by the radio and cinema, then by television. Arguably, too, it was not just the all-pervasiveness of American culture but also its intrinsic superiority that was to win the day. At least, while the ideal of 'a new Soviet man' fell far short of realisation, the continual proclamation of individual freedom constituted a powerful message. Nevertheless, we have to recognise both that it needs to be balanced by a sense of community, and that it has by no means fully existed in or been applied by the countries which proclaim it. Throughout the years of the existence of the Soviet Union, its supporters never tired in their often justified criticism of the USA's shortcomings in this respect both at home, especially regarding race, poverty and violence, and abroad, especially in Latin America.

Towards the future: conclusion

The debate is far from completely along traditional paths: there are new signposts, new sciences, as indicated above. On the other hand, there are those who hold on to the past as a source of reassurance, still insisting on the uniqueness of the civilisation of Russia and the USA, as opposed to the growing realisation of variations in a global process. But we all need to rethink.

In 1976, Gavin and Blakeley reasserted Aristotle's statement that philosophy begins in wonder, and defined the human being as a 'questioning animal'.[29] Nearly a quarter of a century onward, we still have not wondered, or questioned enough. But, at the beginning of a new millennium, we have reached another historical turning point, the full significance of which may take some years to realise. No doubt, the 'world process' and 'civilisation' modes of investigation will continue, as will many forms of human enquiry in different directions.

In conclusion, let us consider briefly some of the problems that could arise in the near future. First, there remains the danger of nuclear annihilation brought about by the arms race of the Cold War. Second, there are the 'green' problems as described in the UN report entitled *Global Environment Outlook 2000* and summarised above, including many different threats to human health. If these are not enough, there are more, as described by Bill Joy, a leading software expert:

> The 21st century technologies – genetics, nanotechnology and robotics – are so powerful that they can spawn whole new classes of accidents and abuses. Most dangerously, for the first time these accidents and abuses are widely within the reach of individuals or small groups. They will not require large facilities or rare raw materials. Knowledge alone will enable the use of them...

For example, there could be no defence against genetically engineered viruses. Meanwhile, nanotechnology, enabling scientists to use individual molecules as circuit elements, could create smart machines small enough to fit inside a blood vessel and able to reproduce themselves like computer viruses; robotics could make human beings superfluous by producing superintelligent machines. 'Once an intelligent robot exists, it is only a small step to a robot species – to an intelligent robot that can make evolved copies of itself', writes Joy. 'The only realistic alternative I see is relinquishment: to limit development of the technologies that are too dangerous by limiting our pursuit of certain kinds of knowledge.'[30]

Here again we meet the problem of generation parallax. Computing science, like lyric poetry and mathematics, is more creatively approached by the young, who also tend to be impatient with stories of yesteryear told them by older teachers. There have been some woeful predictions of the complete loss of a sense of the past. In view of the crimes against humanity with which the record is littered, some might say good riddance. On the other hand, as argued above, without some understanding of previous millennia, we will find a sense of direction for the new millennium elusive.

Faced with the possibility of the obsolescence of their discipline, historians can do no more than carry on their work in a manner which reflects awareness of it. As far as the subject of this book is concerned, they should be encouraged to stop fighting the battles and celebrating the victories of the Cold War, however influential their own experiences of them. For triumphalism in the USA certainly provokes a powerful reaction in Russia.[31] In the pursuit of objectivity, they can draw encouragement from the words of a colleague written at an earlier critical time, in the early 1940s. Having served in the First World War and still emerging from the shock of France's sudden defeat in the Second World War, Marc Bloch worked on *The Historian's Craft*, still incomplete at the time of his execution as a leader of the Resistance in 1944. Bloch observed:

> When all is said and done, a single word, 'understanding', is the beacon light of our studies. Let us not say that the true historian is a stranger to emotion: he has that, at all events. 'Understanding', in all honesty, is a word pregnant with difficulties, but also with hope. Moreover, it is a friendly word. Even in action, we are far too prone to judge. It is so easy to denounce. We are never sufficiently understanding. Whoever differs from us – a foreigner or a political adversary – is almost inevitably considered evil. A little more understanding of people would be necessary merely for guidance, in the conflicts which are unavoidable; all the more to prevent them while there is yet time.

For Marc Bloch, 'the only true history, which can advance only through mutual aid, is universal history'. This book is intended as a contribution to this kind of history.[32]

Indeed, at a time when superficial calm disguises great danger, human societies will not progress through praise of themselves or blame of others, but through understanding of what unites them. In particular, within the universal context, the relationship between the USA and Russia will remain of key significance in any foreseeable future. They could through collaboration make a vast contribution to the world's continuance. Their enmity could yet produce global destruction. After the presumed end of the Cold War, then, the question about the legacy of the twentieth-century superpowers remains open: death or rebirth?

Notes

1 Inheritance: nations and empires, before 1898

1 [Joseph G. Whelan], *Soviet Diplomacy and Negotiating Behavior: Emerging New Context for U.S. Diplomacy*, Washington, DC, 1979.

2 For example, see W.H. Parker, *The Super-Powers: The United States and Soviet Union Compared*, London, 1972; Denis J.B. Shaw, *Russia in the Modern World: A New Geography*, Oxford, 1999.

3 Edward Keenan, 'Muscovite Political Folkways', *The Russian Review*, vol. 45, no. 2, 1986, pp. 118, 125, 128, 135, 167. For criticisms of Keenan's article, see *Russian Review*, vol. 46, no. 4, 1987. One of Keenan's severest critics, Richard Hellie, had already offered an alternative view of a 'garrison state' in 'The Structure of Modern Russian History: Towards a Dynamic Model', *Russian History*, vol. 4, no. 1, 1977, pp. 1–22. On the Mongols, see, for example, C. Halperin, *Russia and the Golden Horde: The Mongol Impact on Medieval Russian History*, Bloomington, Ind., 1985.

4 Keenan, 'Muscovite Political Folkways', p. 118.

5 Dmitry Obolensky, *Byzantium and the Slavs: Collected Studies*, London, 1971, p. 35. Arnold Toynbee wrote that 'the Soviet Union of today, like the Grand Duchy of Moscow in the fourteenth century, reproduces the salient features of the mediaeval East Roman Empire' ('Russia's Byzantine Heritage', *Civilization on Trial*, Oxford, 1948, pp. 181–2).

6 Alan Macfarlane, 'Socio-economic Revolution in England and the Origin of the Modern World', in Roy Porter and Mikulas Teich (eds), *Revolutions in History*, Cambridge, 1986, pp. 145–66, especially 147, 163. For a spirited defence of the traditional view of British liberties stretching back to Magna Carta, see the letters of J.H. Hexter to *The Times Literary Supplement*, 2 September and 28 October 1983.

7 Richard Hakluyt, *The Principal Navigations...*, vol. 2, Glasgow, 1903, pp. 209–10, 297–8 (spelling modernised).

8 ibid., vol. 8, 1904, p. 138.

9 David Cressy, 'Elizabethan America: "God's Own Latitude?"', *History Today*, July 1986, pp. 44–50, especially from p. 50. See also David Cressy, *Coming Over: Migration and Communication between England and New England in the Seventeenth Century*, Cambridge, 1987.

10 Cressy, 'Elizabethan America', p. 50.

11 Jane Ohlmeyer, ' "Civilizinge of those Rude Partes"; Colonization within Britain and Ireland, 1580s-1640s' in Nicholas Canny (ed.), *The Origins of Empire: British Overseas Enterprise to the Close of the Seventeenth Century*, Oxford, 1998.

12 Marc Raeff, *The Well-Ordered Police State: Social and Institutional Change through Law in the Germanies and Russia*, New Haven, Conn., 1983, pp. 5, 23, 31.

13 G. Schmoller, *The Mercantile System and Its Historical Significance*, New York, 1902, quoted by Albion W. Small, *The Cameralists: The Pioneers of German Social Polity*, Chicago, 1909, pp. 9–10.

14 Lindsey Hughes, *Russia in the Age of Peter the Great*, London, 1998.

15 Walter LaFeber, *The American Age: United States Foreign Policy at Home and Abroad since 1750*, New York, 1989, pp. 7–9.

16 Peter Kolchin, *Unfree Labor: American Slavery and Russian Serfdom*, Cambridge, Mass., 1987, pp. 30–1.

17 Bernard Bailyn, *The Peopling of North America: An Introduction*, New York, 1986, p. 112.

18 David Lovejoy, *The Glorious Revolution in America*, New York, 1972.

19 Webster quoted and Johnson and others discussed in Daniel J. Boorstin, *The Americans: The Colonial Experience*, New York, 1958, pp. 278–83, 295. See also Robert Lawson-Peebles, *Landscape and Written Expression in Revolutionary America*, Cambridge, 1988; Jack P. Greene, *The Intellectual Construction of America: Exceptionalism and Identity from 1492 to 1800*, London, 1993.

20 N.N. Bashkina and others (eds), *The United States and Russia: The Beginnings of Relations, 1765–1815*, Washington, DC, 1980. The works of Bolkhovitinov have charted the early history of US–Russian relations with great thoroughness. *The Beginnings of Russian-American Relations, 1775–1815*, London, 1975, is available in English.

21 J.C. Miller, *Triumph of Freedom, 1775–1783*, Boston, 1948, p. 586.

22 Paul Dukes, 'Some Cultural Aspects of the Context of Von Grimm's Prediction', in A.G. Cross, R.P. Bartlett and K. Rasmussen (eds), *Russia and the World of the Eighteenth Century*, Columbus, Ohio, 1988, pp. 45–57.

23 Joseph L. Shulim, 'The United States Views Russia in the Napoleonic Age', *Proceedings of the American Philosophical Society*, vol. 102, no. 2, pp. 148–59. There were pro-Russian statements in the USA at this time, too, views both for and against often reflecting domestic party political differences.

24 Richard W. Leopold and Arthur S. Link (eds), *Problems in American History*, Englewood Cliffs, N.J., 1957, pp. 178–9; Dexter Perkins, *The Monroe Doctrine, 1867–1907*, Baltimore, 1937.

25 Walter LaFeber, *The American Age*, New York, 1989, pp. 96–7.

26 R.W. Emerson, *Works*, Edinburgh, 1906, p. 949.

27 LaFeber, *The American Age*, p. 95.

28 R.W. Emerson, *Essays*, Glasgow, n.d., pp. 288–9.

29 Mark Bassin, *Imperial Visions: Nationalist Imagination and Geographical Expansion in the Russian Far East, 1840–1865*, Cambridge, 1999 evokes the failed dream of the Amur as an 'Asian Mississippi', and much else besides.

30 Paul Dukes, *A History of Russia c.882–1996*, London, 1998, p. 130.

31 Bristed, Everett and Chevalier all from Theodore Draper, 'The Idea of the "Cold War" and Its Prophets', *Encounter*, February 1979, pp. 34–5. See also David Griffiths, 'Soviet Views of Early Russian-American Relations', *Proceedings of the American Philosophical Society*, vol. 116, no. 2, 1972.

32 Karl Marx, *Secret Diplomacy of the Eighteenth Century*, London, 1969, p. 121. This work, first appearing in book form in 1899, originated in articles published in the

London *Free Press* from 1856 to 1857. See also J.H. Gleason, *The Genesis of Russophobia in Great Britain: A Study of the Interaction of Policy and Opinion*, Cambridge, Mass., 1950.

33 Frank A. Golder, 'Russian-American Relations during the Crimean War', *American Historical Review*, vol. 31, 1926, pp. 464–5, 474. See more generally Alan Dowty, *The Limits of American Isolation: The United States and the Crimean War*, New York, 1971.

34 For a suggestion that the relationship of Europe to America and Russia might be viewed as a cultural pH test, see Paul Dukes, *History and World Order: Russia and the West*, London, 1996, pp. 43, 44, 76, 78, 106, 136–7, 144.

35 L.A. Rand, 'America Views Russian Serf Emancipation', *Mid-America*, vol. 50, 1968, pp. 43–4, 47–8. See also Kolchin, *Unfree Labor*, pp. 359–75.

36 Albert A. Woldman, *Lincoln and the Russians*, Westport, Conn., 1952, pp. 9, 270–6.

37 E.A. Adamov, 'Russia and the United States at the Time of the Civil War', *Journal of Modern History*, vol. 2, 1930, 594. There were among the demagogues a few honest men, conceded de Stoeckl, notably Lincoln.

38 Alexander Kucherov, 'Alexander Herzen's Parallel between the United States and Russia', in J.S. Curtiss (ed.), *Essays in Honor of G. T. Robinson*, Leiden, 1963, pp. 34–47.

39 Quoted in Public Record Office, Correspondence respecting Central Asia, c.704, London, 1873, pp. 72–5.

40 N.N. Bolkhovitinov, *Russko-amerikanskie otnosheniia i prodazha Aliaski 1834–1867*, Moscow, 1990, is the most scholarly treatment from the Russian side. Bolkhovitinov does not share the view of some of his fellow-countrymen that Alaska should be returned to Russia.

41 LaFeber, *The American Age*, pp. 162, 248; see also Chapter 2, note 3.

42 Vladimir Trofimov and others, *Staryi Vladivostok – Old Vladivostok*, Vladivostok, 1992, n.p., items 26, 37. See also Norman E. Saul, *Concord & Conflict: The United States & Russia 1867–1914*, Lawrence, Kansas, 1996, pp. 46–7. For the preceding period, see Norman E. Saul, *Distant Friends: The United States and Russia, 1763–1867*, Lawrence, Kansas, 1991.

43 John J. Stephan, *The Russian Far East: A History*, Stanford, Cal., 1994, pp. 87, 89.

44 E.H. Zabriskie, *American-Russian Rivalry in the Far East, 1895–1914*, Philadelphia, 1946.

45 LaFeber, *The American Age*, pp. 151–4, in a chapter entitled 'Laying the Foundations for "Superpowerdom"'.

46 Dukes, *A History of Russia*, pp. 187–8, 192–4.

47 Colin White, *Russia and America: The Roots of Economic Divergence*, London, 1987, with quotations from pp. 13, 97.

48 See Catriona Kelly and David Shepherd (eds), *Constructing Russian Culture in the Age of Revolution: 1881–1940*, Oxford, pp. 193–7 on the pre-revolutionary Russian women's movement.

49 George Steiner, *Tolstoy or Dostoevsky*, Harmondsworth, 1967, pp. 35, 38.

50 W.J. Gavin and T.J. Blakeley, *Russia and America: A Philosophical Comparison: Development and Change from the 19th to the 20th Century*, Dordrecht and Boston, 1976, pp. 101–2.

2 Conception: the First World War and revolution, 1898–1921

1 In the Introduction to his *Russia: People and Empire, 1552–1917*, London, 1997, p. xix, Geoffrey Hosking writes of his theme as how *Rossiia* ('grandiose, cosmopolitan, secular and pace grammarians, masculine') obstructed the flowering of *Rus'* ('humble,

homely, sacred and definitely feminine'). In their *Zemlyanin-1: The Emerging Global Citizen: Essays on the Evolution of Human Consciousness*, Moscow–San Francisco, 1995, A.I. Gostev and J.C. Tucker refer to Russia as a country of the female symbol and the USA as a country of the male symbol.

2 Stephen Kern, *The Culture of Time and Space, 1880–1918*, Boston, Mass., 1983, pp. 12–15. A.J.P. Taylor, *War by Timetable*, London, 1969.

3 David Thomson (ed.), *The New Cambridge Modern History*, vol. XII, *The Era of Violence, 1898–1945*, Cambridge, 1960, pp. 8, 309, 320, 325, 471, 476, 536.

4 Woodrow Wilson, *The State: Elements of Historical and Practical Politics*, Boston, 1899, pp. 620, 624.

5 J.F. Rusling, 'Interview with President McKinley', *The Christian Advocate*, no. 78, January 1903, pp. 137–8.

6 Dexter Perkins, *The Monroe Doctrine, 1867–1907*, Baltimore, 1937, pp. 408–12.

7 J.A. White, *The Diplomacy of the Russo-Japanese War*, Princeton, N.J., 1964.

8 See, for example, H.D. Mehlinger and J.M. Thompson, *Count Witte and the Tsarist Government in the 1905 Revolution*, Bloomington, Ind., 1971.

9 Walter LaFeber, *The American Age: United States Policy at Home and Abroad since 1750*, New York, 1989, pp. 189, 248–9, 253–68.

10 A.F. Pollard, 'The World War', *Encyclopaedia Britannica*, Twelfth Edition, vol. 32, London and New York, 1922, p. 1075. Among other excellent older publications is C.R.M.F. Crutwell, *A History of the Great War 1914–1918*, Oxford, 1934.

11 Pollard, 'The World War', p. 1081.

12 Pollard, 'The World War', pp. 1081–2.

13 Brian Pearce, *How Hague Saved Lenin*, London, 1987.

14 James B.Scott, *President Wilson's Foreign Policy*, New York, 1918, pp. 354–63.

15 R.K. Debo, *Revolution and Survival: The Foreign Policy of Soviet Russia, 1917–1918*, Toronto, 1979.

16 Edward M. House, 'Paris, Conference of', *Encyclopaedia Britannica*, Thirteenth Edition, vol. III, London and New York, 1926, p. 57.

17 A. Lentin, *Guilt at Versailles: Lloyd George and the Pre-History of Appeasement*, London, 1984, p. 74. See also A.J. Mayer, *Politics and Diplomacy of Peacemaking: Containment and Counter-Revolution at Versailles, 1918–1919*, New York, 1967; J.M. Thomson, *Russia, Bolshevism and the Versailles Peace*, Princeton, N.J., 1966.

18 E.H. Carr, *The Bolshevik Revolution*, vol. 3, London, 1966, pp. 127–32.

19 Lev Davidovich Trotsky, 'Lenin, Vladimir Ilyich Ulyanov', *Encyclopaedia Britannica*, Thirteenth Edition, vol. II, pp. 700–1; Orlando Figes, *A People's Tragedy*, London, 1996, p. 179.

20 Thomson, *The New Cambridge Modern History*, vol. XII, pp. 16–23.

21 Samuel Eliot Morison and Henry Steele Commager, *The Growth of the American Republic*, vol. II, New York, 1955, pp. 364, 910–11; Paul Dukes, *A History of Russia, c.882–1996*, London, 1998, pp. 187–8. V.S. Smirnov, 'Ekonomika v predrevoliutsionnoi Rossii v tsifrakh i faktakh', *Otechestvennaia istoriia*, 1999, No. 2, p. 4 suggests that in some respects of its social structure Russia in 1913 lagged behind the USA in 1820.

22 Dukes, *A History*, p. 195; Thomson, *The New Cambridge Modern History*, vol. XII, pp. 24–5; Peter Gatrell, *Government, Industry and Rearmament in Russia, 1900–1914*, Cambridge, 1994, pp. 323, 328–9. For more analysis of the Russian predicament, see Peter Gatrell, *The Tsarist Economy, 1815–1917*, London, 1986; *Government, Industry and Rearmament in Russia, 1900–1914*, Cambridge, 1994.

23 R.W. Davies, *Soviet Economic Development from Lenin to Khrushchev*, Cambridge, 1998, pp. 22–3; LaFeber, *The American Age*, pp. 297, 326–9.

24 Neil Harding, *Lenin's Political Thought*, 2 vols., London, 1977, 1981; V.I. Lenin, *Imperialism: The Highest Stage of Capitalism*, Moscow, 1970, pp. 117–19.

25 John M. Blum, *Woodrow Wilson and the Politics of Morality*, Boston, 1956, pp. 20, 86, 95; *The Papers of Woodrow Wilson*, vol. 65, Princeton, N.J., 1991, p. 70.

26 *The Times*, 4 April 1913, pp. 7–8.

27 See *Encyclopaedia Britannica*, Thirteenth Edition: George Dodds, 'Singing', vol. III, pp. 552–4; Richard Stites, *Russian Popular Culture: Entertainment and Society since 1900*, Cambridge, 1993, pp. 19–20; Bronislaw Malinowski, 'Anthropology', vol. I, pp. 131–40, quotation from p. 139.

28 Thomson, *The New Cambridge Modern History*, vol. XII, p. 100.

29 James Melvin Lee, 'Newspapers', *Encyclopaedia Britannica*, Thirteenth Edition, vol. II, pp. 1054–7.

30 Louise McReynolds, *The News under Russia's Old Regime: The Development of a Mass-Circulation Press*, Princeton, N.J., 1991, pp. 122, 282, unpaginated appendix. For an 'optimistic' view, see Caspar Ferenczi, 'Freedom of the Press under the Old Regime', Olga Crisp and Linda Edmondson (eds), *Civil Rights in Imperial Russia*, Oxford, 1989, pp. 191–214.

31 V.I. Lenin, 'Eshche odin pokhod na demokratiiu', *Polnoe sobranie sochinenii*, Moscow, 1976, vol. 22, p. 83. See also 'Newspaper Journalism in Pre-Revolutionary Russia', *Soviet Studies in History*, vol. 25, 1986.

32 Jeffrey Brooks, *When Russia Learned to Read: Literacy and Popular Literature, 1861–1917*, Princeton, N.J., 1985, p. 356.

33 Brooks, *When Russia Learned*, pp. 144, 169, 244, 355.

34 James D. Hart, *The Popular Book: A History of America's Literary Taste*, New York, 1950, pp. 219–21. 'Postal Sleigh' and 'Endless Road' were equivalents in urbanising Russia. See Stites, *Russian Popular Culture*, pp. 13, 15.

35 J.C.W. Reith (Later Lord Reith and Director of the BBC), 'Broadcasting', *Encyclopaedia Britannica*, Thirteenth Edition, vol. I, pp. 451, 454. As early as 1900–07, half a million gramophones were sold in Russia. See Richard Stites, *Russian Popular Culture*, p. 15.

36 D.S. Mirsky, 'Russian Literature', *Encyclopaedia Britannica*, Thirteenth Edition, vol. III, pp. 435–8.

37 Howard Zinn, *A People's History of the United States*, New York, 1980, pp. 314–15. And see Paul Fussell, *The Great War and Modern Memory*, Oxford, 1975.

38 John L. Heaton, *Cobb of 'The World'*, New York, 1924, pp. 268–70.

39 A.B. Hart, 'United States', *Encyclopaedia Britannica*, Twelfth Edition, vol. XXXII, p. 896.

40 Guy Stanton Ford, 'Censorship', *Encyclopaedia Britannica*, Twelfth Edition, vol. XXX, pp. 595–6; Zinn, *A People's History*, p. 362.

41 Quoted in David S. Fogelson, *America's Secret War against Bolshevism*, Chapel Hill, N.C., 1995, p. 1.

42 Paul Dukes, *October and the World: Perspectives on the Russian Revolution*, London, 1979, pp. 123–5.

43 Guy Stanton Ford, 'Censorship', *Encyclopaedia Britannica*, Twelfth Edition, vol. 30, pp. 595–6. The global impact of the Russian Revolution is described in Dukes, *October and the World*.

44 D.S. Mirsky, 'Russian Literature', *Encyclopaedia Britannica*, Thirteenth Edition, vol. III, pp. 437–9.

45 Peter Kenez and David Shepherd, '"Revolutionary" Models for High Literature: Resisting Poetics', in Catriona Kelly and David Shepherd (eds), *Russian Cultural Studies: An Introduction*, Oxford, 1998, pp. 22–3.

46 Lenin, quoted in Paul Miliukov, *Outlines of Russian Culture*, vol. 2, New York, 1960, p. 82.

47 Mirsky, as in note 44 above.

48 Miliukov, *Outlines*, vol. 3, pp. 88, 94–8; Harvey Wiley Corbett, 'Architecture', *Encyclopaedia Britannica*, Thirteenth Edition, vol. I, pp. 199, 206: In America, 'old buildings give way to new, new buildings seem to rise almost over night'. 'The years 1914–1923 were a period of stagnation for Russian architecture. Only purely theoretical and experimental work was being done…'

49 H.L. Mencken, 'Americanism', *Encyclopaedia Britannica*, Thirteenth Edition, vol. I, pp. 104–5.

50 Virginia Woolf, 'American Fiction', in Andrew McNeillie (ed.), *The Essays of Virginia Woolf*, vol. 4, 1925–1928, London, 1994, p. 278.

3 Gestation: new world orders and the Second World War, 1921–45

1 Charles Seymour, 'Harding, Warren Gamaliel', *Encyclopaedia Britannica*, Thirteenth Edition, vol. II, pp. 314–6.

2 E.H. Carr, *The Bolshevik Revolution*, vol. 2, Harmondsworth, 1966, p. 277.

3 Harold J. Goldberg, *Documents of Soviet-American Relations*, vol. 2, *Propaganda, Economic Affairs, Recognition, 1917–1933*, Gulf Breeze, Flo., 1995, pp. 223–4; vol. 1, *Intervention, Famine Relief, International Affairs*, Gulf Breeze, Flo., 1993, p. 263.

4 Goldberg, *Documents*, vol. 1, pp. 275–7.

5 Goldberg, *Documents*, vol. 1, pp. 278–9. See also David S. Fogleson, 'Keeping Faith with Russia: Ambassador Boris Bakhmeteff and U.S. Efforts to Restore "Democracy"', Chapter 3 of *America's Secret War against Bolshevism*, Chapel Hill, N.C., 1995.

6 Goldberg, *Documents*, vol. 1, pp. 287–94.

7 Arnold J. Toynbee, 'Genoa, Conference of', *Encyclopaedia Britannica*, Thirteenth Edition, vol. II, p. 166.

8 'Rapallo, Treaty of', *Encyclopaedia Britannica*, Thirteenth Edition, vol. III, p. 298; Goldberg, *Documents*, vol. 1, pp. 294–5.

9 Goldberg, *Documents*, vol. 1, pp. 296–8, 300–1.

10 Goldberg, *Documents*, vol. 1, pp. 301–4.

11 Gustav Stresemann, 'Locarno, Pact of', *Encyclopaedia Britannica*, Thirteenth Edition, vol. II, pp. 723–4.

12 Goldberg, *Documents*, vol. 1, pp. 308–12.

13 Walter LaFeber, *The American Age: United States Foreign Policy at Home and Abroad since 1750*, New York, 1989, pp. 326–45, with quotation from Hoover on p. 339.

14 Mark Mazower, *Dark Continent: Europe's Twentieth Century*, Harmondsworth, 1998, pp. 69–71, 141–8.

15 Goldberg, *Documents*, vol. 2, pp. 412–35; Hugh D. Phillips, 'Rapprochement and Estrangement: The United States in Soviet Foreign Policy in the 1930s', *Soviet–US Relations 1933–1942*, Moscow, 1989, pp. 12, 14. See also John Richman, *The United States & The Soviet Union: The Decision to Recognize*, Chapel Hill, NC, 1980; Thomas R.

Maddux, *Years of Estrangement: American Relations with the Soviet Union, 1933–1941*, Tallahassee, Flo., 1980.

16 Edward M. Bennett, 'Soviet–American Relations, 1939–1942: Searching for Allies in a Threatening World'; J. Garry Glifford, 'The Isolationist Context of American Foreign Policy toward the Soviet Union in 1940–1941'; Warren F. Kimball, 'Crisis Diplomacy, June–December 1941'; Grigory Sevostianov, 'The USSR and the USA: Two Courses in World Politics, 1933–1938', all from *Soviet–US Relations*, pp. 29–39, 40–52, 53–71, 160–95; and note 15 above.

17 *The Memoirs of Cordell Hull*, vol. 1, London, 1948, pp. 81–2.

18 LaFeber, *The American Age*, p. 362–6.

19 Jonathan Haslam, *The Soviet Union and the Threat from the East, 1933–1941*, London, 1992, pp. 97–8.

20 Alvin D. Coox, *Nomonhan*, 2 vols, Stanford, Cal., 1985; and Philip Snow, 'Nomonhan – the Unknown Victory', *History Today*, July 1990.

21 Zinovy Sheinis, *Maxim Litvinov*, Moscow, 1990, pp. 294–7, including, in a speech of 31 October 1939, Molotov's introduction of a new critical concept of 'primitive anti-fascism'.

22 Mazower, *Dark Continent*, p. 171.

23 Bennett, 'Soviet–American Relations', p. 33.

24 Harold J. Goldberg, *Documents of Soviet–American Relations*, vol. 3, *Diplomatic Relations, Economic Relations, Propaganda, International Affairs, Neutrality, 1933–1941*, Gulf Breeze, Flo., 1998, pp. 314–26.

25 Warren F. Kimball, 'Crisis Diplomacy: June–December 1941', pp. 63–4. And see note 16 above.

26 LaFeber, *The American Age*, pp. 401–2; Lloyd C. Gardner, 'A Tale of Three Cities: Tripartite Diplomacy and the Second Front, 1941–1942'; Oleg Rzheshevsky, 'Formation of the anti-Hitler Coalition and the Quest for Solving the Problem of the Second Front, 1941–1942', *Soviet–US Relations*, pp. 104–20, 259–73.

27 LaFeber, *The American Age*, p. 406.

28 This promise was made at Yalta, to be discussed in the next chapter.

29 John Erickson, 'Soviet War Losses: Calculations and Controversies', in J. Erickson and D. Dilks (eds), *Barbarossa: The Axis and the Allies*, Edinburgh, 1994, p. 257, points out that for the 'global loss' including the 'natural loss' due to wartime diminution of the birth rate, 'there is something of a consensus … in the order of 47–50 million'.

30 Douglass C. North, *Growth and Welfare in the American Past: A New Economic History*, Englewood Cliffs, N.J., 1966, p. 166.

31 R.W. Davies, *Soviet Economic Development from Lenin to Khrushchev*, Cambridge, 1998, pp. 23–37.

32 Thomas Nixon Carver, 'The Reasons for American Prosperity', *Encyclopaedia Britannica*, Thirteenth Edition, vol. III, pp. 889–90.

33 Stuart Chase, Robert Dunn and Rexford Guy Tugwell (eds), *Soviet Russia in the Second Decade: A Joint Survey by the Technical Staff of the First American Trade Union Delegation*, New York, 1928, pp. 4, 13.

34 Chase, *Soviet Russia*, pp. 55, 58, 59–61, 73, 75, 98, 102.

35 Chase, *Soviet Russia*, pp. 14–15, 17–19, 25–7, 28, 33–6, 44–6, 49–50, 53–4. Henry Ford, *Moving Forward*, London, 1931, pp. 245–6.

36 Mark Harrison, 'Why did NEP fail?', *Economics of Planning*, vol. 16, 1980, p. 66.

37 J.V. Stalin, 'The Tasks of Business Executives', *Works*, vol. 13, pp. 40–1; Davies, *Soviet Economic Development*, pp. 43–58.

38 J.A. Getty and O.V. Naumov (eds), *The Road to Terror: Stalin and the Self-Destruction of the Bolsheviks, 1932–1939*, London, 1999, pp. xiii–xiv. See also A. Nove, S. Wheatcroft and others, in J.A. Getty and R. Manning (eds), *Stalinist Terror: New Perspectives*, Cambridge, 1993. Elena Zubkova, *Russia after the War: Hopes, Illusions, and Disappointments, 1945–1957*, London, 1998, p. 164, considers 'our best approach to a realistic figure' for political prisoners between 1921 and 1953 is V.P. Popov's, based on the records of the Ministry of Internal Affairs, of 4.1 million.

39 North, *Growth and Welfare*, p. 174.

40 Davies, *Soviet Economic Development*, pp. 43–58, 63–4; A. Nove, *An Economic History of the USSR*, London, 1988, pp. 280 agrees that 'The West contributed much more to road transport' than to armaments, before going on to suggest that 'rail transport, however, remained the key, and performed remarkably well in the face of truly formidable handicaps'. And see the detailed analysis by Mark Harrison, *Accounting for War: Soviet Production, Employment, and the Defence Burden, 1940–1945*, Cambridge, 1996, pp. 126–54. At a conference on the results of the Second World War in St Petersburg, 27–28 April 2000, veteran academics put the overall share of Lend-Lease in the wartime Soviet economy at 4–5 per cent, and complained of the quality of some of the supplies sent, condemning the jeeps as death traps.

41 J.L. Garvin, 'Prefatory Note', *Encyclopaedia Britannica*, Thirteenth Edition, vol. I, pp. vii–xiii.

42 Albert Einstein, 'Space-Time', *Encyclopaedia Britannica*, Thirteenth Edition, vol. III, p. 611; Francis William Aston, 'Atomic Energy', vol. I, p. 267.

43 Stephen E. Hanson, *Time and Revolution: Marxism and the Design of Soviet Institutions*, London, 1997, makes no mention of Einstein and relativity.

44 V.G. Bogoraz, *Einshtein i religiia: primenii printsipa otnositelnykh issledovaniiu religioznykh iavlenii*, Moscow–Petrograd, 1923, p. 4.

45 Sigmund Freud, 'Psychoanalysis: Freudian School', *Encyclopaedia Britannica*, Thirteenth Edition, vol. III, pp. 253–5.

46 J.V. Stalin, 'The Foundations of Leninism', *Problems of Leninism*, Moscow, 1953, p. 112.

47 V.I. Lenin, 'The Immediate Tasks of the Soviet Government', *Selected Works*, Moscow, 1975, pp. 413–14.

48 John B. Watson, 'Behaviourism', *Encyclopaedia Britannica*, Thirteenth Edition, vol. I, pp. 345–7; David Cohen, *J. B. Watson, The Founder of Behaviourism: A Biography*, London, 1979, p. 241.

49 Peter Gay, *Freud for Historians*, New York, 1985, p. 193, n.11.

50 For a critique, see Bernard Doray, *From Taylorism to Fordism: A Rational Madness*, London, 1988.

51 Yevgeny Zamyatin, *We*, London, 1993, pp. 3, 34.

52 John Gould Fletcher, *Europe's Two Frontiers: A Study of the Historical Forces at Work in Russia and America as They Will Increasingly Affect European Civilization*, London, 1930, p. 351.

53 Fletcher, *Europe's Two Frontiers*, pp. 358–60, 361–3, 365, 367, 372–3.

54 Catriona Kelly and David Shepherd (eds), *Constructing Russian Culture in the Age of Revolutions, 1881–1940*, Oxford, 1998, p. 232.

55 Peter Kenez, *The Birth of the Propaganda State: Soviet Methods of Mass Mobilization, 1917–1929*, Cambridge, 1985, p. 106; Kelly and Shepherd, *Constructing Russian Culture*, p. 171.

56 Richard Stites, *Russian Popular Culture: Entertainment and Society since 1900*, Cambridge, 1993, pp. 81–3.

57 Chase, *Soviet Russia*, p. 240.

58 Samuel Eliot Morison and Henry Steele Commager, *The Growth of the American Republic*, vol. 2, New York, 1955, pp. 572–4.

59 I. Deutscher, *Stalin: A Political Biography*, Oxford, 1949, p. 458; H. Fireside, *Icon and Swastika: The Russian Orthodox Church under Nazi and Soviet Control*, Cambridge, Mass., 1971, p. 168; A. Werth, *Russia at War, 1941–1945*, London, 1964, pp. 400–3.

60 Caroline F. Ware, *The Consumer Goes to War: A Guide to Victory on the Home Front*, New York, 1942, pp. 1–3; Henry Wallace, *The Century of the Common Man*, New York, 1943, pp. 14–5.

61 Wendell L. Wilkie, *One World*, London, 1943, pp. 69, 72, 85. Like many Democrats, the Republican Wilkie believed in the ideals of Woodrow Wilson. See, for example, Sumner Welles, *The Time for Decision*, London, 1944.

4 Youth: Cold War and decolonisation, 1945–68

1 Ernest V. Pannell, 'Super-Power', *Encyclopaedia Britannica*, Thirteenth Edition, vol. III, pp. 681–3.

2 William T.R. Fox, 'The Super-Powers Then and Now', *International Journal*, vol. 35, 1979–80, pp. 417–30.

3 *Foreign Relations of the United States: The Conference of Malta and Yalta, 1945*, Washington, DC, 1955, pp. 571, 612, 664–9, 718, 844, 970, 972, 975, 987. Some use made of *The Tehran, Yalta and Potsdam Conferences: Documents*, Moscow, 1974.

4 *Foreign Relations of the United States: The Conference of Berlin (The Potsdam Conference), 1945*, 2 vols, Washington, DC, 1960, vol. 2, pp. 1481–7.

5 N. Gordon Levin, *Woodrow Wilson and World Politics: America's Response to War and Revolution*, New York, 1968, p. 260.

6 Terry H. Anderson, *The United States, Great Britain and the Cold War, 1944–1947*, London, 1981, p. 5.

7 Anderson, *The United States*, p. 11.

8 Alec Nove, *An Economic History of the USSR, 1917–1991*, Harmondsworth, 1992, p. 323.

9 Alexander Werth, *Russia at War, 1941–1945*, London, 1964, pp. 879–80. The French General Delattre de Tassigny did accept the invitation.

10 George Clare, *Berlin Days, 1946–1947*, London, 1990, p. 94. And see generally David E. Murphy, Sergei A. Kondrashev, George Bailey, *Battleground Berlin: CIA vs KGB in the Cold War*, London, 1997. The part played by the KGB in Soviet life is well-known. For less well-known aspects of the significance of its counterpart, see Rhodri Jeffreys-Jones, *The CIA and American Democracy*, London, 1989.

11 Gar Alperovitz, *The Decision to Use the Atomic Bomb and the Architecture of an American Myth*, London, 1995, pp. 3–7, 643–68.

12 Thomas G. Paterson, *Soviet–American Confrontation: Postwar Reconstruction and the Origins of the Cold War*, Baltimore, 1973, pp. 8-9.

13 John Barber and Mark Harrison, *The Soviet Home Front, 1941–1945: A Social and Economic History of the USSR in World War II*, London, 1991, p. 40, write of 27 to 28 million excess deaths as 'an emerging consensus among Soviet demographers', adding 'a maximum scholarly estimate of up to 40 million (one-fifth of the prewar Soviet population) ... cannot be excluded.' Compare Chapter 3, note 29 above.

14 Paterson, *Soviet–American Confrontation*, pp. 8–9.

15 Walter LaFeber, *America, Russia, and the Cold War, 1945–1996*, New York, 1997, pp. 22–3; Daniel Yergin, *Shattered Peace: The Origins of the Cold War and the National Security State*, London, 1978, p. 80.

16 George F. Kennan, 'The Sources of Soviet Conduct', *Foreign Affairs*, vol. XXV, 1947, pp. 566–82; LaFeber, *America, Russia*, p. 63. David S. Fogleson, 'Roots of "Liberation": American Images of the Future of Russia in the Early Cold War, 1948–1953', *International History Review*, 1998, p. 65, observes: 'In the late 1940s and early 1950s, Kennan habitually described the historic relationship between Russia and the West in terms of "darkness" and "light". … From that long-range view, the cold war frequently seemed merely the latest episode in the Christian West's crusade to redeem the Byzantine or Oriental East.'

17 Eugene Varga, 'Anglo-American Rivalry and Partnership: A Marxist View', *Foreign Affairs*, vol. XXV, 1947, pp. 592–3. Varga was later removed from office for challenging the dogma that the Western capitalism would soon collapse. Novikov and Roberts telegrams both from Kenneth M. Jensen (ed.), *Origins of the Cold War: The Novikov, Kennan and Roberts 'Long Telegrams' of 1946*, Washington, DC, 1995, pp. 3–16 and 33–67 respectively.

18 W. LaFeber, *The American Age: United States Foreign Policy at Home and Abroad since 1750*, New York, 1989, pp. 514, 544.

19 Vannevar Bush, *Modern Arms and Free Men: A Discussion of the Role of Science in Preserving Democracy*, New York, 1949, p. 113; Nickolai Krementsov, *Stalinist Science*, Princeton, N.J., 1997, pp. 289–91. For apprehension, see P. Blackett, *War, Fear and the Bomb*, London, 1949; J.U. Nef, *War and Human Progress*, London, 1950; and see note 64 below.

20 Truman, Marshall and Vyshynsky all from J.L. Black (ed.), *A Handbook of Interpretations, Propaganda, 'Red' and 'White' Scares*, Laurentian University Social Science Research Publication No. 3, 1972, pp. 64–73.

21 Compare Michail M. Narinskii, 'The Soviet Union and the Berlin Crisis, 1948–9', in Francesca Gori and Silvio Pons, *The Soviet Union and Europe in the Cold War, 1943–53*, London, 1996, pp. 57–75, with Vojtech Mastny, *The Cold War and Soviet Insecurity: The Stalin Years*, Oxford, 1996, pp. 47–53, 63–7.

22 Jenny Pearce, *Under the Eagle: US Intervention in Central America and the Caribbean*, London, 1982, pp. 28–31. In 1999, the USA apologised to Guatemala for its earlier behaviour.

23 D.K. Fieldhouse, 'The Labour Governments and the Empire Commonwealth 1945–51', in R. Ovendale (ed.), *The Foreign Policy of the British Labour Governments 1945–51*, Leicester, 1984, p. 89. See John Kent, *British Imperial Strategy and the Origins of the Cold War*, London, 1993, on Bevin's idea of the British Empire and Commonwealth as a Third Force.

24 R.C. Bridges *et al.* (eds), *Nations and Empires: Documents on the History of Europe and on its Relations with the World since 1648*, pp. 309–12. More generally, see Lloyd C. Gardner, *Approaching Vietnam: From World War II through Dienbienphu, 1945–1954*, New York, 1988.

25 Daniel Yergin, *Shattered Peace: The Origins of the Cold War and the National Security State*, London, 1978, pp. 404–5; Lloyd C. Gardner, *Approaching Vietnam: From World War II through Dienbienphu*, New York, 1988, pp. 78–82; Donald S. Zagoria, *The Sino-Soviet Conflict, 1956–1961*, Princeton, N.J., 1962, pp. 14–20.

26 Yergin, *Shattered Peace*, pp. 401–3; Vladislav Zubok and Constantine Pleshakov, *Inside the Kremlin's Cold War: From Stalin to Khrushchev*, London, 1996, pp. 67–72. See also

Michael J. Hogan, *Cross of Iron: Harry S. Truman and the Origins of the National Security State, 1945–1954*, Cambridge, 1998; Melvyn P. Leffler, *A Preponderance of Power: National Security, the Truman Administration, and the Cold War*, Stanford, Cal., 1992.

27 Bridges, *Nations and Empires*, p. 320.

28 János Radványi, *Hungary and the Superpowers: The 1956 Revolution and Realpolitik*, Stanford, Cal., 1972, pp. 3–20; V.K. Volkov *et al.* (eds), *Sovetskii Soiuz i vengerskii krizis 1956: Dokumenty*, Moscow, 1998, pp. 196, 337.

29 Bridges, *Nations and Empires*, p. 323.

30 Stephen E. Ambrose, *Eisenhower*, vol. 2, *The President*, New York, 1984, pp. 179–80.

31 Zagoria, *The Sino–Soviet Conflict*, pp. 160, 168–9.

32 Michael R. Beschloss, *Kennedy v. Khrushchev: The Crisis Years, 1960–3*, London, 1991; Alexander Fursenko and T.J. Naftali, *One Hell of a Gamble: Khrushchev, Castro, Kennedy and the Cuban Missile Crisis, 1958–1962*, London, 1999. I myself was teaching US history at the SAC base at Fairford, Gloucestershire, which was on red alert, and have rarely been so terrified.

33 See Chapter 5, note 10.

34 Raymond L. Garthoff, *Détente and Confrontation: American–Soviet Relations from Nixon to Reagan*, Washington, DC, 1994.

35 Alec Nove, *An Economic History*, pp. 291–2. And see generally S. Linz (ed.), *The Impact of World War II on the Soviet Union*, Totowa, N.J., 1985.

36 Anderson, *The United States*, pp. 13, 54.

37 Paterson, *Soviet–American Confrontation*, pp. 147, 153.

38 V. Batiuk and D. Estafiev, *Pervye zamorozki: sovetsko-amerikanskie otnosheniia v 1945–1950gg.*, Moscow, 1995, pp. 78–9, 82; Paterson, *Soviet–American Confrontation*, pp. 37–9, 49.

39 Batiuk, Estafiev, *Pervye zamorozki*, pp. 89, 98; Paterson, *Soviet–American Confrontation*, 22, 47–56, 159, 262.

40 V.M. Molotov, *Problems of Foreign Policy: Speeches and Statements, April 1945–November 1948*, Moscow, 1949, pp. 210–6.

41 Nove, *An Economic History*, 306, 322, 323, 358–9.

42 LaFeber, *The American Age*, p. 513.

43 S. Ambrose, *Eisenhower*, vol. 2, pp. 611–13.

44 LaFeber, *The American Age*, 513–16; 579–82.

45 Alexander Tarn, 'A Comparison of Dollar and Ruble Values of the Industrial Output of the USA and USSR', *Soviet Studies*, vol. 19, no. 4, 1968, p. 500.

46 Fred Halliday, *The Making of the Second World War*, London, 1983, p. 5, for the quotation from Don John Manuel; A.J.P. Taylor in review, 'Mapping the Cold War', in *The Observer*, 19 April 1981; Arnold Toynbee, 'Russia's Byzantine Heritage', *Civilization on Trial*, Oxford, 1948, pp. 181–2.

47 Howard Zinn, *A People's History of the United States*, New York, 1980, p. 405.

48 Archibald MacLeish, *Freedom is the Right to Choose: An Inquiry into the Battle for the American Future*, London, 1952, pp. viii, 79–81, 84, 87–8.

49 Signi Lenea Falk, *Archibald MacLeish*, New York, 1965, p. 155.

50 Ilya Ehrenburg, *Men, Years – Life*, vol. 6, *Post-War Years, 1945–1954*, London, 1966, pp. 79–81.

51 LaFeber, *America, Russia*, p. 39.

52 G.F. Alexandrov and others, *Joseph Stalin: A Short Biography*, Moscow, 1949, pp. 202–3.

53 A.A. Zhdanov, *On Literature, Music and Philosophy*, London, 1950, pp. 108–9; Black, *A Handbook*, pp. 76–7.

54 Molotov, *Problems*, p. 214. On cultural offensives and responses, see Walter L. Hixson, *Parting the Curtain: Propaganda, Culture, and the Cold War, 1945–1961*, London, 1998; Scott Lucas, *Freedom's War: The US Crusade against the Soviet Union, 1945–56*, Manchester, 1999; V.S. Lelchuk and E.I. Pivovar, 'Mentalitet sovetskogo obshchestva i "kholodnaia voina"', *Otechestvennaia istoriia*, 1993, No. 6; V.O. Pechatnov, '"Strelba kholostymi": sovetskaia propaganda na Zapad v nachale kholodnoi voiny, 1945–1947', in I.V. Gaiduk *et al.* (eds), *Stalin i kholodnaia voina*, Moscow, 1998; J.L. Black, '*Kanada – Votchina Amerikanskogo Imperializma*: Canadian and Candian Communists in the Soviet "Coming War" Paradigm, 1946–1951', in Greg Donaghy (ed.), *Canada and the Early Cold War, 1943–1957*, Ottowa, 1998.

55 Frances Stonor Saunders, *Who Paid the Piper? The CIA and the Cultural Cold War*, London, 1999, pp. 27–8, 33–4.

56 Saunders, *Who Paid the Piper?*, pp. 101, 159–60, 171.

57 Saunders, *Who Paid the Piper?*, pp. 60–3.

58 Conyers Read, 'The Social Responsibilities of the Historian', *American Historical Review*, vol. 55, no. 2, 1950, pp. 283–4.

59 Stephen J. Whitfield, *The Culture of the Cold War*, London, 1992, p. 55.

60 Saunders, *Who Paid the Piper?*, pp. 221, 223, 245–50, 253–4, 285, 287.

61 Reinhold Niebuhr, 'Power and Ideology in National and International Affairs', in William T.R. Fox (ed.), *Theoretical Aspects of International Relations*, Notre Dame, Ind., 1959, p. 118; Saunders, *Who Paid the Piper?*, p. 281.

62 Hogan, *A Cross of Iron*, pp.440–3; *Times Literary Supplement* 2 April 1999; Joel Kovel, *Red Hunting in the Promised Land: Anticommunism and the Making of America*, London, 1997, p. 112; Saunders, *Who Paid the Piper?*, p. 204.

63 ibid., pp. 303, 305–6.

64 Joseph Rotblat, *Science and World Affairs: History of the Pugwash Conferences*, London, 1962.

65 Frank Ellis, 'The Media as Social Engineer', in Catriona Kelly and David Shepherd, *Russian Cultural Studies: An Introduction*, Oxford, 1998, p. 215.

5 Maturity: Cold War and the Third World, 1968–91

1 Walter LaFeber, *The American Age: United States Foreign Policy at Home and Abroad since 1750*, New York and London, 1989, pp. 579–80.

2 LaFeber, *The American Age*, p. 602.

3 *The Current Digest of the Soviet Press*, The Joint Committee on Slavic Studies, New York, vol. XX, No. 14, 1968, pp. 13–18. Soon, although on the basis of border disputes as well as ideological differences, Harrison Salisbury was to write *The Coming War between Russia and China*, London, 1969.

4 *The Current Digest*, vol. XX, No. 34, 1968, p. 19; vol. XX, No. 39, 1968, pp. 12–13.

5 Immanuel Wallerstein, '1968: Revolution in the World-System', *Geopolitics and Geoculture: Essays on the Changing World-System*, Cambridge, 1991, pp. 13–14, 65–83. Wallerstein's italics.

6 Fred Halliday, *The Making of the Second Cold War*, London, 1983, p. 3 argues that there were four major phases in post-1945 history: the First Cold War, 1946–53; Oscillatory Antagonism, 1953–69; Detente, 1969–79; and the Second Cold War, 1979–. In his discussion of the Second Cold War, he made special use of his expertise on the Middle East and Central Asia. See also his *Cold War, Third World: An Essay on Soviet–American Relations*, London, 1989.

7 W. LaFeber, *America, Russia, and the Cold War, 1945–1996*, New York, 1997, pp. 244–5.

8 Robert D. Schlesinger, *Henry Kissinger: Doctor of Diplomacy*, New York, 1989, pp. 131–40.

9 Richard Nixon, *1999: Victory without War*, London, 1988, p. 123 insists that his Doctrine 'was not a formula for getting America *out* of the Third World, but for providing the only sound basis for America to stay *in* the Third World'.

10 Leslie H. Gelb and Richard K. Betts, *The Irony of Vietnam: The System Worked*, Washington, DC, 1979, p. 169n. write: 'With all the notorious data on how many more bombs were dropped on Southeast Asia than in all of World War II, most observers find it hard to comprehend how military leaders could keep straight faces in ascribing their failure to administrative restraints.'

11 Schlesinger, *Kissinger*, p. 75 writes: 'Kissinger's greatest achievement was the opening of relations between the United States and the People's Republic of China.'

12 LaFeber, *The American Age*, p. 616.

13 [Joseph G. Whelan], *Soviet Diplomacy and Negotiating Behavior: Emerging New Context for U.S. Diplomacy*, Washington, DC, 1979, pp. 462–92.

14 Daniel Yergin, *The Prize: The Epic Quest for Oil, Money and Power*, London, 1991, pp. 555–8, 606–32.

15 Erwin C. Hargrove, *Jimmy Carter as President: Leadership and the Politics of the Public Good*, London, 1988, pp. 99–101, 111–59.

16 Jenny Pearce, *Under the Eagle: U.S. Intervention in Central America and the Caribbean*, London, 1982, pp. 205–50.

17 Halliday, *The Making*, pp. 94, 187, 217, 227–8.

18 Halliday, *The Making*, pp. 90–9, 151–9; Henry S. Bradsher, *Afghanistan and the Soviet Union*, Durham, NC, 1983, pp. 56–7, 74–61, 98–100, 169–89.

19 Bradsher, *Afghanistan*, pp. 222–4.

20 M. Heller and A. Nekrich, *Utopia in Power: A History of the USSR from 1917 to the Present*, London, 1985, pp. 691–3.

21 Garry Wills, *Reagan's America: Innocents at Home*, London, 1988, pp. 348–50.

22 Michael Schaller, *Reckoning with Reagan: America and Its President in the 1980s*, New York, 1992, p. 120.

23 M. Lewin, *The Gorbachev Phenomenon: A Historical Phenomenon*, Berkeley, Cal., 1988, p. 147.

24 A. Brown, *The Gorbachev Factor*, Oxford, 1996, p. 175.

25 Brown, *The Gorbachev Factor*, p. 212.

26 Jonathan Schell, *The Gift of Time: The Case for Abolishing Nuclear Weapons Now*, London, 1998, p.123, quotes Helmut Schmidt: 'the INF treaty was the end of the Cold War.'

27 Brown, *The Gorbachev Factor*, pp. 221–2. See also John Gooding, 'Gorbachev and Democracy', *Soviet Studies*, vol. 42, 1990.

28 John Morrison, *Boris Yeltsin: From Bolshevik to Democrat*, London, 1991, pp. 142–3. See also Stephen White, *Russia's New Politics: The Management of a Postcommunist Society*, Cambridge, 2000, pp. 91–5.

29 Alec Nove, *An Economic History of the USSR, 1917–1991*, London, 1992, pp. 378–92; M.E. Ruban, 'The Consumer Economy', H.-J. Veen (ed.), *From Brezhnev to Gorbachev: Domestic Affairs and Social Policy*, New York, 1987, pp. 16–21.

30 LaFeber, *America, Russia*, pp. 314–5.

31 *Guidelines for the Economic and Social Development of the USSR for 1986–1990 and for the Period ending in 2000*, Moscow, 1985, p. 12. Alfred Zauberman, *The Mathematical Revolution in Soviet Economics*, Oxford, 1975, provides clear evidence of Soviet expertise with

numbers and concepts. But the mathematical revolution was not followed by an IT revolution. For the Soviet economic predicament in a wider context, see C. Maier, 'The Collapse of Communism: Approaches for a Future History', *History Workshop*, no. 31, 1991.

32 White, *Russia's New Politics*, pp. 123–4; Stephen White, *Russia Goes Dry: Alcohol, State and Society*, Cambridge, 1995; V. Mau, *Ekonomika i vlast: politicheskaia istoriia ekonomicheskoi reformy v Rossii, 1985–1994*, Moscow, 1995.

33 LaFeber, *The American Age*, pp. 671–2, 675–6; Schaller, *Reckoning with Reagan*, pp. 126–32; White, *Russia's New Politics*, p. 33.

34 Paul Kennedy, *The Rise and Fall of the Great Powers: Economic Change and Military Conflict from 1500 to 2000*, New York and London, 1988, pp. xxii–xxiv; Paul Kennedy's italics.

35 Kennedy, *The Rise and Fall*, pp. 515, 521, 525–6.

36 Nove, *An Economic History*, pp. 418–19; R.W. Davies, *Soviet Economic Development from Lenin to Khrushchev*, Cambridge, 1998, pp. 80–1. On the basis of the remarks of Davies and Nove, an interesting comparison could perhaps be made with the economies of China and some of the Asian 'tigers'.

37 Herbert Marcuse, *One Dimensional Man: The Ideology of Industrial Society*, London, 1968, pp. 13, 26, 59, 71.

38 Marcuse, *One Dimensional Man*, pp. 80, 86–7.

39 Marcuse, *One Dimensional Man*, pp. 86–7, 99, 105, 137, 159.

40 Marcuse, *One Dimensional Man*, pp. 177, 192–3, 194, 200–1.

41 L.S. Leonova, 'Evoliutsiia politicheskikh vozzrenii V.I. Vernadskogo', in S.A. Baibakov *et al.*, *Rossiiskoe gosudarstvo i obshchestvo: XX/ vek*, Moscow, 1999, pp. 460–518. See also Kendall E. Bailes, *Science and Russian Culture in an Age of Revolutions: V.I. Vernadsky and his Scientific School*, Bloomington, Ind.,1990.

42 William Vogt, *Road to Survival*, London, 1949, pp. v–vi, 16–7; Rachel Carson, *Silent Spring*, London, 1962.

43 R.W. Davies, *Soviet History in the Gorbachev Revolution*, London, 1989; Ronald Radosh, CThe Bare-Knuckled Historians', *The Nation*, 2 February 1970.

44 D. Remnick, 'Sakharov's Testament: New Soviet Constitution', *The Guardian Weekly*, 24 December 1989; A. Solzhenitsyn, '"Russkii vopros" k kontsu XX veka', *Novyi mir*, no. 7, 1994.

45 Harrison E. Salisbury (ed.), *Sakharov Speaks*, London, 1974, pp. 112–14.

46 Frank Ellis, 'The Media as Social Engineer', in Catriona Kelly and David Shepherd (eds), *Russian Cultural Studies*, Oxford, 1998, pp. 210–20.

47 Ellis, 'The Media', pp. 220–2.

48 Laurie Garrett, *The Coming Plague: Newly Emerging Diseases in a World out of Balance*, London, 1995, p. 476.

6 The legacy: death or rebirth? 1991–

1 Jonathan Schell, *The Gift of Time: The Case for Abolishing Nuclear Weapons Now*, London, 1998, p. 123.

2 Schell, *The Gift*, p. 7.

3 Richard Dean Burns, 'Foreword', in J.L. Black, *Origins, Evolution and Nature of the Cold War: An Annotated Bibiliographical Guide*, Oxford, 1986, p. xx.

4 K. Shteppa, *Russian Historians and the Soviet State*, New Brunswick, N.J., 1962, pp. 220–3, 233, 234–5, 326.

5 John Lewis Gaddis, 'The Emerging Post-Revisionist Synthesis on the Origins of the Cold War', *Diplomatic History*, vol. 7, No. 2, Summer 1983, pp. 180–1.
6 John Lewis Gaddis, *We Now Know: Rethinking Cold War History*, Oxford, 1997, pp. 51–2, 294.
7 Gaddis, *We Now Know*, pp. viii, 1–4.
8 Melvyn P. Leffler, 'The Cold War: What Do "We Now Know"?', *American Historical Review*, vol. 104, No. 2, 1999, p. 513. Quotation from Elena Zubkova, *Russia after the War: Hopes, Illusions and Disappointments, 1945–1957*, London, 1998, p. 12. Gaddis, *We Now Know*, p. 13, writes (with his own italics): 'The Soviet leader, too, sought security after World War II: his country lost at least 27 million of its citizens in that conflict; he could hardly have done otherwise. But no tradition of *common* or *collective* security shaped postwar priorities as viewed from Moscow, for the very good reason that it was no longer permitted there to distinguish between state interests, party interests, and those of Stalin himself.'
9 Leffler, 'The Cold War', pp. 502–3.
10 A.O. Chubarian, 'Novaia istoriia "Kholodnoi Voiny"', *Novaia i noveishaia istoriia*, No. 6, 1997, pp. 8–9.
11 Richard Pipes, 'Misinterpreting the Cold War: The Hard-Liners Had it Right', *Foreign Affairs*, vol. 74, January/February, 1995. In a letter to the *New York Review of Books*, 8 April 1999, a group of nineteen academics and journalists complained about the assumption that the revisionist view of Cold War historiography had been 'discredited by archival records in Moscow', recommending as an antidote Melvyn P. Leffler's essay 'Inside Enemy Archives: The Cold War Reopened', *Foreign Affairs*, vol. 75, July/August 1996.
12 Chubarian, 'Novaia istoriia', p. 12.
13 Chubarian, 'Novaia istoriia', pp. 12–22.
14 Leffler, 'The Cold War', p. 523.
15 Francis Fukuyama, *The End of History and the Last Man*, Harmondsworth, 1992, pp. xiii, 51, 66, 126, 152, 283.
16 Samuel P. Huntington, *The Clash of Civilizations and the Remaking of World Order*, New York, 1996, pp. 20–1, 31–2, 164, 301–21. Vladimir Batyuk, 'The End of the Cold War: A Russian View', *History Today*, April, 1999, p. 28 argues that 'the Cold War was fundamentally about ideology not geopolitics'. On p. 33, he comments: 'So far, however, the traditionalists have failed to produce any new holy creed which would cement the new empire.'
17 A.S. Akhiezer, 'Samobytnost Rossii kak nauchnaia problema', with others in 'Rossiia – raskolotaia tsivilizatsiia?', *Otechestvennaia istoriia*, 4–5, 1994. Compare Lorina Repina, 'The Russian Revolutions in the Light of New Theoretical Models of Universal History', *International Politics*, vol. 33, no. 4, 1966, pp. 379–84.
18 L.N. Gumilëv, *Drevniaia Rus i Velikaia step*, Moscow, 1989, pp. 29, 217, 530; Bruno Naarden, '"I am a genius, but no more than that": Lev Gumilëv (1912–1992), Ethnogenesis, the Russian Past and World History', *Jahrbücher für Geschichte Osteuropas*, vol. 44, no. 1, 1996.
19 N.B. Ter-Akopian, 'O kategorii "razdelenie truda"'; V.S. Ovsiannikov, 'V poiskakh novykh podkhodov k istoricheskim issledovaniiam', *Novaia i noveishaia istoriia*, no. 4, 1996.
20 M.Ya. Gefter and V.L. Malkov, 'Reply to an American Scholar', *Soviet Studies in History*, vol. V, 1966–7.

21 M. Vilchek, *Proshchanie s Marksom: Algoritmy istorii*, Moscow, 1993, pp. 70, 121–2, 187–8, 210–12, 213–20.

22 Igor M. Diakonoff, *The Paths of History*, Cambridge, 1999, pp. xi, 1–9, 324–38.

23 Schell, *The Gift*, p. 120; Zbigniew Brzezinski, *The Grand Chessboard: American Primacy and Its Geostrategic Imperatives*, New York, 1997, pp. 24, 30, 44.

24 Richard Nixon, *1999: Victory without War*, London, 1988. Brzezinski, *The Grand Chessboard*, p. 44, suggests that 'China is already a significant regional power and is likely to entertain wider aspirations, given its history as a major power and its view of the Chinese state as the global center'.

25 *Global Environment Outlook 2000*, London, 1999, pp. xx–xxii, 26, 102–6, 138–40, 154.

26 Arthur M. Schlesinger, Jr, *The Vital Center: The Politics of Freedom*, Boston, 1949, pp. 241–2.

27 Compare the well-known observation of Ralph Waldo Emerson: 'We are not free to use today or to promise tomorrow because we are already mortgaged to yesterday.'

28 Valentin Kudrov, *Soviet Economic Performance in Retrospect: A Critical Re-examination*, Moscow, 1998, pp. 52, 71–2, 92, 123–4. According to one calculation, if the installation of telephones had continued at the rate achieved in the USSR in the last twenty years of its existence, to reach the same level as the USA in 1989 would have taken 160 years. V.S. Smirnov, 'Ekonomika predrevoliutsionnoi Rossii v tsifrakh i faktakh', *Otechestvennaia istoriia*, 1999, no. 2, p.10.

29 W.J. Gavin and T.J. Blakeley, *Russia and America: A Philosophical Comparison: Development and Change of Outlook from the 19th to the 20th Century*, Boston, 1976, pp. 101–2.

30 James Bone, 'New sciences "threaten end of humanity"', *The Times*, 15 March 2000. James Bone points out that Bill Joy's article, entitled 'Why the Future Doesn't Need Us' and published in *Wired* magazine, has been compared to Einstein's letter of 1939 to President Roosevelt warning about the possibility of a nuclear bomb.

31 A. Ia. Froianov, *Pogruzhenie v bezdnu*, St Petersburg, 1999. Froianov, a medieval historian, complains of Russia's 'plunge into the abyss' but foresees the possibility of national revival along lines similar to those set out by Solzhenitsyn.

32 Marc Bloch, *The Historian's Craft*, Manchester, 1967, pp. 47, 143–4.

Bibliography

Babey, A. M., *Americans in Russia, 1776–1917: A Study of the American Travelers in Russia*, New York, 1938.

Bailey, T.A., *America Faces Russia: Russian-American Relations from Early Times to Our Own Day*, Ithaca, NY, 1950.

Bashkina, N.N. *et al.* (eds), *The United States and Russia: The Beginnings of Relations, 1765–1815*, Washington, DC, 1980.

Black, J.L. (ed.), *Origins, Evolution and the Nature of the Cold War: An Annotated Bibliographic Guide*, Oxford, 1986.

Bolkhovitinov, N.N., *The Beginnings of Russian-American Relations, 1775–1815*, Cambridge, Mass., 1975. (Translation of *Stanovlenoe russko-amerikanskikh otnoshenii, 1775–1815*, Moscow, 1966.)

—— *Russko-amerikanskie otnosheniia, 1815–1832*, Moscow, 1975.

—— *Russko-amerikanskie otnosheniia i prodazha Aliaski, 1834–1867*, Moscow, 1990.

Brewster, D., *East–West Passage: A Study in Literary Relationships*, London, 1954.

Brzezinski, Zbigniew and Huntington, Samuel P., *Political Power: USA–USSR*, New York, 1964.

Crockatt, Richard, *The Fifty Years' War: The United States and the Soviet Union in World Politics, 1941–1991*, London, 1995.

Cronin, James E., *The World the Cold War Made: Order, Chaos, and the Return of History*, London, 1996.

Dukes, Paul, *The Emergence of the Super-Powers: A Short Comparative History of the USA and the USSR*, London, 1970.

—— *The Last Great Game: USA versus USSR: Events, Conjunctures, Structures*, London, 1989.

Dulles, F.R., *The Road to Teheran: The Story of Russia and America, 1781–1943*, Princeton, N.J., 1944.

Filene, P.G. (ed.), *American Views of Soviet Russia*, Homewood, Ill., 1968.

Fletcher, John G., *Europe's Two Frontiers: A Study of the Historical Forces at Work in Russia and America as they will increasingly affect European Civilization*, London, 1930.

Gaddis, John Lewis, *Russia, the Soviet Union and the United States: An Interpretive History*, New York, 1978.

—— *We Now Know: Rethinking Cold War History*, Oxford, 1997.

Garrison, M. and Gleason, A., *Shared Destiny: Fifty Years of Soviet–American Relations*, Boston, Mass., 1985.

Garthoff, Raymond L., *The Great Transition: American–Soviet Relations and the End of the Cold War*, Washington, DC, 1994.

Gavin, W.J. and Blakeley, T.J., *Russia and America: A Philosophical Comparison: Development and Change of Outlook from the Nineteenth to the Twentieth Century*, Boston, Mass., 1976.

Halperin, J.J. and English, R.D., *The Other Side: Soviets and Americans Perceive Each Other*, New Brunswick, NJ, 1988.

Hasty, O. P. and Fusso, S. (eds), *America through Russian Eyes, 1874–1926*, New Haven, Conn., 1988.

Hecht, D., *Russian Radicals look to America*, Cambridge, Mass., 1947.

Hildt, J.C., *Early Diplomatic Negotiations of the United States with Russia*, Baltimore, 1906.

Hobsbawm, E., *Age of Extremes: The Short Twentieth Century*, London, 1994.

Hollander, Paul (ed.), *American and Soviet Society: A Reader in Comparative Sociology and Perceptions*, Englewood Cliffs, N.J., 1969.

Jones, Mervyn, *Big Two: Life in America and Russia*, London, 1962.

Kolchin, Peter, *Unfree Labor: American Slavery and Russian Serfdom*, Cambridge, Mass., 1987.

LaFeber, Walter, *America, Russia, and the Cold War, 1945–1996*, New York, 1997.

—— *The American Age: United States Foreign Policy at Home and Abroad since 1750*, New York, 1989.

Laserson, M.M., *The American Impact on Russia, Diplomatic and Ideological, 1784–1917*, London, 1962.

Lebow, Richard Ned and Stein, Janice Gross, *We All Lost The Cold War*, Princeton, N.J., 1994.

Leffler, Melvyn P. and Painter, David S., *Origins of the Cold War: An International History*, London, 1994.

Manning, C. A., *Russian Influence on Early America*, New York, 1953.

McGwire, Michael, *Perestroika and Soviet National Security*, Washington, DC, 1991.

Nikoljukin, A. (ed.), *A Russian Discovery of America*, Moscow, 1986.

Painter, David S., *The Cold War: An International History*, London, 1999.

Parker, W.H., *The Super-Powers: The United States and Soviet Union Compared*, London, 1972.

Saul, Norman E., *Distant Friends: The United States and Russia, 1763–1867*, Lawrence, Kansas, 1991.

—— *Concord and Conflict: The United States and Russia, 1867–1914*, Lawrence, Kansas, 1996.

Sivachev, N.V., and Yakovlev, N.N., *Russia and the United States*, Chicago, 1979.

Sorokin, P.A., *Russia and the United States*, London, 1950.

Stephan, John J. (ed.), *Soviet–American Horizons on the Pacific*, Honolulu, 1986.

Tarsaidze, A., *Czars and Presidents: The Story of a Forgotten Friendship*, New York, 1958.

Thomas, B.P., *Russo–American Relations, 1815–1867*, Baltimore, 1930.

[Whelan, Joseph G.], *Soviet Diplomacy and Negotiating Behavior: Emerging New Context for US Diplomacy*, Washington, DC, 1979.

White, Colin, *Russia and America: The Roots of Economic Divergence*, London, 1987.

Williams, William A., *American–Russian Relations, 1781–1947*, New York, 1972.

Woodrow Wilson Center, *Cold War International History Project Bulletin*, Washington, DC, 1992.

Zubok, Vladislav and Pleshakov, Constantine, *Inside the Kremlin's Cold War: From Stalin to Khrushchev*, Cambridge, Mass., 1996.

Index